THE AutoCAD 3D Book

George O. Head

Charles A. Pietra

Kenneth J. L. Segal

Ventana Press
Chapel Hill, North Carolina

The AutoCAD 3D Book, First Edition. Copyright © 1989 by George O. Head, Charles A. Pietra, Kenneth J.L. Segal.

Library of Congress Catalog No.: 89-050054
ISBN: 0-940087-18-9

Book design by David M. Kidd, Oakland, CA.

Cover design by Holly Russell, Durham, NC.

Typesetting by Johnna Webb and Wendy Wegner, Pixel Plus Desktop Publishing, Chapel Hill, NC.

Technical Editing by Greg Malkin, Cleveland, OH.

First Edition, First Printing
Printed in the United States of America

Ventana Press, Inc.
P.O. Box 2468
Chapel Hill, NC 27515
919/942-0220
FAX 919/942-1140

Limits of Liability and Disclaimer of Warranty

Trademark Acknowledgments

AutoCAD, AutoLISP and AutoSHADE are registered trademarks of Autodesk, Inc. Any representation of the AutoCAD name and logo throughout this book and related promotion is not to be construed as an endorsement on the part of Autodesk, Inc.

dBASE is a registered trademark of International Business Machines Corporation.

Microsoft, MS-DOS and Multiplan are registered trademarks of Microsoft Corporation.

WordStar is a registered trademark of MicroPro International Corporation.

About the Authors

George O. Head is president of Associated Market Research, a business and management consulting firm for architects and engineers, based in Austin, Texas. He is the developer of Integrated Management Systems, a project management and financial accounting software package for architects and engineers. He is also author of *AutoLISP in Plain English* (Ventana Press). He may be reached at:

Associated Market Research
3755 Capital of Texas Hwy. South
Suite 380
Austin, TX 78704
512/445-6482

Charles A. Pietra is owner of MicroCAD Managers, an educational computer consulting company in Syracuse, New York, which specializes in CAD/CAE training services. A veteran AutoCAD trainer and curriculum developer, he has conducted workshops and lectures on AutoCAD and computer graphics. He may be reached at:

MicroCAD Managers
5858 E. Molloy Rd.
Pickard Building. #121
Syracuse, NY 13211
315/454-9360

Kenneth J.L. Segal is a consultant in Philadelphia specializing in 3D modeling, animation and scene simulation. He may be reached at 215/341-9999.

Acknowledgments

The authors and publisher wish to express appreciation to the following individuals:

Bill Kramer
Bob Bradlee
Tony Vincent
Sidney and Norma Segal
Bob Mader
Cecelia Robinson
Ann Elizabeth Luoma Segal
Jennie Pietra
Clare Pietra
Mary Votta
Brenda Williams

Contents

Introduction

Chapter One Basic Features

Chapter Two Learning the Ropes

Chapter Three Dynamic View

Chapter Four AutoCAD's User Coordinate System

Chapter Five Surfaces and Meshes

Chapter Six Putting It All Together

Chapter Seven New Twists to Old Commands

Chapter Eleven Third-Party Software and the Future

The AutoCAD 3D Library

List of Figures

CONTENTS

CONTENTS

Introduction

WHO NEEDS 3D?

With AutoCAD's new Release 10, you'll never draw the same way again. Why? Because everything you draw will be in 3D. Entities now have a Z coordinate in addition to the usual X and Y; your drawings may look the same as before, but in reality entities have been created in 3D space, opening up vast new opportunities for managing almost any design or project more productively.

Release 10's new 3D features enhance efficiency and productivity by giving you the tools you need to produce multiple views, elevations, perspectives, surfaces, meshes and renderings. But it really goes beyond efficiency and productivity. Just as using CAD instead of a drawing board created vast new opportunities, drawing — indeed *thinking* — in 3D has implications for nearly every AutoCAD professional — whether for 2D or 3D applications. And the possibilities are just being tapped.

Engineers now can build computer-generated models as prototypes to check tolerances, fits and more, thus avoiding time-consuming and expensive production of real prototypes. Architects can also create realistic models, thus avoiding the cost of building miniatures. In addition, they can let AutoCAD show how a structure might look from the street, or quickly walk a client through a building. And all AutoCAD professionals will appreciate the many new vistas Release 10 offers in terms of multiple windows, dynamic viewing and the new User Coordinate System.

Each AutoCAD user will decide which 3D tools fit his or her needs. However, anyone who's ever drawn more than one view of the same object can benefit from the increase in efficiency and productivity provided by AutoCAD's new 3D tools. And, with some practice and patience, drawing in 3D will become even easier than drawing in 2D.

WHAT IS 3D?

3D isn't a feature, as you might think of **OBJECT SNAP** or **ZOOM**. Rather, it's a series of tools that let you draw entities in 3D space, view them from any angle, manipulate them in entirely new ways and produce realistic computer models of objects quickly and inexpensively.

In normal 2D drafting, you were forced to draw an object up to five times to create a representation of various views. With Release 10, instead of drawing five different views of the same object, you draw it once, then rotate the object or viewpoint to access your desired views.

Look beyond the traditional ideas of 3D to the enhancements of AutoCAD for the purpose of 3D design. A few examples:

AutoCAD's new User Coordinate System lets anyone who needs to work with more than one coordinate system at a time—civil and structural engineers, surveyors—define an unlimited set of coordinates. Even if you're drawing in plan view, you can set a variety of coordinate systems for entities and groups of entities. These coordinate systems can be rotated—even in plan view. This means you can maintain the original coordinates while the entire coordinate system is shifted. You can also translate coordinates between coordinate systems.

DYNAMIC VIEW (DVIEW) was developed for 3D to let you view an object from any angle and plane. But it has other outstanding features. The **ZOOM** is what might be considered a hardware zoom. By moving the cursor, you dynamically increase or decrease the magnification. A new, dynamic **PAN** lets you "drag" the object rather than point to displacements. Even in plan view, an object can be rotated in any direction and viewed from any angle.

One of the most alluring aspects of 3D is its ability to maintain multiple windows on the same drawing—useful for 2D as well as 3D applications. With Release 10's multiple viewports, you can switch between windows effortlessly. You can draw and edit in any window and the others are updated immediately. In addition to saving and restoring views and windows, you can even plot from each window individually.

These are only a few of the things you can do with Release 10's powerful new 3D tools. The purpose of this book is to make learning and using of these tools as easy and painless as possible. It will take a little effort, but you took the first step when you bought AutoCAD in the first place!

WHAT'S INSIDE?

The AutoCAD 3D Book teaches you how to use the powerful new tools now available with AutoCAD's Release 10. Chapters One through Eight take you step by step through the creation of a wire frame 3D drawing, then through the process of adding surfaces and meshes.

Chapters Nine through Eleven introduce you to the basics of rendering with AutoSHADE, and under what circumstances it's most useful. Also discussed are important third-party 3D applications that will lead to future productivity leaps.

Finally, *The AutoCAD 3D Library* is a set of 25 AutoLISP routines that help smooth out the rough edges of Autodesk's ambitious new update. All users will benefit from the simpler programs; more advanced users will be able to revise many of the AutoLISP programs for additional power and performance. An optional diskette, containing all the programs found in the book, can save you considerable time over typing.

Veteran users will appreciate Chapter Seven, "New Twists to Old Commands," which discusses numerous new quirks to commands you've been using for years. And Chapter Eight, "3D Tips and Tricks," gives everyone a head start with dozens of hands-on techniques and shortcuts for using 3D most effectively.

HOW WELL SHOULD YOU KNOW AUTOCAD?

This book assumes you understand the basics of CAD or AutoCAD, including commands such as **LINE**, **ARC**, **CIRCLE**, **OBJECT SNAP** and **LAYER**. You need not be an expert AutoCAD user, nor is any AutoLISP programming required. You'll learn new concepts to help you draw smarter and faster, and to work effectively with AutoCAD's new dimension.

HOW TO USE THIS BOOK

The AutoCAD 3D Book was written as a hands-on reference to get you "thinking in 3D" as quickly as possible. This book is based on the concept of learning by doing. Of course, you'll also find the book a lasting reference; and it will be the first book you'll turn to for information on the new features of Release 10.

Beginning AutoCAD users should carefully read Chapters One through Eight, taking the time to keyboard the drawings and examples.

If you're a veteran AutoCAD user, you'll find *The AutoCAD 3D Book* contains most of the information necessary to become acquainted with Release 10. Therefore, you may not need to buy the umpteenth edition of your favorite beginning AutoCAD book.

All users will find the material on AutoSHADE and third-party 3D products of value. The AutoSHADE tutorial in Chapters Nine and Ten will be of particular value to those looking into the advantages of rendering software, or to those who've purchased AutoSHADE.

While you're learning 3D, work with the program and computer in front of you. You can receive the most from the tutorial by working through the examples.

Read each explanation as it's presented. Then type, pick and draw as requested. Compare your screen with the illustrations given. Then read the final explanation and tips that follow. Experiment with the different and new constructions relating to each concept.

SOFTWARE AND HARDWARE REQUIREMENTS

1. AutoCAD Release 10 or higher.

2. A computer and operating system that can run AutoCAD. If you have an MS-DOS computer, then 640K RAM memory is the mini-mum recommendation.

3. A graphics board and monitor that can run AutoCAD.

4. A plotter or printer-plotter is valuable, but optional.

5. AutoSHADE isn't required for Chapters One through Eight.

RULES OF THE ROAD

As you know from working with AutoCAD, there are many ways to choose the same command. You can:

Type it from the keyboard,

Pick it from a screen menu,

Pick it from the pull-down menus or dialogue boxes, or

Pick it from the tablet menu.

It's too cumbersome to explain each method for every command each time it's used in this book. Instead, we do the following:

When a new command is first introduced, all the possibilities for choosing the command are given.

After that, the command is shown between angle brackets (< >). Nested or multipart commands are separated by commas. For example, a **ZOOM ALL** is later presented as **< ZOOM, A >**. A **CIRCLE** drawn as a center radius is **< CIRCLE, CEN-RAD >**.

< OS-ENDPOINT > means that you're to set **OBJECT SNAP** to Endpoint or the requested setting.

"Pick" refers to the pick button on your cursor. This is generally button **1**, but it may differ from computer to computer.

"Confirm" refers to several commands that require confirmation. Any time you're asked to select objects, the objects selected are highlighted. You then confirm your selection by **< RETURN >** or, in many cases, the second button on your cursor.

CROSSING or **WINDOW** refers to a method of selecting objects. When you're asked to select objects, you can type **C** or **W** — which lets you encircle the object with a box.

If you're manually typing AutoLISP programs featured in The AutoCAD Reference Library, note the differences between **1**s, **l**s and **i**s, as well as **0**s and **O**s. If you find the AutoLISP programs useful, an optional diskette can get you using these programs immediately and without cumbersome error-checking. Finally,

Type: means to type the designated data in from the keyboard. **< RETURN >** indicates that you're to press the **RETURN** or **ENTER** key. Except with text, you can also press the space bar.

YOU'RE ON YOUR WAY . . .

With Release 10, you can greatly improve the efficiency and quality of your drawings — whether 2D or 3D. AutoCAD's new approach to drawing won't go away with future releases, and you'll come face to face with these new commands at some point down the ever-changing CAD road. Learning something new is best done in increments — so let's take the first step...

Section I

WORKING IN AUTOCAD'S NEW DIMENSION

1 Basic Features

OVERVIEW

Until Release 10, AutoCAD was based on a 2D coordinate system.

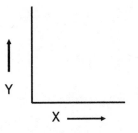

That is, the positive **Y** coordinates go up and the positive **X** coordinates go to the right. But now, AutoCAD's Release 10 provides features for drawing in 3D, which adds the **Z** coordinate. So where is **Z**?

We explain the 3D coordinate system by using what we call the *right-hand rule*. If you point the thumb of your right hand toward positive **X** and point your forefinger toward positive **Y**, then the remaining fingers, held away from your hand, point toward positive **Z**.

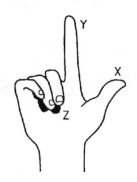

In Figure 1-1, note the direction of the arrows indicating the direction of the **X** and **Y** coordinates. The heavy lines around the square indicate the original 2D plan view. Assuming the square is one unit, the coordinates beginning at the point of origin are **0,0,0**; the top left, **0,1,0**; the upper right, **1,1,0**; and the lower right, **1,0,0**.

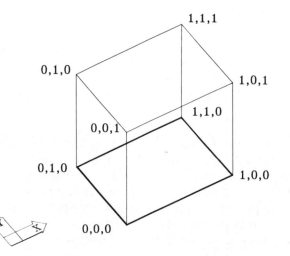

Figure 1-1: The World Coordinate System.

In each case the third coordinate is **0**. This is the **Z** coordinate. Therefore, the point in space one unit above the point of origin is **0,0,1** (and so forth) around the points, one unit above each corner.

OUT WITH THE OLD, IN WITH THE NEW

To understand the features available with Release 10, you need to understand some of the features that became available when AutoCAD first attempted 3D with Version 2.5. At that time, **ELEVATION** and **THICKNESS** were introduced. **ELEVATION** created the default value for the **Z** coordinate, drawing an entity at the default elevation above the **X, Y** plane. This provided a limited way to produce the **Z** coordinate for some entities.

THICKNESS gives you a shortcut for drawing 3D objects. By providing an **ELEVATION** of **0** and a **THICKNESS** of **4** you could draw a square that would *extrude* four units into the **Z** axis. By choosing a 3D **VIEWPOINT**, you could examine wire frame views of the cube from different angles.

Version 2.6 and Release 9 provided three major improvements to this modest beginning: **3DLINE**, **3DFACE** and **3D FILTERS**.

3DLINE has been eliminated and replaced with **LINE**, with full 3D capabilities.

You can think of **3D FILTERS** as the "Gimme a Z" concept. In order to draw a 3D line, you had to pick a point on the **X, Y** plane. AutoCAD then asked for the value of the **Z** coordinate.

3DFACE provided a way to produce the illusion of a solid object and also let you produce hidden lines.

These limited beginnings quickly earned AutoCAD the nickname of "2 1/2 D" by its users. But as rudimentary a beginning as this was, these tools still play an important part in the new procedures of Release 10.

But it's not just the addition of a few commands that have changed AutoCAD from its 2 1/2 D beginnings to a full 3D program; the entire structure of the program and its underlying precepts have changed. Let's briefly examine the new 3D tools you'll be using with Release 10.

AUTOCAD'S USER COORDINATE SYSTEM

The basic problem with any 3D CAD system is that you're using a 2D input and a 2D output device. In other words, the only way you can select all coordinates at one time is through keyboard input. Of course, this is extremely difficult and cumbersome. The more natural way would be to use features such as **SNAP** and **OBJECT SNAP** and point to where you need to draw.

In AutoCAD's 2D world before Release 10, there was only one coordinate system, the **X**, **Y** system described previously. We now call this original system the **World Coordinate System (WCS)**.

Unfortunately, you can pick only two coordinates at a time using a mouse or digitizer. Therefore, you need a simpler way to pick all three coordinates: we call this method the **User Coordinate System (UCS)**.

Because an input device can select only two coordinates at once, a method was devised to choose which two coordinates would be input. By reassigning the directions of **X** and **Y** to reflect only one side of the object, the **Z** is held constant. As a result, you're drawing on only one 2D plane at any one time.

Every side you draw on will require its own **UCS**. Each User Coordinate System can be named, saved and recalled. As a result, you'll always be working with two dimensions somewhere in the drawing.

A NEW WAY TO VIEW

The most frustrating feature of AutoCAD's older 3D views was the **VIEWPOINT**. This "bulls-eye" approach to choosing the angle of view never let you know what was going to be drawn on your screen. The new method, dynamic view or **DVIEW**, is far superior.

DVIEW lets you rotate the object dynamically on the screen so that you can see exactly the angle of view and what you're looking at. Only part of the image is drawn on the screen until the cursor stops moving. You may also rotate only part of a complicated object. When the view is finally selected, the rest of the object rotates into view.

MANY POINTS OF VIEW

One of the most valuable and essential features of Release 10 is the ability to split screens into multiple views (**VPORTS**). When you're drawing dynamically in 3D, it's vital to divide the screen into at least two different angles on the same object. As you begin to draw, you may have your **UCS** incorrectly set and not realize it; your drawing might look perfectly correct on the screen. Splitting the screen between different angles lets you confirm the accuracy of what you're drawing. You can also see when you've made a mistake and are drawing a line out into "deep space," rather than on the object.

But the real reason for multiple viewports is to let you work on the drawing from several views at once. That way, you can toggle from one view to another without rotating the drawing.

WHICH WAY IS UP?

When you first start working with 3D, it's often difficult to visualize where you are. In fact, while working with a wire frame drawing, two people may actually see the object from different vantage points.

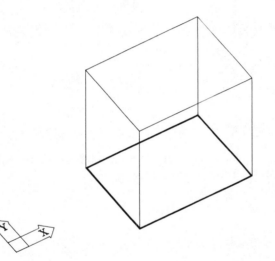

Figure 1-2: Are you on the top or the bottom?

For example, many people may see Figure 1-2 from the top of the box looking down. The heavy lines form the bottom of the box as you look into it. Others may see the box from the bottom, with the heavy lines forming the bottom of the box from underneath. See if you can adjust your eyes to see the box from both angles. As you do, the box will seem to move as your eyes adjust.

As a result, you must develop techniques to create faces and hide selected lines so that you know for sure which side you're actually drawing on.

Now look at Figure 1-3. This is how it would appear if you were looking at it from the bottom with the lines hidden.

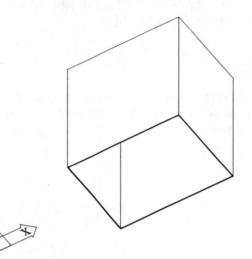

Figure 1-3: From the bottom.

Now look at Figure 1-4. This is how it would appear if you were look-ing at it from the top with the lines hidden.

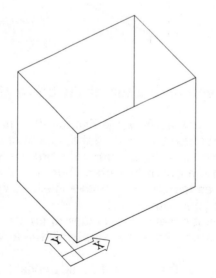

Figure 1-4: From the top.

GIVING SHAPE TO A DRAWING

One of the most powerful and valuable 3D tools is *surface modeling* — models created with Release 10 can be transferred over to AutoSHADE for shading and rendering. But for AutoSHADE to properly do its work, it must know the shape of an object. This is where meshes come in.

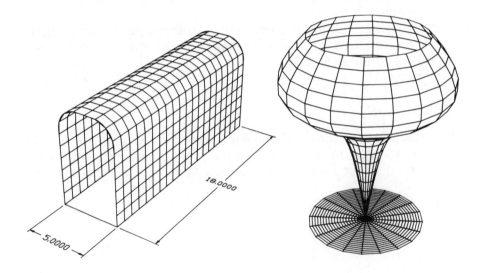

Figure 1-5   **Figure 1-6**

3D meshes are really a series of multiple **3DFACES** applied around the curvature or shape of the object. The density of the meshes is controlled by two system variables, **SURFTAB1** and **SURFTAB2**.

There are four special-purpose meshes and one general-purpose mesh available to you in Release 10.

• **RULESURF** creates a surface mesh between two objects.

- **TABSURF** uses only one entity and extends the surface mesh out from the entity, using its general shape.

- **REVSURF** creates a circular mesh around a central axis.

- **EDGESURF** is used with a figure with exactly four sides or edges. Each side may be a polyline or a 3D polyline.

The **3DMESH** command creates a general-purpose mesh that requires you to assign each vertex to it. This command is more applicable through AutoLISP.

By using each of these commands correctly, you have the tools necessary to shape your models and then use them, with realistic renderings, through AutoSHADE.

MOVING ON

We've given you an idea of some of the powerful new tools available to you with Release 10. The next chapter gets you drawing in 3D right away and gives you a good idea of how to use these important new tools.

So, let's get started.

2 Learning the Ropes

To begin your adjustment to the world of 3D, let's start with a simple exercise. You'll draw a cube with faces added to each side, and each side hatched with a different pattern. By rotating the cube and hiding the lines, you'll learn to visualize the effect of **DVIEW** and other 3D drawing tools.

STARTING YOUR DRAWING

So that you're drawing using the same units, make the following selections. Enter a new drawing (using item number **1** from the main AutoCAD menu). Name it whatever you like.

Once you're in the AutoCAD drawing, type in the following:

Type: `UNITS <RETURN>`

Response: `Enter Choice, 1-5.`

Type: `2 <RETURN>`

This is decimal units.

Response: `Number of digits to right of decimal point (0 to 8).`

Type: 2 <RETURN>

Response: Choice, 1 to 5 (Angle measurement).

Type: 1 <RETURN>

This is decimal angles.

Response: Number of fractional places for display of
angles (0 to 8).

Type: 2 <RETURN>

Response: Enter direction for angle 0.00.

Type: 0 <RETURN>

Response: Do you want angles measured clockwise?

Type: N <RETURN>

Now set your limits.

Type: LIMITS <RETURN>

Response: ON/OFF <Lower left corner.>

Type: 0,0 <RETURN>

Response: Upper right corner.

Type: 10,8 <RETURN>

Type: ZOOM A <RETURN>

Type: GRID 1 <RETURN>

Type: SNAP 1 <RETURN>

ZOOM ALL will ensure that you have a full grid on your screen.

DRAWING THE CUBE

You're now ready to draw the cube. Set **ELEVATION** and **THICKNESS**, then draw a square.

Type: ELEV <RETURN>

Response: New current elevation.

Type: 0 <RETURN>

Response: New current thickness.

Type: 4 <RETURN>

You can also set elevation and thickness from the screen menu by picking **SETTINGS** and then **ELEVATION,** or you can choose elevation and thickness from the pull-down menus. Move your cursor to the top of the pull-down menus and pick **SETTINGS.** Then select a submenu box called **ENTITY CREATION.** This will bring down a dialogue box of entity creation modes.

At the bottom of the dialogue box is **ELEVATION** and **THICKNESS.** You can change these by pointing to **ELEVATION** or **THICKNESS** and changing the number. Remember, when you change a feature in a dialogue box, **CONFIRM** by choosing **OK** or **<RETURN>.**

Now that **ELEVATION** is set to **0** and **THICKNESS** is set to **4,** draw a 4 x 4 square using the **LINE** command (see Figure 2-1). Note the arrows pointing to the **X** and **Y** axes. In all Release 10 drawings, the **UCS** icon will appear in the lower left-hand portion of the screen to indicate where **X** and **Y** are in relation to the User Coordinate System. If the **UCS** and the World Coordinate System (**WCS**) are the same, an additional **W** will appear under the **Y**. If the **UCS** icon doesn't appear on your screen:

> **Type:**   UCSICON <RETURN>

> **Response:**   ON/OFF/All/Noorigin/ORigin.

> **Type:**   ON <RETURN>

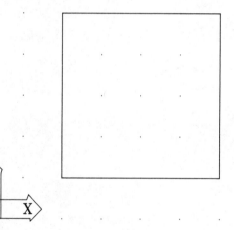

Figure 2-1: Draw object.

Now, in the same manner as before, set **ELEVATION** and **THICK-NESS** back to **0**.

> **Type:**   ELEV <RETURN>

> **Response:**   New current elevation.

Response: New current thickness.

    Type: 0 <RETURN>

USING DVIEW

You're now ready to examine your first view of the cube, using a new Release 10 feature called **DVIEW**. Select **DVIEW** from the screen menu under **DISPLAY**, from the pull-down menus under **DISPLAY**, or type **d v i e w** from the keyboard.

    When you're asked to **SELECT OBJECT**, do so by putting a <CROSSING> around the entire square. Confirm your selection with <RETURN>. Let's try it.

    Type: DVIEW <RETURN>

Response: Select Objects:

<CROSSING> Select entire object and <RETURN> to confirm.

At the command line you'll now see several options:.

CAmera/TArget/Distance/POints/PAn/Zoom/TWist/CLip/Hide/Off/Undo/eXit

To choose these from the screen menu, select **DVIEW OPTIONS**. These options now appear and may be chosen from your screen menu.

<CAmera>

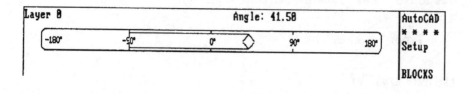

Slide bar in DVIEW.

LIGHTS! CAMERA! ACTION!

Pick the **CAMERA** option. AutoCAD now wants to know the angle from which to view your drawing. On the right-hand side of the screen is a vertical slide bar beginning with **0** in the middle and advancing upward to a maximum of **90** degrees, and descending downward to a minimum of **-90** degrees. This is the angle of inclination from which you'll view the object. You can move your cursor up and down the slide bar to see this inclination dynamically. Make sure your **SNAP** is **OFF**.

When you've reached the desired inclination, pick to stop the rotation. For consistency in this exercise, enter the angles from the keyboard.

    Type: 35 ‹RETURN›

At the top of the screen, you now see a horizontal slide bar that begins with 0 in the middle to a maximum of **180** degrees to the right and a minimum of **-180** degrees to the left. This is the left-right rotation of the object. Move your cursor left and right and watch the cube as it begins to rotate. When you have the desired left-right angle from which to view the object, you can pick and the rotation will stop.

    Type: 50 ‹RETURN›

USING PAN

Chances are the cube may be slightly high on your screen, so let's get the feel of the dynamic **PAN**.

‹PAn›

Position your cursor in the middle of the cube and pick to move it downward. Notice how the cube dynamically moves with you. When it's positioned in the center of your screen, then pick.

While you're in **DVIEW** you may continue to choose any of the options listed. When you're ready for the cube to be permanently positioned at the current view, then confirm with ‹**RETURN**›.

Your screen should now look like Figure 2-2. If it doesn't, go back and begin again.

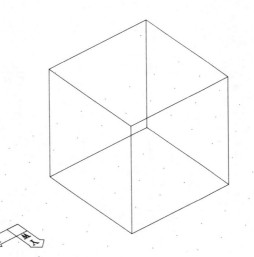

Figure 2-2: DVIEW of square.

WORKING WITH VPORTS

You're now ready to split your screen using the **VPORTS** command. You can choose **VPORTS** from the screen menu with **SETTINGS**.

Because the **SETTINGS** command gives a multiple-screen menu, choose **NEXT**.

```
<VPORTS>
```

You're now asked to select how many views you want.

Type: `2 <RETURN>`

Response: `Horizontal/Vertical.`

Type: `V <RETURN>`

Two views of the cube will now be displayed on your screen, as shown in Figure 2-3.

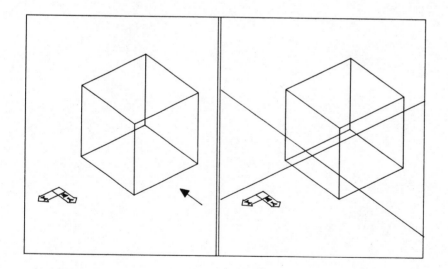

Figure 2-3: You are active in the right window.

By using the pull-down menus and the dialogue box you get a much more visual effect. From the pull-down menus, pick **DISPLAY**. At the bottom is the **VPORTS** option, which is called **SET VIEWPORTS**. You now get an actual picture of how your viewports are going to look. Pick the two vertical windows if you haven't already done so. If you pick

VPORTS from the screen or type it in a second time, the current screen will be further subdivided. This isn't true with the pull-down options. If this happens, simply pick **VPORTS SINGLE** and begin again.

You may be active in only one window at a time. To choose between one window or the other, move your cursor first to the left window. Pick. Crosshairs will now appear. Now move your cursor to the right window, where you'll see an arrow. This indicates that window isn't active. To choose the right window, move your cursor to the right window and pick. The crosshairs are now in your right window, with the arrow in your left.

Pick and make active the left window. Let's rotate the cube in the left window.

Type: DVIEW <RETURN>

Response: Select Objects:

<CROSSING> Select entire object and <RETURN> to confirm.

Type: CAMERA <RETURN>

Response: Enter angle from X-Y plane.

Type: 35 <RETURN>

Response: Enter angle in X-Y plane from X-axis.

Type: 30 <RETURN>

Type: <RETURN>

The second <**RETURN**> confirms the view. You should now have two slightly different views of the same object as shown in Figure 2-4. Notice how you can tell the two different views or angles of the same entity by the different directions of the **X Y UCS** icon. The **W** is still visible, indicating that the **UCS** and the **WCS** are the same.

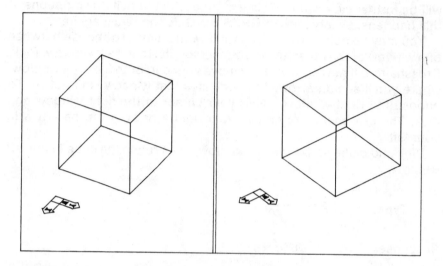

Figure 2.4: Two views of a cube.

Make sure you're active in the left screen. Next, let's put a **3DFACE** on the left side of the cube. When working in 3D, you'll be better off if each face or hatching pattern created is on a different layer.

Type: `LAYER <RETURN>`

Response: `?/Make/Set/New/ON/OFF/Color/Ltype/Freeze/Thaw.`

Type: `M <RETURN>`

Response: `New current layer.`

Type: `FACE1 <RETURN>`

Response: `?/Make/Set/New/ON/OFF/Color/Ltype/Freeze/Thaw.`

Type: C <RETURN>

Response: Color

Type: 1 <RETURN>

Response: Layer name(s) for color 1 (red) <FACE1>.

Type: <RETURN>

Response: ?/Make/Set/New/ON/OFF/Color/Ltype/Freeze/Thaw.

Type: <RETURN>

USING UCS

This "makes" and "sets" you to a layer called **FACE1** with **COLOR 1**. You're now ready to create your first **UCS**.

Type: UCS <RETURN>

Response: Origin/ZAxis/3point/Entity/View/X/Y/Z/Prev/
Restore/Save/Del/?

A variety of options that will be explained later are listed at the command line. For now, the one you want is **3POINT**.

Type: 3POINT <RETURN>

This lets you indicate a beginning origin and direction of the positive **X** and the positive **Y** (see Figure 2-5).

<OS-Intersection>

Pick the point indicated at **X1**. AutoCAD now wants to know the positive direction for the new **X** axis.

```
<OS-Intersection>
```

Pick the point indicated at **X2**. Finally you're asked for a positive direction for the **Y** axis.

```
<OS-Intersection>
```

Pick the point indicated at **Y3**. At that point the new **UCS** is displayed by the **UCS** icon.
You now need to save this **UCS**:

    Type: UCS <RETURN>

Response: Origin/ZAxis/3point/Entity/View/X/Y/Z/Prev/
                    Restore/Save/Del/?

    Type: S <RETURN>

Response: ?/Name of UCS.

    Type: SIDE1 <RETURN>

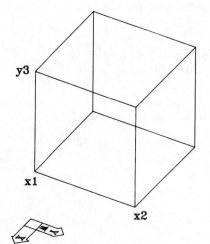

Figure 2-5: UCS 3POINT.

If you'll be picking your **UCS** from the pull-down menu (which is much more convenient), pick **SETTINGS**, then **UCS DIALOGUE**. Then pick **DEFINE NEW CURRENT UCS**. Pick **NAME**. Type **SIDE1** and **<RETURN>**. Then pick **ORIGIN, X AXIS, PLANE**.

This is slightly confusing in that the screen menu and the AutoCAD manual both call this **3POINT**, but the dialogue box calls it **ORIGIN, X AXIS, PLANE**. You then pick the same points as before.

Note also that if you return to the dialogue box, it's much easier to choose which **UCS** you want active at any one time by simply picking the current box beside the name of each **UCS** available to you. Note that the **UCS** icon has been changed.

ABOUT 3DFACE

Now that the **UCS** is set, let's add a **3DFACE**.

      Type: 3DFACE <RETURN>

The easiest place to pick **3DFACE** is from **3D** on the main AutoCAD screen menu, or to type it from the keyboard. You can get to **3DFACE** through the **DRAW** option of the pull-down menus in a roundabout way. Pick **3D CONSTRUCTION**. Pick one of the surfaces such as **Surface of REVOLUTION**. Cancel the command with **CTRL C**. Now the right screen menu with **3DFACE** is available. This is a lot of trouble, so the pull-down menu isn't viable for this command.

Refer to Figure 2-6.

<OS-Intersection>

Pick points **1**, **2**, **3** and **4**.

      Type: <RETURN>

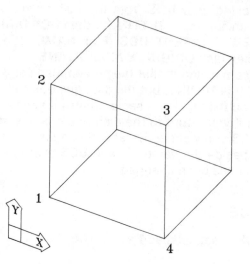

Figure 2-6: Apply 3DFACE.

A **3DFACE** is now in place on that side of your object.

Note how in Screen 2 the face is also outlined, but at a different angle. One reason you need a minimum of two screens is that if a mistake were made at this point, the **3DFACE** or entity drawn might look correct in one screen but be somewhere in outer space on the other! If the two screens both look correct, then you can be reasonably certain that your drawing is accurate.

Now let's see what happens if you hatch this. Make a new layer called **HATCH1** as **COLOR 1**.

```
<Layer, m, hatch1, c, 1, hatch1>
```

   Type: LAYER <RETURN>

Response: ?/Make/Set/New/ON/OFF/Color/Ltype/Freeze/Thaw.

Type: M <RETURN>

Response: New current layer.

Type: HATCH1 <RETURN>

Response: ?/Make/Set/New/ON/OFF/Color/Ltype/Freeze/Thaw.

Type: C <RETURN>

Response: Color.

Type: 1 <RETURN>

Response: Layer name(s) for color 1 (red)   <HATCH1>.

Type: <RETURN>

Response: ?/Make/Set/New/ON/OFF/Color/Ltype/Freeze/Thaw.

Type: <RETURN>
           <Hatch, u, 0, .5, N, L>

Type: HATCH <RETURN>

Response: Pattern (? or name/U, style).

Type: U <RETURN>

Response: Angle for crosshatch lines.

Type: 0 <RETURN>

Response: Spacing between lines.

Type: .5 <RETURN>

Response: Double hatch area?

Type: N <RETURN>

Response: Select Objects:

Type: L <RETURN>

Your **3DFACE** should highlight at this point.

Type: <RETURN>

You should have a hatching pattern in both screens. Your left screen should look like Figure 2-7.

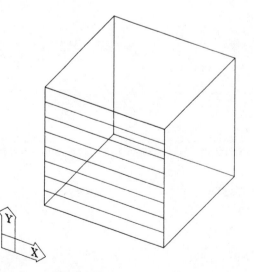

Figure 2-7: Hatch 3DFACE.

If the hatching pattern doesn't occur, it's because you didn't properly set the **UCS**. Go back and make sure the correct points were picked as in Figure 2-5.

You really don't need a **3DFACE** on each side to hide the lines, since **THICKNESS** creates the extrusion. But it's necessary if you want to hatch it, since you're really hatching the **3DFACE** and not the extrusion.

<HIDE>

HIDE your lines at this point and you'll see the effect in Figure 2-8.

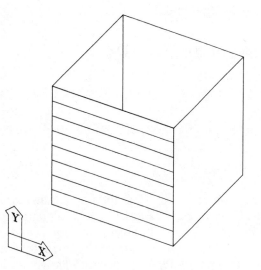

Figure 2-8: Hatch with hidden lines.

Now create a new **LAYER** called **FACE2** as **COLOR 2**.

    Type: LAYER <RETURN>

Response: ?/Make/Set/New/ON/OFF/Color/Ltype/Freeze/Thaw.

    Type: M <RETURN>

Response: New current layer.

Type: `FACE2 <RETURN>`

Response: `?/Make/Set/New/ON/OFF/Color/Ltype/Freeze/Thaw.`

Type: `C <RETURN>`

Response: `Color.`

Type: `2 <RETURN>`

Response: `Layer name(s) for color 2 (yellow) <FACE2>.`

Type: `<RETURN>`

Response: `?/Make/Set/New/ON/OFF/Color/Ltype/Freeze/Thaw.`

Type: `<RETURN>`

   To learn the importance of the **UCS**, let's do a little experiment. Draw a line from point **1** to point **2** in as Figure 2-9. Don't use **OBJECT SNAP**, but try to draw the line as closely along the points indicated as possible. (If **OBJECT SNAP** is used, then you'll correctly **SNAP** to the intersections of two known points in 3D space.) However, let's see what can happen when using a **UCS** that isn't aligned correctly.

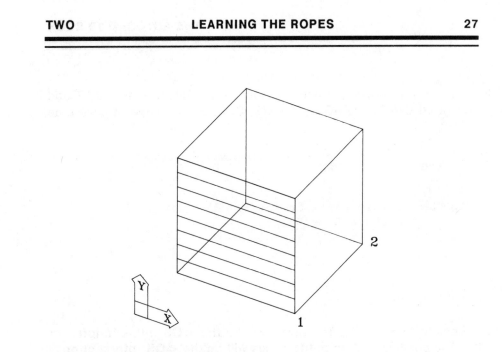

Figure 2-9: Draw a line.

Note Figure 2-10. Even though the line appears to be correctly drawn in Screen 1, it's off sharply in Screen 2. Therefore, you must create a new **UCS** for each side upon which you wish to draw.

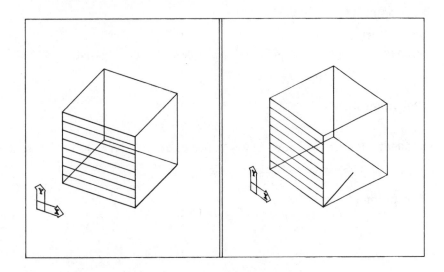

Figure 2-10: Things aren't what they appear to be.

Cancel and erase the line you just drew. Select a new **UCS** and choose **3POINT** or **ORIGIN, X AXIS, PLANE** and name or save it as **SIDE2**.

    Type: UCS <RETURN>

Response: Origin/ZAxis/3point/Entity/View/X/Y/Z/Prev/
            Restore/Save/Del/?

    Type: 3POINT <RETURN>

Response: Origin point.

Look at Figure 2-11. The origin will be the < **OS-Intersection** > of **X1**. The positive portion of the **X** axis will be the < **OS-Intersection** > of **X2**. The positive **X** portion of the **X, Y** plane will be the < **OS-Intersection** > of **Y3**.

<OS-Intersection>

Pick point **X1**.

Response: Point on positive portion of the X-axis.
            <OS-Intersection>

Pick point **X2**.

Response: Point on positive-Y portion of the UCS X-Y plane.
            <OS-Intersection>

Pick point **Y3**.

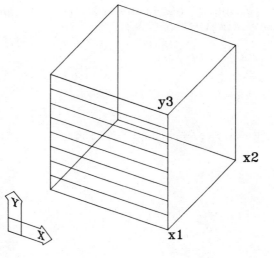

Figure 2-11: UCS 3POINT.

Note how the **UCS** icon has now shifted, with the **Y** pointing upward.

`<3dface>`

Refer to Figure 2-12. Using **< OS-Intersection >**, pick points **1**, **2**, **3** and **4**.

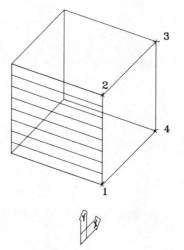

Figure 2-12: Apply 3DFACE.

In order to keep the hatched layers separate from your faces, make a new layer called **HATCH2** as **COLOR 2**.

```
<Layer, m, hatch2, c, 2>
```

Type: LAYER <RETURN>

Response: ?/Make/Set/New/ON/OFF/Color/Ltype/Freeze/Thaw.

Type: M <RETURN>

Response: New current layer.

Type: HATCH2 <RETURN>

Response: ?/Make/Set/New/ON/OFF/Color/Ltype/Freeze/Thaw.

Type: C <RETURN>

Response: Color.

Type: 2 <RETURN>

Response: Layer name(s) for color 2 (yellow) <HATCH2>.

Type: <RETURN>

Response: ?/Make/Set/New/ON/OFF/Color/Ltype/Freeze/Thaw.

Type: <RETURN>

You should now be on layer **HATCH2**. Let's **HATCH** side **2**.

```
<Hatch, hex, 2, 0, L>
Pattern for hatch is HEX.
Scale for pattern is 2.
Angle is 0.
SELECT OBJECTS is LAST and CONFIRM.
```

Type: HATCH <RETURN>

Response: Pattern (? or name/U,style).

Type: HEX <RETURN>

Response: Scale for pattern.

Type: 2 <RETURN>

Response: Angle for pattern.

Type: 0 <RETURN>

Response: Select Objects:

Type: L <RETURN>

Type: <RETURN>

Note how neatly the pattern is hatched on the correct side. If you
HIDE your lines at this point, the cube begins to develop a nice visual
effect (see Figure 2-13).

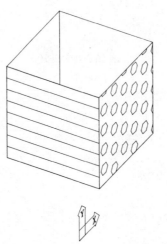

Figure 2-13: Hex hatch 3DFACE.

`<Layer, m, face3, c, 3>`

Make a new **LAYER** as **FACE3**, **COLOR 3**.

    Type: LAYER `<RETURN>`

Response: ?/Make/Set/New/ON/OFF/Color/Ltype/Freeze/Thaw.

    Type: M `<RETURN>`

Response: New current layer.

    Type: FACE3 `<RETURN>`

Response: ?/Make/Set/New/ON/OFF/Color/Ltype/Freeze/Thaw.

    Type: C `<RETURN>`

Response: Color.

Type: 3 <RETURN>

Response: Layer name(s) for color 3 (green) <FACE3>.

Type: <RETURN>

Response: ?/Make/Set/New/ON/OFF/Color/Ltype/Freeze/Thaw.

Type: <RETURN> <Layer, f, h*>

While you're using the **LAYER** command, **FREEZE** all hatching layers. In the exercises these always begin with the letter **H**. You need to do this so that the hatching pattern won't interfere with <**OS-Intersection**>, as it often does; this is one reason to put faces and hatching patterns on separate layers.

Type: LAYER <RETURN>

Response: ?/Make/Set/New/ON/OFF/Color/Ltype/Freeze/Thaw.

Type: F <RETURN>

Response: Layer name(s) to Freeze.

Type: H* <RETURN>

Response: ?/Make/Set/New/ON/OFF/Color/Ltype/Freeze/Thaw.

Type: <RETURN>

Now rotate your object.

Type: DVIEW <RETURN>

Response: Select Objects:

<CROSSING> Select entire object and <RETURN> to confirm.

Type: CAMERA <RETURN>

Response: Enter angle from X-Y plane.

Type: 35 <RETURN>

Response: Enter angle in X-Y plane from X axis.

Type: 160 <RETURN>

Type: <RETURN>

The second <RETURN> confirms the view. This has the effect of rotating the cube to where the straight-line hatch is in front of you and the hex pattern is to your left.

Now let's define a new **UCS**, called **SIDE3**. Using **3POINT** or **ORIGIN, X AXIS, PLANE** pick the points as indicated in Figure 2-14.

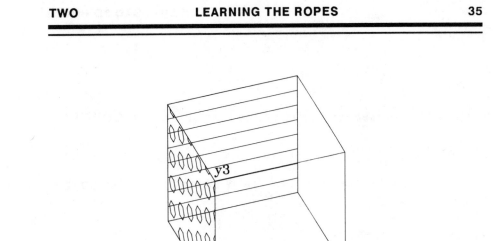

Figure 2-14: UCS 3POINT.

Use < **OS-Intersection** >. The origin point should be **X1**. The positive portion of the **X** axis is **X2** and the positive **Y** portion on the **X,Y** plane is **Y3**.

Now add the **3DFACE**, as illustrated in Figure 2-15.

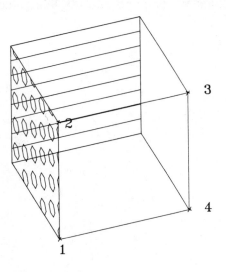

Figure 2-15: Apply 3DFACE.

```
<3DFACE>
```

Use < **OS-Intersection** >. Pick points **1**, **2**, **3** and **4**, then **CONFIRM**.

```
<Layer, t, *>
```

Enter the **LAYER** command and **THAW** all layers. You can do this with the * wild card.

```
<Layer, m, hatch3, c, 3>
```

While using the **LAYER** command, make a new layer called **HATCH3** as **COLOR 3**. You should now be on the **HATCH3** layer.

```
<Hatch, angle, 2, 0, L>
To HATCH the side:
Pattern is ANGLE.
The scale is 2.
The angle is 0.
SELECT OBJECTS is LAST and CONFIRM.
```

When the hatching is complete and the lines hidden, your screen should look like Figure 2-16.

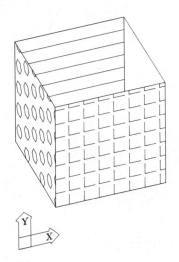

Figure 2-16: Angle hatch 3DFACE.

Rotate your cube one more time.

Type: DVIEW <RETURN>

Response: Select Objects:

<CROSSING> Select entire object and <RETURN> to confirm.

Type: CAMERA <RETURN>

Response: Enter angle from X-Y plane.

Type: 35 <RETURN>

Response: Enter angle in X-Y plane from X axis.

Type: 70 <RETURN>

Type: <RETURN>

The second **<RETURN>** confirms the view.

At this point it's hard to tell which side is which. The optical illusion is at its greatest. **HIDE** your lines to get some idea as to exactly where you are in space.

As you can see, you've simply rotated the view around to the blank side of the cube.

<Layer, m, face4, c, 4>

Make a **LAYER** called **FACE4** as **COLOR 4**.

<Layer, f, h*>
Freeze all HATCH layers by using the H*.
Define a new UCS called SIDE4.
Use 3POINT or ORIGIN, X AXIS, PLANE. Pick the points (Figure 2-17).

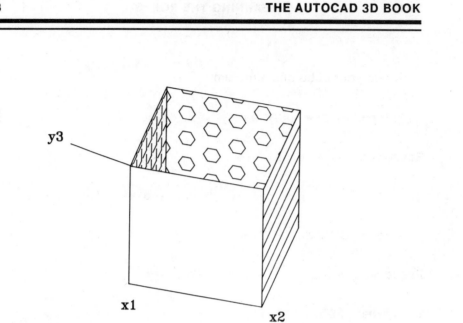

Figure 2-17: UCS 3POINT.

Use **<OS-Intersection>**. The origin point should be **X1**. The positive portion of the **X** axis is **X2** and the positive **Y** portion on the **X,Y** plane is **Y3**.

Add the 3DFACE (as in Figure 2-18).

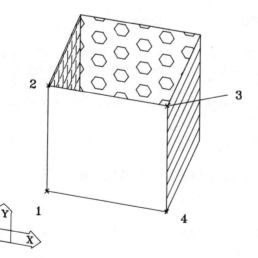

Figure 2-18: Apply 3DFACE.

```
<3DFACE>
```

Use **< OS-Intersection >**. Pick points **1**, **2**, **3** and **4**, then **CONFIRM**.

```
<Layer, t, *>
```

Enter the **LAYER** command and **THAW** all layers. This may be done with the ***** wild card.

```
<Layer, m, hatch4, c, 4>
```

Make a new **LAYER** called **HATCH4** as **COLOR 4**.

```
<Hatch, brick, 3, 0, L>
To HATCH the side:
Pattern is BRICK.
The scale is 3.
The angle is 0.
SELECT OBJECTS is LAST and CONFIRM.
```

Once the lines are hidden, the drawing should look like Figure 2-19.

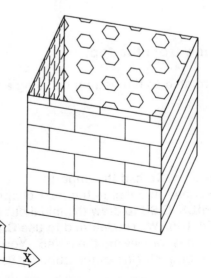

Figure 2-19: Brick hatch 3DFACE.

So far, you've gone around all four sides of the cube. You can insert the top and bottom of the cube the same way by simply rotating the vertical bar and increasing the angle of inclination from **35** degrees to **75** degrees relative to the **WCS**. The left-right rotation angle should be **-75** degrees.

You should produce the illustration found in Figure 2-20. As you can see, after the lines are hidden, you're looking at the top of the box.

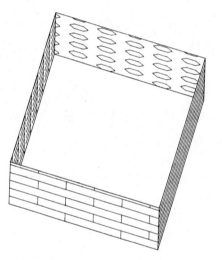

Figure 2-20: View from the top.

The box can be rotated to the bottom by using a negative angle of inclination.

MOVING ON

Through this exercise you've had the opportunity to use several commands that are described in detail in the next chapters. You've used **ELEVATION** and **THICKNESS** to draw the initial cube. The object was rotated into view with **DVIEW**. You learned to use **CAMERA** and **PAN**, only two of many options for viewing the object. You created one type of **UCS** and saved it for each side of the cube by using **3POINT**. You temporarily changed back to **UCS World** and then restored the previous **UCS**. Finally, you added **3DFACES** and hatched the cube's sides.

You should have a basic understanding of a few of the concepts and commands that help you draw in 3D. Now you're ready to learn the details of the most dramatic visual effects in AutoCAD.

3 Dynamic View

One of the most exciting aspects of Release 10 is the dynamic view **(DVIEW)** feature. Unlike the older "bulls-eye" method of viewing a drawing in 3D space, **DVIEW** lets you actually see the object and *dynamically* rotate it in 3D space.

DVIEW's many options let you rotate the drawing precisely to the angle or view that you want to work with and place the target and camera at precisely the correct angles. To maintain a constant reference and relationship to an object in 3D space, you'll need to learn how to use the tools available under **DVIEW**. To understand **DVIEW**'s various options, let's create a simple floor plan and view it from different angles.

SETTING UP YOUR DRAWING

So that you have the same reference point as the illustrations in this chapter, use the following set-up procedure. Create a new drawing using the name you want. Use the following units and limits:

Architectural	4	16th inch
Degrees/minutes/seconds	2	Four units of precision
East	0 degrees	
Angles measured clockwise	No	
Limits are set to lower left-hand corner	0,0	
Upper right-hand corner	144', 96'	

In order to do this:

Type: UNITS <RETURN>

Response: Enter choice, 1 to 5.

Type: 4 <RETURN>

Response: Denominator of smallest fracion to display.

Type: 16 <RETURN>

Response: Systems of angle measure.

Type: 2 <RETURN>

Response: Number of fractional places for display of angles (0 to 8).

Type: 4 <RETURN>

Response: Enter direction for angle 0d0'0".

Type: 0 <RETURN>

Response: Do you want angles measured clockwise?

Type: N <RETURN>

You've now returned to the command line.

Type: LIMITS <RETURN>

Response: ON/OFF/<Lower left corner>.

Type: 0,0 <RETURN>

Response: Upper right corner.

Type: 144', 96' <RETURN>

You've now returned to the command line.

<ZOOM, A>
<GRID, 3'>
<SNAP, 3'>

You should now have **GRID** set to 3' apart with **SNAP** at 3'. Now set **ELEVATION** and **THICKNESS**.

Type: ELEV <RETURN>

Response: New current elevation.

Type: 0 <RETURN>

Response: New current thickness.

Type: 12' <RETURN>

Draw a 45' X 60' rectangle as illustrated in Figure 3-1, using the ordinary **LINE** command. Next, using the **LINE** command, draw three offices, as illustrated in Figure 3-2.

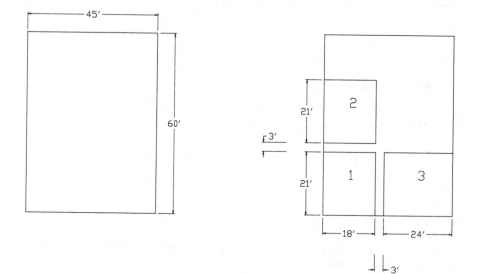

Figure 3-1: Draw office area.   **Figure 3-2: Add offices.**

Office #1	21' X 18'
Office #2	21' X 18'
Office #3	21' X 24'

Each office is separated by a 3' hallway. Don't include dimensions or office numbers in either of these illustrations.

Next, break each room and hallway as illustrated in Figure 3-3, at points **1, 2, 3, 4** and **5**. At points **1** and **2**, when you issue the **BREAK** command, you must first pick the entire line, then type **f** for **first point**. Then pick two points that are 3' apart. If **GRID** and **SNAP** are still set to **3'**, then you'll snap right to the break points. For points **3, 4** and **5**, the beginning break point is **3'** inward from the door, then **1** grid point

(**3'**) away. Thus, each door opening to the hallway and to each of the three rooms is **3'**.

Remember, do not include the numbers in your drawing. Your drawing should look the same as Figure 3-4.

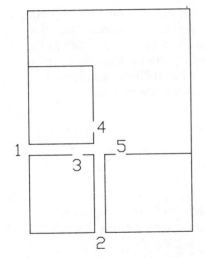

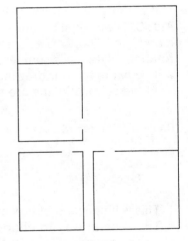

Figure 3-3: Break doors.   **Figure 3-4: Plan view.**

LOOKING AT YOUR DRAWING THROUGH DYNAMIC VIEW (DVIEW)

You can enter **DVIEW** three ways. First, you can:

Type: DVIEW <RETURN>

Response: Select Objects:

<CROSSING> Select entire object and <RETURN> to confirm.

If at this point you simply **<RETURN>** instead of selecting objects, AutoCAD will select its own object. To let you continue with the commands, the AutoCAD selected object is a picture of a house. Whatever rotation, distance, zoom, etc., is performed on the house, the settings will be made to your drawing when you exit the **DVIEW** command.
At the command line are the 12 choices available to you.

CAmera/TArget/Distance/POints/PAn/Zoom/TWist/CLip/Hide/
Off/Undo/<eXit>

Type: CTRL C

This will cancel that command and return you to the command line.
The second way to choose **DVIEW** is to select it from AutoCAD's main screen menu. Pick **DISPLAY**, then pick **DVIEW**.

Response: Select Objects:

<CROSSING> Select entire object and <RETURN> to confirm.

The 12 options are again at the command line. You can also see these options on the screen menu with pick **DVIEW OPTIONS**. Now you can choose any one from the screen menu.

Type: CTRL C

This will cancel and return you to the command line.

The third way is to use pull-down menus. If your screen supports these, move your cursor to the pull-down menu bar and pick **DISPLAY**. Pick **DVIEW OPTIONS**.

You'll now have three options to choose from in the dialogue box. They are **DVIEW CAMERA**, **DVIEW ZOOM** and **DVIEW PAN**. These are three more subcommands of **DVIEW**. Not all of the commands are available through the pull-down menus.

Pick **EXIT**.

Each time you enter **DVIEW**, you'll be given this group of prompts:

Type: DVIEW <RETURN>

Response: Select Objects:

<CROSSING> Select entire object and <RETURN> to confirm.

You should now be in **DVIEW** with the 12 options available to you.

At this point, make sure **SNAP** is **OFF**. You can test this by typing CTRL B one or two times. If **SNAP** is **ON** while you're using **DVIEW**, you won't have total control of the object as you rotate it into view.

Type: CAMERA <RETURN>

Move your cursor to the right until you can move it up and down inside the vertical bar that goes from **-90** to **+90**.

As you slowly move up and down, you'll see the floor plan rotate up and down in front of you. Put the small circle-like bubble on zero (or as close to zero as you can get). Now you're looking straight at the floor plan. Move the pointer to **45** degrees.

You're now at approximately a 45-degree angle, looking down at the floor plan.

Right now, it's difficult to see exactly what the object looks like. If you were to pick now, you'd be taken to the left-right rotation. So that you're using the same degrees used in the illustration in this book, don't pick the cursor at 45 degrees. Instead,

Type: 45 <RETURN>

Notice that the top of the screen shows your angle in the number of degrees.

Now move your cursor left and right, from **-180** degrees to **0** to **+180** degrees. If you move the cursor slowly, the floor plan will start to rotate from left to right. Place your cursor at approximately **45** degrees–about halfway between **0** and **+90** degrees. Instead of picking at this point,

Type: 45 <RETURN>

Now you're still in the **DVIEW** command and all of the options are still available to you. While in the **DVIEW** command,

Type: <HIDE>

This should produce an illustration like Figure 3-5. Notice the **UCS** icon in the lower left-hand portion of your screen. Whenever the **W** appears below the **Y**, the **User Coordinate System** and the **World Coordinate System** are one and the same. Note that from this view you can see where your original **X** and **Y** coordinates were.

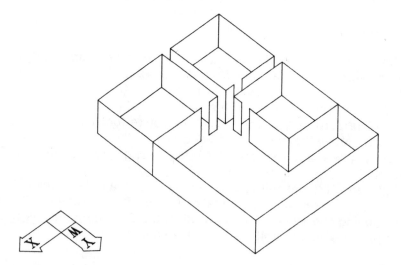

Figure 3-5: View from top (note icon).

Now let's see if you can use **DVIEW** and some of its options.

ROTATING YOUR DRAWING WITH CAMERA (CAMERA)

In each illustration in Chapter Two, you used the **CAMERA** subcommand of **DVIEW**. We're assuming that the object referred to as the "target" by AutoCAD is stationary. The camera moves in a vertical motion above or below the object, and then left and right, rotating around the object. In Figure 3-5, your vertical inclination was **+45** degrees.

Note: In each of the following examples you'll be using a **DVIEW** subcommand. At the beginning of each example, you'll begin as though you were *not* in **DVIEW**, so that you can exit the tutorial and re-enter it whenever you want. If you're doing all the examples in one session, then you can stay in **DVIEW** without reissuing the **DVIEW** command.

Type: DVIEW <RETURN>

Response: Select Objects:

<CROSSING> Select entire object and <RETURN> to confirm.

Type: CAMERA <RETURN>

Response: Enter angle from X-Y plane.

Your vertical inclination was **+45** degrees above the object. To explore the use of vertical inclination, move your cursor to approximately **-45** degrees (notice that the exact angle is displayed at the top of the screen). Move your cursor very slowly, and as you pass **0** on the way down to **-45** degrees, notice how the picture changes.

It's hard to imagine exactly what's happening, because the lines are not constantly being hidden; in a complex drawing, this would be nearly impossible to visualize. Place your cursor at approximately **-45** degrees and pick, or:

Type: -45 <RETURN>

Response: Enter angle in X-Y plane from X axis.

Let's keep the left-right rotation constant (as in the previous example) at **+45** degrees.

Type: 45 <RETURN>

Now you can make the rotation permanent:

Type: <RETURN>

<HIDE>

Notice that once the lines are hidden it becomes obvious that by changing the inclination of the camera from **+45** degrees to **-45** degrees you're now looking at the object from below. Therefore, by using the subcommand **CAMERA** (by changing the angle of the inclination from positive to negative) you're keeping the target still and seeing the object either from above or below.

Many times with complex objects it's hard to know whether you're looking at the object from the top down or from the bottom up. The **UCS** icon provides a solution. If the arrows crisscross at the corner, you're looking from the top down. If the arrows don't cross, you're looking from the bottom up. Notice the difference in the **UCS** icon Figures 3-5 and 3-6.

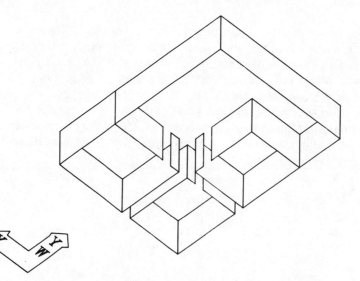

Figure 3-6: View from bottom (note icon).

Now look at the object from another angle:

Type: DVIEW <RETURN>

Response: Select Objects:

<CROSSING> Select entire object and <RETURN> to confirm.

Type: CAMERA <RETURN>

Response: Enter angle from X-Y plane.

Type: 45 <RETURN>

Response: Enter angle in X-Y plane from X axis.

Note that by sliding the bar back and forth, you can rotate the object a full **360** degrees, by going from **-180** degrees on one side to **+180** degrees on the other.

Type: -100 <RETURN>

Type: <RETURN> again to confirm the angle.

<HIDE>

As you can see from Figure 3-7, this gives you a view from a 45-degree angle. You're looking at the object almost as if it were drawn using **WCS** as indicated from the **UCS** icon.

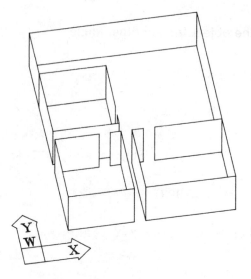

Figure 3-7: View without perspective.

ADDING PERSPECTIVE THROUGH DISTANCE (DISTANCE)

As you can see from Figure 3-7, you've been able to control both the camera angle's inclination and the camera's left-right rotation around the object. This is fine, but as you view the floor plan it's obvious that something just doesn't look right: the perspective is off.

If you could view a real room from a given height or distance, its foreground would appear larger and then the lines on each side of the floor plan would merge together the farther away the object was. Even though the distance between the lines doesn't really change, it's this optical illusion that gives the object a real-life look of depth. This is called *perspective.*

AutoCAD controls **PERSPECTIVE** under **DVIEW** and through the subcommand **DISTANCE**.

Type: DVIEW <RETURN>

Response: Select Objects:

<CROSSING> Select entire object and <RETURN> to confirm.

Type: DISTANCE <RETURN>

Response: New camera/target distance.

Now you're presented with a horizontal bar at the top of the screen. This bar goes from **0x** on the right to **16x** on the left. **1x** is your current distance from camera to target. If you move to **4x**, then the distance from camera to target is increased by a factor of four, etc., on up to **16x**. As you move to a larger number, the distance from camera to target increases, making the object look smaller or farther away. You can also type in a distance at the command line.

Type: 125' <RETURN>

Type: <RETURN>

<HIDE>

The object on your screen should look like Figure 3-8. Note how the wall lines tend to meet, making the lines at the farther end of the drawing look closer together; this gives the drawing true perspective.

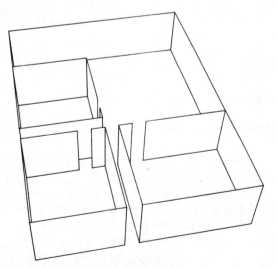

Figure 3-8: View with perspective.

In the bottom left-hand corner of your screen, the **UCS** icon has been replaced with an oblong box. This indicates that **PERSPECTIVE** is **ON**. You can't draw or edit by pointing with **PERSPECTIVE ON**. The perspective is only a view of that particular drawing. When you begin to draw or edit, you can do so as long as you enter coordinates through the keyboard, not by pointing. Pointing and zooming aren't allowed until **PERSPECTIVE** is turned **OFF**.

To save this perspective view of the drawing so that you can view it after editing, use the **VIEW, SAVE** command. After editing, use **VIEW, RESTORE**. This returns you to the saved perspective, complete with any edits.

One final word of caution. The **DISTANCE** command is intended to let you add perspective to a drawing, to give it a realistic depth. Don't use it to simply get closer to the drawing in order to perform closer, detailed work. To do this, use the **ZOOM** subcommand of **DVIEW**.

ZOOMING IN AND OUT (ZOOM)

The **ZOOM** command works differently as a subcommand of **DVIEW** than it does as an ordinary command.

    Type: `DVIEW <RETURN>`

Response: `Select Objects:`

`<CROSSING>  Select entire object and <RETURN> to confirm.`

    Type: `ZOOM <RETURN>`

Response: `Adjust zoom lens.`
                 `or`
                 `Adjust zoom scale factor.`

The bar at the top is the same option bar as in **DISTANCE**. **1x** is the current distance to the object, increasing to **4x**, **9x** and **16x**. You may also type the actual distance to the object at the command line. The information entered at the command line through the keyboard performs two functions, depending on whether **PERSPECTIVE** is **ON** or **OFF**. **PERSPECTIVE** is **ON** if there is a box in the lower left-hand corner of the screen. If the **UCS** icon is present, then **PERSPECTIVE** is **OFF**.

If **PERSPECTIVE** is **ON**, enter a number that corresponds to what AutoCAD calls the camera's "lens length." If you entered 30, this would be a simulation of what you would see through a 35mm camera with a 30mm lens. Increasing the size of the lens has a similar effect to changing to a telephoto lens, thereby increasing the size of the object and bringing it closer to you. Decreasing the size of the lens makes the object seem smaller and puts it farther from the camera.

Figure 3-9 illustrates what might be seen through a 200mm lens.

Figure 3-9: Zoom with 200mm lens.

If **PERSPECTIVE** is **OFF**, **ZOOM** is the equivalent of a **ZOOM, CENTER** command. This lets you **ZOOM** at a factor of the last view. Therefore, each **ZOOM** is measured as a factor times the previous **ZOOM's** view. Thus, if you increased the factor to **2**, then did another **ZOOM** and increased the factor again by **3**, the last view would be **6** times the original **ZOOM**. Practically speaking, it's better to use the sliding bar at the top so that you can see the exact required level of **ZOOM**.

Pick an appropriate zoom level.

Type: <RETURN> to confirm the view.

POSITIONING THE TARGET (TARGET)

AutoCAD considers the object you are drawing — such as a floor plan — as the target. There is a focal point on the target, which is an actual X Y Z coordinate. Imagine now that your camera is at a given distance from the target point; these are the beginning relative positions of the target and camera. But you can change either or both of these, since you already know how to move the camera in relation to the target.

The **TARGET** option works like **CAMERA**, except that the target moves instead of the camera. The camera remains stationary, which has the effect of reversing the positive and negative inclinations.

Under **CAMERA,** if the camera moved to a positive, 45-degree inclination, it would be on top of the object, looking down. If the camera moved to a negative, 45-degree inclination, it would be below the object, looking up.

But if you use **TARGET** and give it a positive, 45-degree inclination, then the target is moved **45** degrees above the camera and the camera is looking up at it from below. If, on the other hand, the target is given a negative, 45-degree inclination, then it is moved below the camera and the angle of view is from the top.

POSITIONING TARGET AND CAMERA (POINTS)

POINTS is a way to position two variables, the camera and the target, in relation to each other. It also has two different effects, depending on whether **PERSPECTIVE** is **ON** or **OFF**.

For this exercise, re-create the view used in Figure 3-5:

Type: DVIEW <RETURN>

Response: Select Objects:

<CROSSING> Select entire object and <RETURN> to confirm.

Response: Enter angle from X Y plane.

   Type: 45 <RETURN>

Response: Enter angle in X Y plane from X axis.

   Type: 45 <RETURN>

   At this point, your drawing may be off the screen. If so, use **ZOOM** and **PAN** to bring the object into view at the center of the screen.
   Assuming that you're still in the **DVIEW** subcommands, let's look at the effect of **POINTS**. First make sure that **PERSPECTIVE** is **OFF**. This can be confirmed by:

<OFF>

   This will turn **PERSPECTIVE OFF** at any time. The oblong box should not appear at the bottom of the screen.

   Type: POINTS <RETURN>

Response: Enter target point.

   The **POINTS** subcommand will ask you to enter a target point, then a camera point. This lets you position yourself anywhere within the object from any angle and elevation. Look at Figure 3-10.

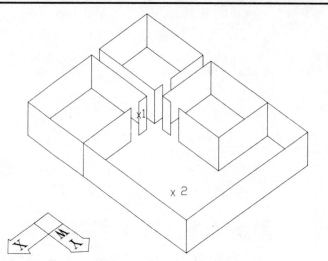

Figure 3-10: Reposition target and camera.

Pick a point at approximately point **1**.

Response: Enter camera point.

To get a position of about six feet elevation (about eye level), use a **FILTER** command. A **FILTER** command lets you pick any two coordinates with the cursor and then key in the third from the keyboard. Access to the **FILTER** commands is **.XY** if the two picked points are **X** and **Y**. **Z** will be requested from the keyboard. If you're picking two other coordinates, precede them with a decimal point.

   Type: .XY <RETURN>

Pick a point at about point 2.

Response: Need Z.

   Type: 6' <RETURN>

   Type: <RETURN>

Refer to Figure 3-11. It's not much to look at, is it? In fact, you could have done the same thing using either the **CAMERA** or **TARGET** subcommands. Save this view so that you can use it later.

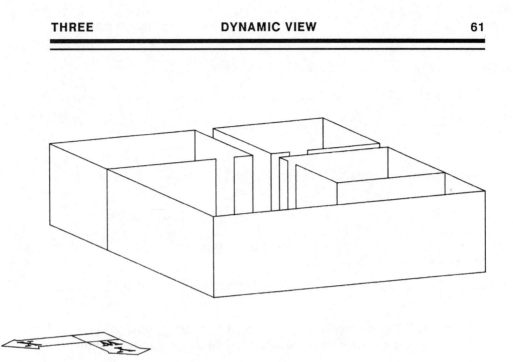

Figure 3-11: With PERSPECTIVE OFF, DISTANCE not changed.

Because **PERSPECTIVE** is **OFF**, only the angle of view is changed. The distance from camera to target remains unchanged; that's why you're still looking at the object from 125'. This is still the distance you set previously.

    Type: VIEW <RETURN>

Response: Delete, Restore, Save, Window.

    Type: S <RETURN>

Response: View name to save.

    Type: V1 <RETURN>

Return now to the view in Figure 3-10. This is the view selected with **< DVIEW, CAMERA, 45, 45 >**.

Now turn **PERSPECTIVE ON**. If you're in the **DVIEW** subcommands,

Type: `<DISTANCE>`

Response: `New camera/target distance.`

Type: `<RETURN> to accept the current distance.`

This will give you the same view, but in perspective. Make sure that **PERSPECTIVE** is **ON**.

`<POINTS>`

PERSPECTIVE is temporarily turned **OFF**. Your current target is already chosen by default and permits a rubberband to the new target point.

Response: `Enter target point.`

Type: `<RETURN>`

You want to keep the same target point as before.

Response: `Enter camera point.`

Again, use the **XY** filter.

Type: `.XY`

Pick a point at about point **2** in Figure 3-10.

Response: `(Need Z).`

Type: `6' <RETURN>`

`<ZOOM>`

ZOOM back and forth until you get your desired perspective. The effect now is quite dramatic, as shown in Figure 3-12. Note that you've placed yourself inside the room at point **2**. The difference between choosing points with **PERSPECTIVE ON** or **OFF** doesn't change the previous distance to the point of the camera and therefore puts you outside the figure, looking at the target point only from the angle indicated by point **2**. With **PERSPECTIVE ON**, the distance is changed to the point of the camera. You're actually placed at point **2** so that you can enter the floor plan. Then you can create dramatic effects, such as walkthroughs.

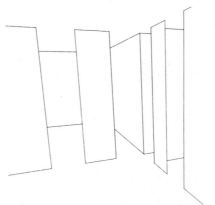

Figure 3-12: PERSPECTIVE ON, DISTANCE changed.

ROTATE THE DRAWING LEFT AND RIGHT (TWIST)

Return to the view that you previously saved.

Type: VIEW <RETURN>

Response: Delete, Restore, Save, Window.

Type: R <RETURN>

Response: View name to restore.

Type: V1 <RETURN>

You should have on your screen a view that resembles Figure 3-11.
The **TWIST** subcommand simply lets you rotate the view.

Type: DVIEW <RETURN>

Response: Select Objects:

<CROSSING> Select entire object and <RETURN> to confirm.

Type: TWIST <RETURN>

Response: New view twist.

Now, using your cursor, tilt the object from left to right. At a rotation
of **26** degrees, you could produce Figure 3-13. Rotate the object back
to **0** degrees and **CONFIRM**.

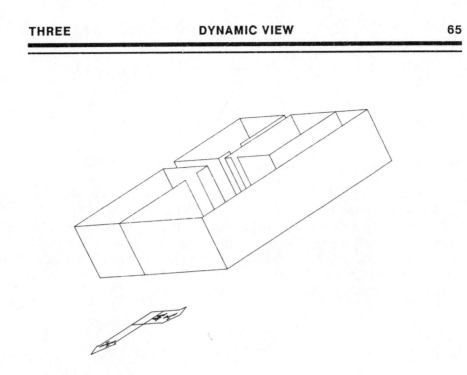

Figure 3-13: Twist the object.

REMOVING THE FRONT AND BACK CLIP

The last **DVIEW** option is **CLIP**, which lets you peel away objects from the front or back, as in Figure 3-11. Of course, if you wanted to get inside the floor plan, an easier way would be to use **POINTS**, with **PERSPECTIVE ON**.

On the other hand, the front wall of the floor plan can simply be peeled away.

> **Type:** DVIEW ‹RETURN›

> **Response:** Select Objects:

> ‹CROSSING› Select entire object and ‹RETURN› to confirm.

> **Type:** CLIP ‹RETURN›

> **Response:** Back/Front/Off.

Type: F <RETURN>

Response: Eye/OFF/ON/distance from target.

   If you choose the **EYE** command, then the front clipping plane is
placed at the camera (this is generally the default).

   By moving the slide bar from left to right, you see part of the front of
the wall begin to disappear. The farther to the right you push the slide bar,
the more the front disappears. Note the image that was created in Figure
3-14. By moving closer to the object and by increasing the clipping plane,
you can move inside the floor plan, as shown in Figure 3-15.

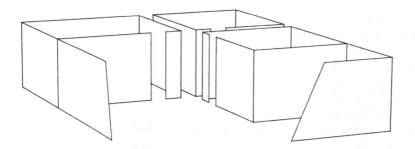

Figure 3-14: Front clipping.

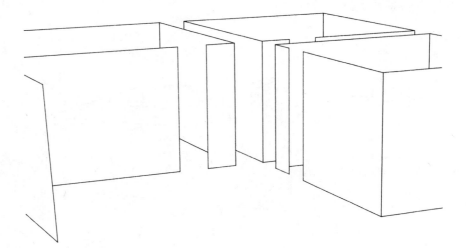

Figure 3-15: A closer look.

Now turn clipping **OFF**.

    Type: CLIP <RETURN>

Response: Back/Front/Off.

    Type: B <RETURN>

By moving the side bar to the left, you can begin stripping away part of the back of the floor plan, as shown in Figure 3-16. You can also **CLIP** both the back and the front one at a time, as in Figure 3-17.

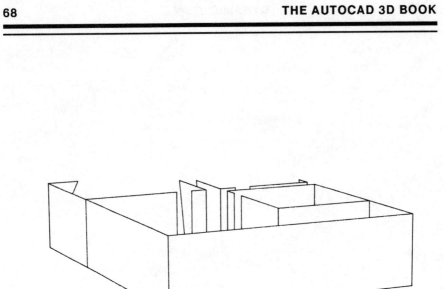

Figure 3-16: Back clipping.

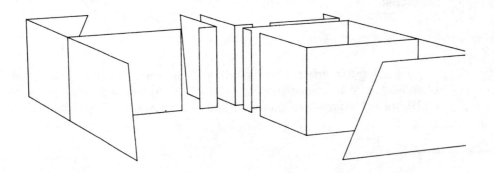

Figure 3-17: Simultaneous front and back clipping.

MISCELLANEOUS POINTS

Often, you won't need to see all of a large, complicated object. AutoCAD lets you rotate *only* the area of the object you want to view. You do this by simply selecting the object with a **WINDOW** or by choosing only those entities you want to view. **CAMERA, TARGET, POINTS,** etc., let you select the angle from which you wish to view. When you **CONFIRM,** the entire object is rotated to the view selected. This also keeps AutoCAD from being burdened with the overhead of the entire object while it executes **DVIEW** commands.

MISCELLANEOUS POINTS

4 AutoCAD's User Coordinate System

Before Release 10, AutoCAD had only one coordinate system, composed of two basic parts: 1) the point of origin, and 2) a series of straight lines relative to each other that formed the **X**, **Y** and **Z** axis at 90-degree angles. Now, the point of origin is in the center. If you're looking down on a piece of graph paper, positive **X** is to the right of the point of origin, positive **Y** is at the top of the paper, and positive **Z** is pointing straight at you.

AutoCAD now calls this basic system the **World Coordinate System (WCS)**. In the **WCS**, any point can be described in terms of **X**, **Y** and **Z**.

Beginning with Release 10, this coordinate system can be redefined, depending on your needs and on drafting problems. Whenever the **WCS** is redefined, it's then called the **User Coordinate System (UCS)**.

AutoCAD not only lets you redefine the **UCS** in a variety of ways, it also lets you save the current **UCS** by name and recall it at any time.

To demonstrate the **UCS**'s many benefits and features, we'll show you how to draw a 3D widget and then revise it from several viewpoints. This should give you a better understanding of the different **UCS** options.

SETTING UP YOUR DRAWING

Begin a new drawing using any name you want.

Type: UNITS <RETURN>

Response: Enter choice, 1 to 5.

Type: 3 <RETURN>

This is an engineering measure, in feet and inches.

Response: Number of digits to right of decimal point (0 to 8).

Type: 4 <RETURN>

Response: Systems of angle measure.

Type: 2 <RETURN>

Response: Number of fractional places for display of angles (0 to 8).

Type: 4 <RETURN>

Response: Enter direction for angle 0d0'0".

Type: 0 <RETURN>

Response: Do you want angles measured clockwise?

Type: N <RETURN>

Now set your limits.

Type: LIMITS <RETURN>

Response: ON/OFF/<Lower left corner>

Type: 0,0 <RETURN>

Response: Upper right corner.

Type: 36,24 <RETURN>

Type: ZOOM a <RETURN>

Type: GRID 1 <RETURN>

Type: SNAP 1 <RETURN>

You should now be using engineering units with degrees, minutes and seconds. Your limits should be set to 36,24. **SNAP** and **GRID** are both set to **1**.

Type: ELEV <RETURN>

Response: New current elevation.

Type: 0 <RETURN>

Response: New current thickness.

Type: .25 <RETURN>

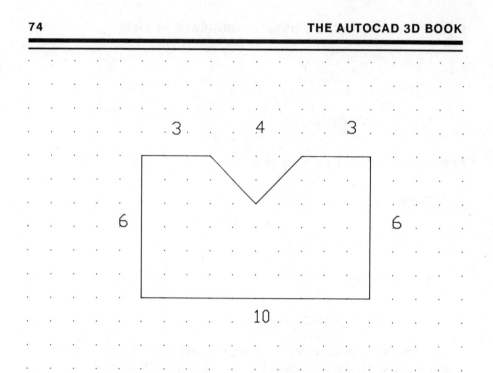

Figure 4-1: Draw object.

Draw the figure shown in Figure 4-1. Don't include the annotated numbers; they're just to help you construct the illustration properly. When the illustration is drawn,

      Type: FILLET <RETURN>

Response: Polyline/Radius/<Select two objects>

      Type: R <RETURN>

Response: Enter fillet radius.

      Type: 2 <RETURN>

      Type: <RETURN>

Response: FILLET Polyline/Radius/<Select two objects>

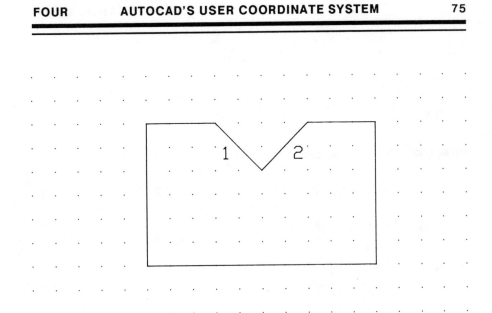

Figure 4-2: Fillet lines 1 and 2.

Pick lines **1** and **2** as shown in Figure 4-2. Your drawing should now look like Figure 4-3. Now look at your drawing using **DVIEW**.

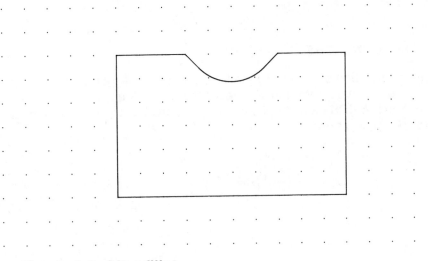

Figure 4-3: After fillet.

\<DVIEW\>

Response: Select Objects:

\<CROSSING\> Select entire object and \<RETURN\> to confirm.

   Type: CAMERA \<RETURN\>

Response: Enter angle from X-Y plane.

   Type: 25 \<RETURN\>

Response: Enter angle in X-Y plane from X axis.

   Type: -25 \<RETURN\>

   Type: \<RETURN\>

POSITIONING THE UCS ICON

Note the position of the **UCS** icon in relation to your object, as shown
in Figure 4-4. Also note that whenever the letter **W** appears below the
letter **Y** in the **UCS** icon, it indicates that the **UCS** is equal to the **World
Coordinate System**.

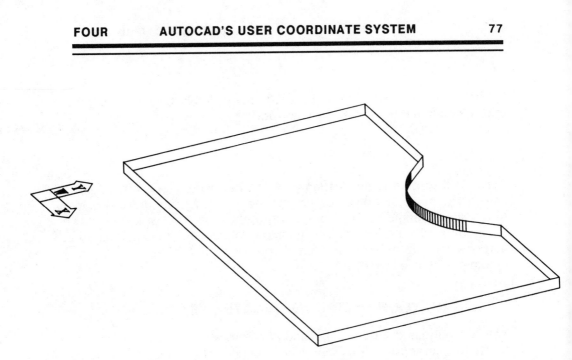

Figure 4-4: DVIEW of object.

It's often useful to attach the **UCS** icon to the object at the point of origin. Use the following command:

Type: UCSICON <RETURN>

Response: All/Noorigin/ORigin/OFF/ON

UCSICON is also a menu item on the screen menu, under **SETTINGS**. The **ON** and **OFF** options let you turn the **UCS** icon on and off at your discretion. The **ALL** option determines whether the **UCS** icon is re-adjusted in all the viewports when more than one screen is available.

Noorigin puts the **UCS** icon in the lower left portion of your screen, where it is now. The **ORigin** option places the **UCS** icon at the point of origin.

Type: A <RETURN>

Response: Noorigin/ORigin/OFF/ON

Nothing will appear to happen. The **A** option simply says that the following command is active for all viewports.

Type: OR <RETURN>

The **ALL** option is *not* a toggle switch. It's simply activated right before you make any other selection. Therefore, if you didn't choose **ALL** before changing **ORigin** or **Noorigin,** then the viewports wouldn't be readjusted automatically. Remember to use the **ALL** command before selecting the other options if you want the **UCS** icon to move automatically in all windows.

CHANGING YOUR USER COORDINATE SYSTEM

You can choose the **UCS** command several ways: through keyboard entry, the screen menu or pull-down menus. First, let's look at the screen menu. Pick **UCS** from the AutoCAD main menu.

Response: Origin/ZAxis/3point/Entity/View/X/Y/Z/Prev/
                 Restore/Save/Del/?

These are the options available to you whenever you choose **UCS**.

Type: CTRL C

This will cancel the command. Next, if pull-down menus are available on your machine, pick **SETTINGS**. Now you have several options:

UCS DIALOGUE
UCS OPTIONS
UCS PREVIOUS

Pick **UCS DIALOGUE.**

You should now have a dialogue box called **MODIFY UCS**.

Pick **DEFINE NEW CURRENT UCS.**

This takes you to a secondary dialogue box, which gives you the various **UCS** options:

```
NEW ORIGIN
NEW ORIGIN Z AXIS
ORIGIN, X AXIS, PLANE
ROTATE ABOUT X AXIS
ROTATE ABOUT Y AXIS
ROTATE ABOUT Z AXIS
ALIGN WITH VIEW
ALIGN WITH ENTITY
```

You also have the option to enter a name at the top of the dialogue box under which the current **UCS** will be saved. If you're not using pull-down menus, then you can save a **UCS** by first creating it, then issuing the **SAVE** option. The dialogue box, on the other hand, wants you to name the **UCS** *before* you choose the options. If you forget to choose a name at this time, you can save the name manually by using the screen menu or keyboard. Pick **CANCEL.**

Response: You're returned to the previous dialogue box.

Pick **CANCEL** again to get out of the dialogue boxes.

Type: UCS <RETURN>

Response: Origin/ZAxis/3point/Entity/View/X/Y/Z/Prev/
Restore/Save/Del/?

Type: O <RETURN>

Response: Origin point.

AutoCAD now asks you to pick a new origin. The **ORIGIN** command lets you change the point of origin at any time. Changing the point of origin doesn't change the relative position of the **X**, **Y** or **Z**.

```
<OS-Intersection>
```

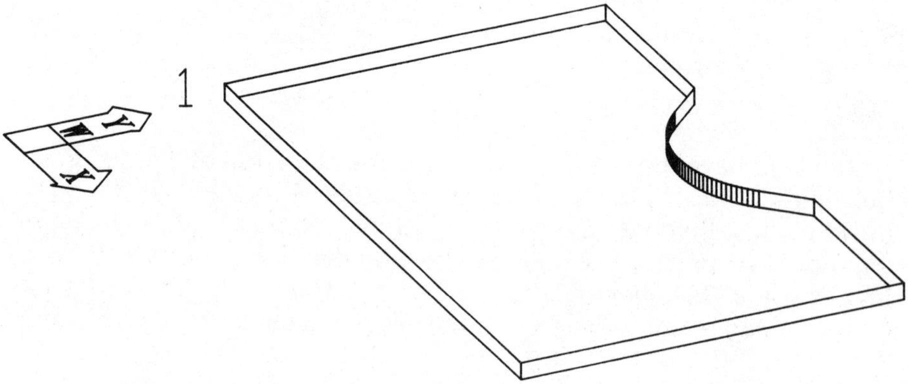

Figure 4-5: Change origin.

Pick point **1**, as shown in Figure 4-5. Note how the **UCS** icon attaches itself to the point of origin of your object. In many situations, you might want to have the **UCS** icon attached at the point of origin in order to get a better orientation of **X-Y**.

POINTING TO THE POSITIVE Z AXIS (ZAxis)

In Figure 4-6, the **X** axis goes to the right and the **Y** axis goes toward the top of the object. Use the right-hand method as discussed in Chapter One, with your fingers pointing out. The **Z** axis is pointing toward the extrusion or the thickness of the object, as though it were pointing toward you while you were looking down at the object.

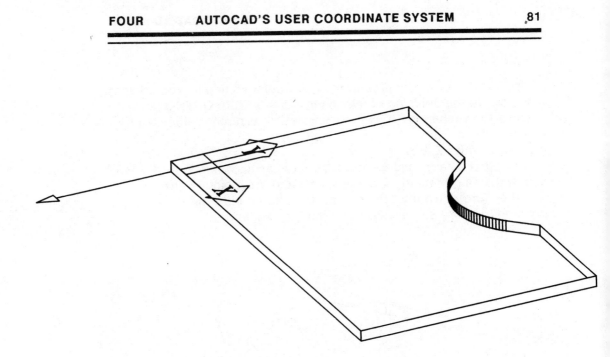

Figure 4-6: UCS ZAxis (positive Z axis).

However, you can redefine the positive direction of the **Z** axis.

    Type: UCS <RETURN>

Response: Origin/ZAxis/3point/Entity/View/X/Y/Z/Prev/
                 Restore/Save/Del/?

    Type: ZA <RETURN>

Response: Origin point <0,0,0>

    Type: <RETURN>

   You want your point of origin to be the same; therefore, **< RETURN >** here.

Response: Point on positive portion of Z axis.

You'll now see a rubberband from the point of origin. You should now point to the direction of the positive **Z** axis. Turn **ORTHO** on.

Move the rubberband toward what would currently be considered negative **Y** (i.e., move it below the object) and pick. This will become the new positive **Z** axis.

Note what's happened to your **UCS** icon, as shown in Figure 4-7. **X** is now pointing to the right of the object and **Y** is pointing straight up. **Z** is therefore down from the object, toward the older negative **Y**. By pointing to a new **Z**, you've caused the **X** and **Y** to rotate.

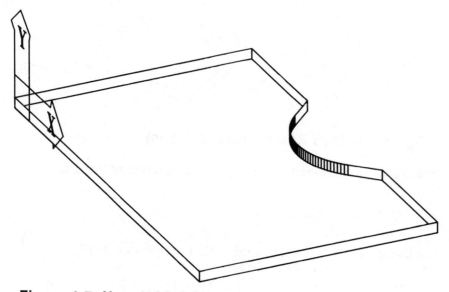

Figure 4-7: Note UCSICON rotation.

Rotating the **UCS** with **Y** pointing up can be very useful. If you wanted to copy the object on top of the original, you now know which way is "up." You simply copy @ distance and < (angle) of 90 degrees, the direction of now positive **Y**.

SAVING YOUR UCS

You can save the current **UCS** in two different ways, depending on whether you're using your screen and keyboard or the pull-down menus. If you're using the dialogue box, enter the name of the **UCS** *before* defining the **UCS**. However, you can save any current **UCS** after the fact. Let's save the current **UCS**.

> **Type:** UCS <RETURN>

> **Response:** Origin/ZAxis/3point/Entity/View/X/Y/Z/Prev/ Restore/Save/Del/?

> **Type:** UCS <RETURN>

> **Response:** ?/Name of UCS name.

If you enter ? **<RETURN>**, all currently saved **UCS**'s are displayed along with coordinate information.

> **Type:** U1 <RETURN>

POINTING TO A NEW X AND Y (3POINT)

The most common **UCS** definition you'll use is **3POINT**. This can be a bit confusing since *The AutoCAD Reference Manual* and the screen menus refer to this option as **3POINT**. But the dialogue box refers to it as **ORIGIN, X AXIS, PLANE**. They're the same thing.

Regardless of what it's called, **3POINT** lets you designate three points: the point of origin, the direction of the positive **X** axis and the direction of the positive **Y** axis.

Now make a copy of the object and place it four inches above the current object. Since you've rotated the **Z** axis, positive **Y** is now pointing above the object.

> **Type:** COPY <RETURN>

> **Response:** Select Objects:

`<CROSSING>` Select entire object and `<RETURN>` to confirm.

Response: Base point or displacement:

    Type: 0,0,0 `<RETURN>`

Turn **ORTHO OFF** and move your cursor around. You'll see that you can move a copy of the object around and above the original. You want to be precise, so use the relative coordinate system for placing the object four inches above the existing object. Because this is the equivalent of moving straight up the **Y** axis,

    Type: @4<90 `<RETURN>`

As you can see, **90** degrees is the normal entry you would use to point straight up in plan view. Since the **X-Y** axis has been rotated, **Y** is now above the object. **90** degrees now points to the new **UCS Y** axis.

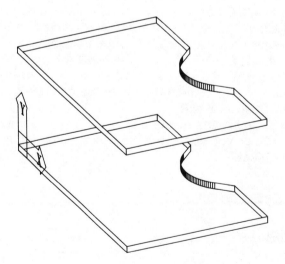

Figure 4-8: Copy in direction of positive Y.

Your drawing should now look like Figure 4-8. Split your screen so that you can view the object from two different angles.

Type: VPORTS <RETURN>

Response: Save/Restore/Delete/Join/Off/?/2/3/4

Type: 2 <RETURN>

Response: Horizontal/Vertical.

Type: V <RETURN>

Pick and make the left window active.

<DVIEW>

Response: Select Objects:

<CROSSING>   Select entire object and <RETURN> to confirm.

Now use **TWIST** to rotate the object **75** degrees.

Type: TW <RETURN>

Response: New view twist.

Type: 75 <RETURN>

Type: <RETURN>   (This makes the view permanent.)

Your drawing should now look like the illustration in Figure 4-9. To help you with your orientation, if you were to rotate Figure 4-9 a quarter-turn clockwise, it would be the same as in Figure 4-8. You would then see that the **UCS** icon is pointing in the same direction.

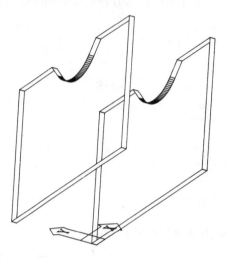

Figure 4-9: Twist object.

Compare Figure 4-9 with Figure 4-8. Look at the left and right view screens: Note that in the right view screen (Figure 4-8), the point of origin is on the bottom object with the **Y** axis pointing to the top object. In the left view screen (Figure 4-9), the object on your right is the bottom object.

Notice that the **Y** axis is pointing to the object on the top. These two screens are looking at the object from the same inclined angle, but you've twisted the rotation **75** degrees.

Just remember that in the screen on the left, the object at the right is on the bottom. It's very important for you to get this visual orientation.

Let's see what happens if you draw a circle with an elevation of **0** and a thickness of **4**, using your current **UCS**.

Type: ELEV <RETURN>

Response: New current elevation.

Type: 0 <RETURN>

Response: New current thickness.

Type: 4 <RETURN>

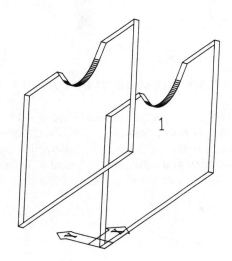

Figure 4-10: Pick center point of circle.

Draw a circle with a small radius, with the center at point **1** on the bottom object as in Figure 4-10.

<Circle, r>

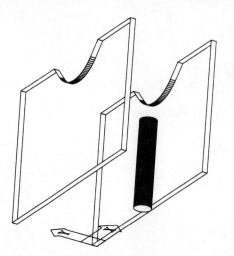

Figure 4-11: Note direction of extrusion (THICKNESS).

Pick point **1** and draw a small radius. Figure 4-11 represents the left
screen and Figure 4-12 represents what you should be viewing in the right
screen. Note the same relative position of the cylindrical bar. You had previously set the elevation at **0** with a thickness of **4**. The cylinder was drawn
from the bottom object and extrudes toward the current **Z** axis.

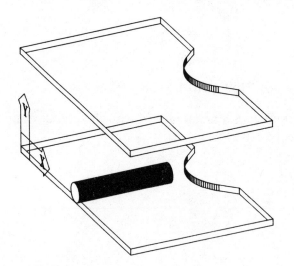

Figure 4-12: Other viewport.

But what if you wanted the cylindrical bar to connect the two objects? You could give AutoCAD enough coordinates to draw the cylinder connecting the bottom object with the top — a difficult task. It's easier to simply redefine the **UCS**.

Before continuing, erase the cylinder you've drawn.

<ERASE, L>

  Type: UCS <RETURN>

Response: Origin/ZAxis/3point/Entity/View/X/Y/Z/Prev/
     Restore/Save/Del/?

  Type: 3 <RETURN>

You'll now change the **UCS**, using the **3POINT** option.

Response: Origin point.

<OS-Intersection>

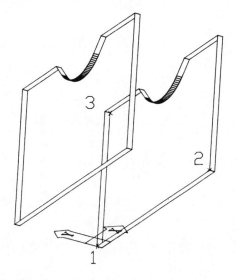

Figure 4-13: UCS 3POINT.

`<OS-Intersection>`

Pick the intersection as indicated by point **1** of Figure 4-13.

Response: `Point on positive portion of the X-Axis.`

`<OS-Intersection>`

Pick the intersection of point **2** as indicated in Figure 4-13. This is the direction of positive **X**.

Response: `Point on positive-Y portion of the UCS X-Y plane.`

Now that the **X** plane has been chosen, AutoCAD wants to know the direction of positive **Y**.

`<OS-Intersection>`

Pick point **3** as indicated in Figure 4-13. Now draw the circle.

`<CIRCLE, R>`

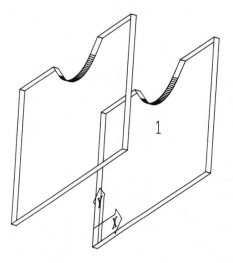

Figure 4-14: Pick center point of circle.

Pick the center point at point 1, as in Figure 4-14, and draw a small radius of not more than 1/8 inch. Note the two views in the left screen (Figure 4-15) and the right screen (Figure 4-16).

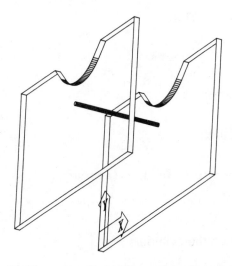

Figure 4-15: Now note direction of extrusion (THICKNESS).

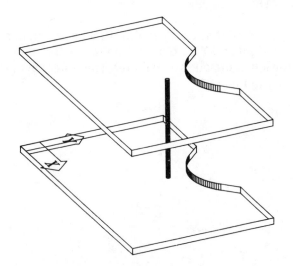

Figure 4-16: Other viewport.

Now copy the cylindrical bar one inch to the left of the current bar.

Type: COPY ⟨RETURN⟩

Response: Select Objects:

Type: L ⟨RETURN⟩

Type: ⟨RETURN⟩

Response: Base point or displacement.

⟨OS-Center⟩

Pick any place on the cylinder.

Response: Second point of displacement.

Type: @l⟨180 ⟨RETURN⟩

Notice in Figure 4-16 that because the **UCS** has been changed, with **X** pointing to the right and **Y** pointing to the top of the object, then **180** degrees is to the left of the current cylinder. The object in the left screen should look like Figure 4-17.

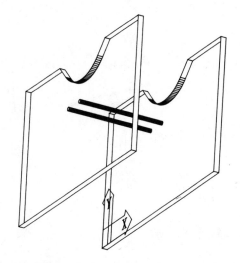

Figure 4-17: Copy cylinder <180.

ROTATING AROUND X, Y AND Z

The last options let you rotate the **UCS** icon around the **X**, **Y** or **Z** axis. Refer to Figure 4-17. If you were to rotate **180** degrees around the **Y** axis, then the current **X** (which is pointing to the right) would flip and point to the left. The **Y** would remain constant and the rotation would be around the **Y** axis. Give it a try.

Type: UCS <RETURN>

Response: Origin/ZAxis/3point/Entity/View/X/Y/Z/Prev/
Restore/Save/Del/?

Type: Y <RETURN>

Response: Rotation angle about Y axis.

Type: 180 <RETURN>

The results are confirmed in Figure 4-18. Note that the **X** arrow is now pointing to the left.

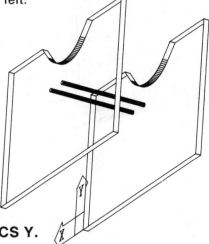

Figure 4-18: UCS Y.

You'll often make mistakes, especially in the beginning when you're just learning to use the **UCS**. And, hard as you try, you'll have a difficult time getting the **UCS** icon to point in the right direction. As you gain experience, this will become easier. But often you'll almost get there only to find that your **X** or **Y** is going in the wrong direction. By using **X**, **Y** or **Z** and rotating **90** or **180** degrees, you can often flip the **X** or the **Y** in the right direction.

Now that **X** is pointing to the left and **Y** remains constant (pointing up), what happened to **Z**? Remember the right-hand rule. Instead of pointing up toward the object on the left, **Z** is now pointing below the object on the bottom, because the orientation of **X** and **Y** have changed. Now rotate **Y** around **X**.

Type: UCS <RETURN>

Response: Origin/ZAxis/3point/Entity/View/X/Y/Z/Prev
/Restore/Save/Del/?

Type: X <RETURN>

Response: Rotation angle about X axis.

Type: 180 <RETURN>

In Figure 4-19, the **Y** axis is now rotated 180 degrees around the **X** axis and is pointing down. Again, where is **Z**? Remembering the right-hand rule, turn the book upside down so that **X** is pointing to the right and **Y** is pointing straight up. Then point your hand with the thumb going in the direction of **X** and the forefinger in the direction of **Y**. The other fingers are the direction of **Z**.

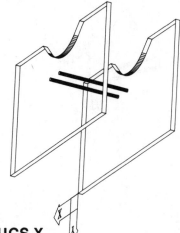

Figure 4-19: UCS X.

Before reading on, see if you can figure out what will happen when you rotate **180** degrees around the **Z** axis.

Type: UCS <RETURN>

Response: Origin/ZAxis/3point/Entity/View/X/Y/Z/Prev/
Restore/Save/Del/?

Type: Z <RETURN>

Response: Rotation angle about Z axis.

Type: 180 <RETURN>

Did you figure it out? Note that in Figure 4-20, you're now back where you started. The **Z** axis remained constant, still pointing toward the object on the upper left. The **X** and **Y** rotated **180** degrees counterclockwise.

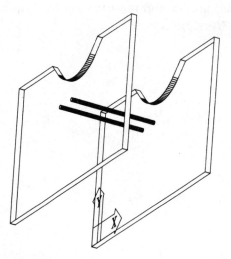

Figure 4-20: UCS Z.

Now let's put a **3DFACE** on the object. You might be tempted at this point to change your **UCS**. Although you can create a new **UCS** at any time, it's not always required. If you'll be snapping to real objects that already have coordinates in 3D space, you don't need to change the **UCS**.

In the following example, you'll use **3DFACE** to connect the intersections of four points.

Type: 3DFACE <RETURN>

Response: First point.

<OS-Intersection>

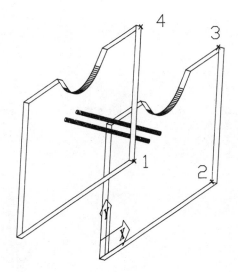

Figure 4-21: Apply 3DFACE.

Pick point 1 on Figure 4-21.

Response: Second point.

<OS-Intersection>

Pick point 2 on Figure 4-21.

Response: Third point.

<OS-Intersection>

Pick point 3 on Figure 4-21.

Response: Fourth point.

<OS-Intersection>

Pick point 4 on Figure 4-21.

Type: <RETURN>

<HIDE>

Note the effect of **3DFACE** as illustrated in Figure 4-22. Before you proceed, **SAVE** this view.

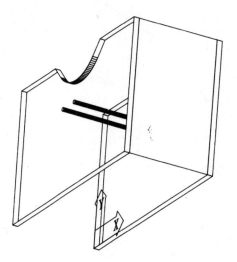

Figure 4-22: Hide lines.

Type: VIEW <RETURN>

Response: ?/Delete/Restore/Save/Window

Type: SAVE <RETURN>

Response: View name to save.

Type: V1 <RETURN>

To get a good view of this object, look at it from the other side:

<DVIEW>

Response: Select Objects:

<CROSSING> Select entire object and <RETURN> to confirm.

Type: PO <RETURN>

Response: Enter target point.

<OS-Intersection>

Pick point 3 in Figure 4-21.

Response: Enter camera point.

<OS-Intersection>

Pick the intersection of one of the back legs of the object. You should be looking at the object from behind. Your view of the object may differ from Figure 4-23, depending on the position of **TARGET** and **CAMERA**.

Figure 4-23: Back view.

Now, save your drawing; you'll use it again in Chapter Six.

    Type: SAVE <RETURN>

Response: File name.

    Type: WIDGET <RETURN>

PLACING TEXT IN THE DRAWING

Text normally goes in the direction of positive **X**. This can be really troublesome, depending on the **UCS** you've defined. Therefore, the best way to use text is to define the **UCS** as **VIEW**.

   The **VIEW** option sets **X** and **Y** parallel to your screen, making the grid look normal. **X** goes to the right and positive **Y** is up, as in plan view. Your text thus comes out flat against the drawing.

Type: UCS <RETURN>

Response: Origin/ZAxis/3point/Entity/View/X/Y/Z/Prev/
Restore/Save/Del/?

Type: V <RETURN>

You may now type your text. The text should appear as in Figure 4-24.

The text
should
appear
normal.

Figure 4-24: Using text.

One word of caution when using the **VIEW** option with text: As you can see from the screen on the right, the text went crazy. The **VIEW** option will only create a **UCS** parallel to your screen. As a result, the text's location relative to the **WCS** and the rest of your object is unpredictable. Therefore, you might want to save a view of the object and put the text on a separate layer so you can turn it off.

MISCELLANEOUS HINTS

Five other options are available with **UCS: ENTITY, PREV RESTORE, SAVE** and **DEL**.

ENTITY lets you line up the **UCS** by selecting an entity. This guarantees that the **X-Y** plane of the new **UCS** is parallel to the **X-Y** plane in effect when the entity was created.

PREV (previous) lets you bring back a **UCS** that was previously defined. As a result, you can temporarily define a **UCS** view and return with **UCS PREVIOUS < RETURN >**. AutoCAD will save ten of these previous definitions so that you can go back through them as needed.

RESTORE lets you restore a previously saved **UCS**. However, be aware that **RESTORE** won't return you to the view that was in effect when the **UCS** was saved. One trick you can use is to save a view using **< VIEW, S >** under the same name as the **< UCS, S >**. That way, you can recall the view at the same time you **RESTORE** the **UCS**.

The **SAVE** option lets you save **UCS** definition so that you can return to it later. The name you choose may be up to 32 characters long and may contain letters, numbers, $, dash (–) and underline (_) symbols. The name can be in upper- or lower case. AutoCAD converts all names to upper case.

DEL (delete) lets you delete one or more saved **UCS** definitions.

Finally, **WORLD** is always the default for any **UCS** command. Any time you enter **UCS** and **< RETURN >**, the **UCS** will be defined as the **WCS**.

VIEWING FROM PLAN

The basic definition of plan view is the view from **Z** looking straight at the **X-Y** plane. But, as you've seen, the **X-Y** plane can be redefined by the **UCS**. Therefore, if you issue the **PLAN** command, you can choose **WORLD**, current **UCS** or name the saved **UCS**. Either **UCS** will let you look straight at the newly defined **X-Y** plane.

MOVING ON

UCS will seem a little confusing at first. After working through the examples in this chapter, you should be familiar now with the workings of the **UCS** and how to change it to accommodate any 3D problem that might arise.

The trick of working with **UCS** is to be constantly aware of **Z**'s location. If you ever get confused, hold your right hand out and use the right-hand rule. If things still seem to be going backwards, chances are it's not your **UCS** that's in error, but that the object is turned around. This can often occur if the lines aren't hidden and you think you're looking at the object from a completely different angle. The key to **UCS** is to work with it and keep practicing.

Now let's add a little shape to our models with **3D MESHES**.

5 Surfaces and Meshes

The 3D mesh commands available in AutoCAD Release 10 give you the chance to produce some of the most dramatic visual effects available in 3D. They also let you give shape and body to your drawings and transfer the shape of an object to AutoSHADE for rendering.

First, let's define what we mean by *surface* and *mesh*. If you draw a simple rectangle in 3D space, assuming no thickness, the rectangle is considered to be transparent. That is, the lines simply form the outline of a rectangular object. No lines can be hidden, because there's no surface to the rectangle. On the other hand, you can take the same rectangle and add a **3DFACE**, thus producing a solid surface behind which lines can be hidden. The **3DFACE** command is very useful for flat, rectangular objects. However, once curved surfaces are added to an object, the **3DFACE** command isn't as suitable.

Assume that **3DFACE** was the only surface modeling command available. The problem facing you involves placing a surface on a circular object. You could draw enough **3DFACES** to approximate the fill of the circle. As you reached the outer areas of the circle, you could reduce the size of each **3DFACE** so that when plotted it would come close to the fill of the circle. But as you can see, this would take a long time, and each entity would be a separate **3DFACE**.

A *mesh* lets you easily provide a 3D surface for curved entities, or any entity whose face is a single entity.

WHAT IS A 3D MESH?

A *3D mesh* is a single entity that tries to put multiple **3DFACES** on the surface of an object. It's also a series of lines or cross-grids, consisting of columns and rows. The *AutoCAD User Reference Manual* defines a cross-grid as a matrix of **M** by **N**: **M** and **N** designate columns and rows.

AutoCAD lets you determine the relative spacing (resolution) between grids and lines. Two system variables let you control the resolution of the 3D mesh: **SURFTAB1** and **SURFTAB2**. (*Resolution* is the distance between the columns and rows). AutoCAD has four 3D meshes: **RULESURF**, **TABSURF**, **REVSURF** and **EDGESURF**.

The differences between these types of meshes depend on the types of objects connecting the surfaces. **RULESURF** creates a surface connecting two known objects. **TABSURF** extends a surface in the exact shape of a single object. **REVSURF** creates a surface in the shape of a single object revolving around a center point. **EDGESURF** creates a series of vertices that connect along four sides in the shape and contour of the lines that created the four edges (sides); this may be used with curve-fitted polylines.

The system variable **SURFTAB1** controls the density of any 3D mesh generated by **RULESURF** and **TABSURF**. **REVSURF** and **EDGESURF** are controlled by both **SURFTAB1** and **SURFTAB2** to determine the density. The reason for this is that **RULESURF** and **TABSURF** aren't cross-grids. They're actually single lines forming the mesh from one point to another. However, **REVSURF** and **EDGESURF** create a cross-grid mesh that requires control of the density of the columns and rows.

You'll have to see what density you need; generally, you need a greater density if the objects are more curved than linear. The two system variables may be changed at any time and affect only the next 3D mesh drawn. However, system response slows as the density increases.

RULED SURFACES (RULESURF)

Let's set **LIMITS** to **12** by **9** and **UNITS** to **DECIMAL**. Draw two arcs like those in Figure 5-1.

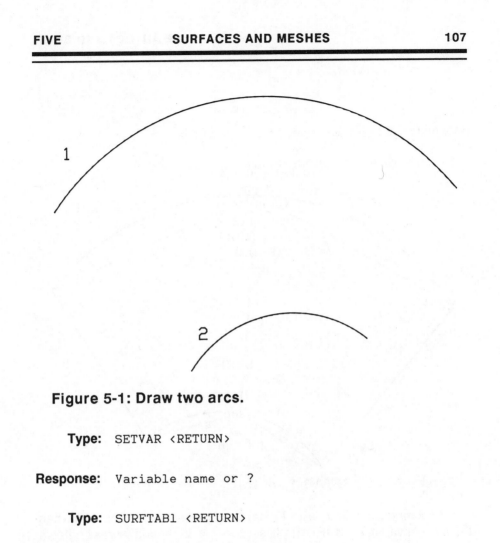

Figure 5-1: Draw two arcs.

Type: SETVAR <RETURN>

Response: Variable name or ?

Type: SURFTAB1 <RETURN>

Response: New value for SURFTAB1.

Type: 2 <RETURN>

RULESURF is one of the simplest of the 3D meshes. It forms a 3D mesh connecting two entities.

Type: RULESURF <RETURN>

Response: Select first defining curve.

Pick the arc at the top at point 1.

Response: Select second defining curve.

Pick the arc at the bottom at point **2**.

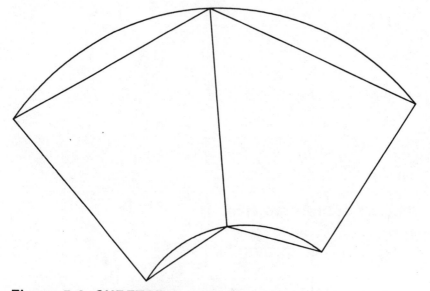

Figure 5-2: SURFTAB 1 set to 2.

It's not much to look at, is it? Figure 5-2 represents what happens when the system variable **SURFTAB1** is set too low. What you've really drawn here are two **3DFACES**. Now set **SURFTAB1** to a better density.

Type: SETVAR <RETURN>

Response: Variable name or ?

Type: SURFTAB1 <RETURN>

Response: New value for SURFTAB1.

Type: 20 <RETURN>

Type: ERASE L <RETURN>

Type: <RETURN>

This erases the 3D mesh just drawn.

Type: RULESURF <RETURN>

Response: Select first defining curve. Pick the arc at the top at point 1.

Response: Select second defining curve, then pick the arc at the bottom at point 2.

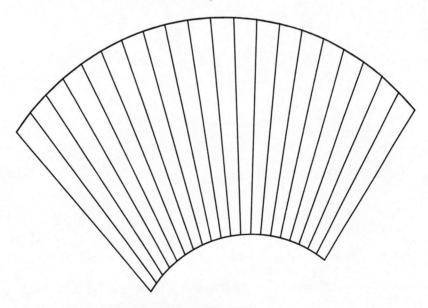

Figure 5-3: SURFTAB 1 set to 20.

Your screen should look like Figure 5-3. Now erase all entities on your screen. Remember that **RULESURF** lets you place a 3D mesh connecting any two entities; but you must have two entities. Instead of using arcs, draw two straight lines as in Figure 5-4. Don't put in the letters.

One of the peculiar aspects of **RULESURF** is that it tries to connect the vertices closest to the end points of the entities selected. Thus, the correct way to do a **RULESURF** on the two entities in Figure 5-4 is to pick a point on the larger line somewhere close to point **B** and on the smaller line close to point **A**. The two points don't actually have to be the end points of the lines. Let's see what happens if you do it the wrong way.

Figure 5-4: Draw two lines.

Type: RULESURF <RETURN>

Response: Select first defining curve.

Pick a point somewhere on the larger line toward point **C**. It needn't be the exact end point.

Response: Select second defining curve.

Pick the smaller line toward the end at point **A**. The result should look like Figure 5-5.

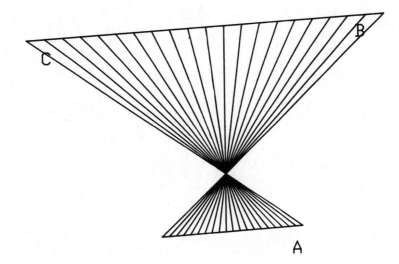

Figure 5-5: Be careful how you pick the points.

```
<ERASE L>
```

This erases the 3D mesh.

Type: `RULESURF <RETURN>`

Response: `Select first defining curve.`

Pick the smaller line toward the end at point **A**.

Response: `Select second defining curve.`

Pick the larger line toward the end at point **B**. This is the proper way to do a **RULESURF**, as shown in Figure 5-6. Now, erase your entire screen.

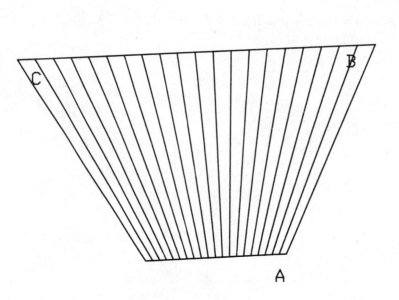

Figure 5-6: The right way.

Remember when using **RULESURF** that the larger the first entity is compared to the second, the closer the lines will merge at the smaller entity. Let's use **DVIEW** to illustrate.

Type: DVIEW <RETURN>

Response: Select Objects.

Type: <RETURN>

Response: CAmera/TArget/DIstance/POints/PAn/Zoom/TWist/
              CLip/Hide/Off/Undo/eXit

Note that because no object was selected, AutoCAD supplies you with the image of a house.

Type: CA <RETURN>

Response: Enter angle from X-Y plane.

Type: 35 <RETURN>

Response: Enter angle in X-Y plane from X axis.

Type: 35 <RETURN>

Type: <RETURN>

Draw a circle at the bottom of the screen and a point at the top of the screen as shown in Figure 5-7. Use the **POINT** command. Now connect the two entities with a **RULESURF**.

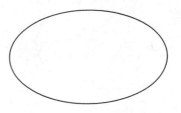

Figure 5-7: Draw a circle and a point.

Type: RULESURF ⟨RETURN⟩

Response: Select first defining curve.

Pick the circle.

Response: Select second defining curve.

Pick the point.

Your drawing should look like Figure 5-8. Notice that once the **RULESURF** is added, the circle seems to be outlined more with straight line segments. This is because of the interval you selected using the system variable **SURFTAB1**. If you increase the variable to **50** from the current setting of **20**, then the 3D mesh will more closely approximate the circle.

Figure 5-8: Connect the point and circle.

Erase your entire screen.

Type: PLAN <RETURN>

Response: Current UCS/UCS/World.

Type: W <RETURN>

This takes you back to the plan view in **WCS**.

TABULATED SURFACES (TABSURF)

Unlike **RULESURF**, **TABSURF** doesn't require or connect to a second entity. **TABSURF** needs only one entity, thus creating a surface extrusion from that entity; but **TABSURF** *does* need a direction vector. This is a second entity somewhere in the drawing that points toward the direction of, and is the same length as, the 3D mesh to be drawn. Remember that the direction vector must be an entity such as a line or polyline.

Type: PLINE <RETURN>

Now draw a series of polylines as in Figure 5-9 and **CONFIRM**.

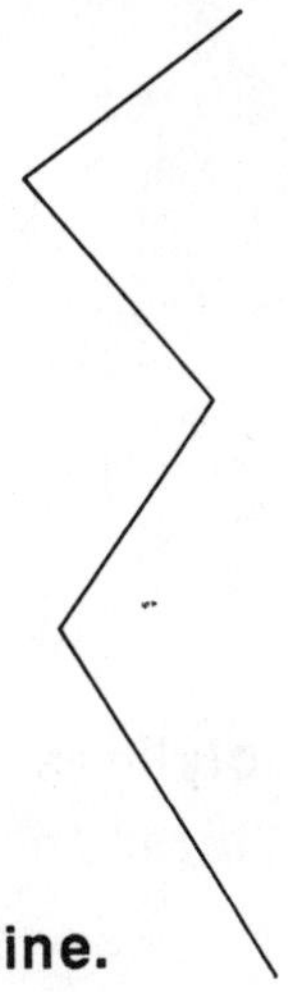

Figure 5-9: Single polyline.

Type: PEDIT <RETURN>

Response: Select polyline.

Type: L <RETURN>

Type: F <RETURN>

This will curve-fit the polyline.

Type: X <RETURN>

This exits from the **PEDIT** commands. Using the regular **LINE** command, draw a line for the direction vector as shown in Figure 5-10.

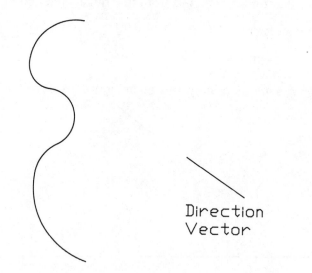

Direction
Vector

Figure 5-10: Curve-fit polylines.

Type: TABSURF <RETURN>

Response: Select path curve.

Pick the curve-fitted polyline.

Response: Select direction vector.

Pick the line drawn as the direction vector, and be sure which side you pick. If you picked the side closer to the left-end point, then the 3D mesh would be drawn to the right of the polyline. However, if you picked the side closer to the right-end point, then the 3D mesh would be drawn to the left of the polyline. The result of the **TABSURF** is shown in Figure 5-11.

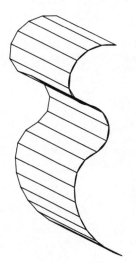

Direction
Vector

Figure 5-11: TABSURF.

SURFACES OF REVOLUTION (REVSURF)

REVSURF is a more complicated 3D mesh because it uses both columns and rows to form a complete matrix cross-grid. The key to using **REVSURF** is to remember that the surface will revolve around a fixed axis similar to a circular (polar) array.

Before proceeding, let's be sure that the second system variable, **SURFTAB2**, is properly set.

Type: SETVAR <RETURN>

Response: Variable name or ?

Type: SURFTAB2 <RETURN>

Response: New value for SURFTAB2.

Type: 20 <RETURN>

Both **SURFTAB1** and **SURFTAB2** are now set at **20**. Let's draw a simple object to demonstrate how **REVSURF** revolves a 3D mesh around a fixed axis.

Figure 5-12: Draw a line and an arc.

Draw an arc and a straight line, as shown in Figure 5-12. During the
REVSURF command you'll be asked for the path curve and the axis of
revolution. The path curve is the entity you wish to revolve around the
axis. The axis of revolution is the center point around which the entity
will revolve. In our case, it's the straight line.

Type: REVSURF <RETURN>

Response: Select path curve.

Pick the arc.

Response: Select axis of revolution.

Pick the straight line.

Response: Start angle <0>

You can now supply the angle at which the 3D mesh will begin. The
default is **0**. If you're going to do a full circle, it doesn't matter what you
put here.

Type: ¿ <RETURN>

Response: Included angle (+=ccw, -=cw) <Full circle>

You can now specify how many degrees around the axis the 3D mesh
will revolve. If you **<RETURN>**, the default is **Full circle**.

Type: 280 <RETURN>

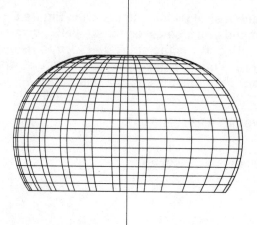

Figure 5-13: 280 degrees around the axis.

For this example, you'll draw the 3D mesh only **280** degrees around the axis so that you can see exactly what's happening. Your screen should look like Figure 5-13.

```
<DVIEW, CAMERA, 35, 20>
```

From the current view, you can't tell exactly what's happening. But by changing the view using **DVIEW**, you get a different point of view, as shown in Figure 5-14.

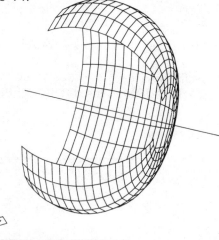

Figure 5-14: DVIEW of REVSURF.

Figure 5-14 is shown here with hidden lines. Be aware that hiding lines can take some time, depending on the speed of your computer.

As you can see, the 3D mesh revolved around the selected axis by **280** degrees. Also, it matters where you pick the axis of revolution. Look at Figures 5-15, 5-16 and 5-17. Each end of the line representing the axis of revolution is labeled **A** or **B**. In Figure 5-16, the axis of revolution was picked toward letter **A**.

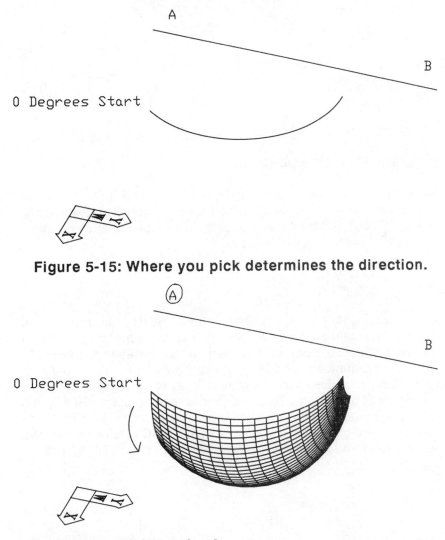

Figure 5-15: Where you pick determines the direction.

Figure 5-16: Pick a point A.

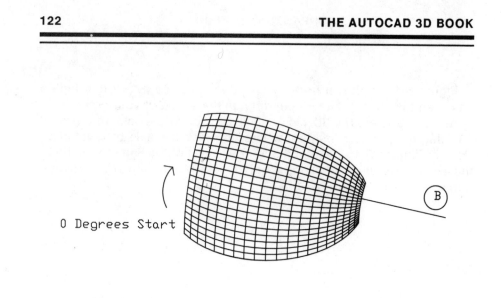

0 Degrees Start

Figure 5-17: Pick a point B.

Remember that it doesn't actually have to be the end point. In Figure 5-17, the axis of revolution was picked toward letter **B**. Note that the direction in which the 3D mesh proceeds to generate change depends on which end of the axis was chosen.

SPECIAL MODELS

You can draw nice-looking patterns with **REVSURF**, but don't forget that one of the main purposes of meshes is to fit a surface to an object for 3D modeling. These objects can then be transferred to AutoSHADE.

In many illustrations for 3D, you see bowls, glasses, goblets or teapots. But you're rarely shown what it takes to draw them.

Drawing a goblet, for example, is a simple series of steps. First, using **PLINE**, draw Figure 5-18. The curved area is a simple polyline that's been curved using **SPLINE**. If you have an AutoCAD version earlier than Release 9, you'll need to provide more points and use **FIT CURVE**.

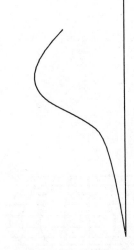

Figure 5-18: How to draw a goblet.

The straight line represents the axis of revolution around which the 3D mesh will revolve and will later be erased.
Once the figure is drawn,

    Type: REVSURF <RETURN>

Response: Select path curve.

    Pick the curved object.

Response: Select axis of revolution.

    Pick the straight line.

Response: Start angle <0>

Type: ‹RETURN›

Response: Included angle (+=ccw, -=cw) ‹Full circle›

Type: ‹RETURN›

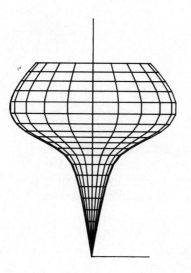

Figure 5-19: Add the base.

When your drawing looks like Figure 5-19, draw a short straight line at the bottom. You'll now use this straight line as the rotated object.

Type: REVSURF ‹RETURN›

Response: Select path curve.

Pick the small straight line you just drew.

Response: Select axis of revolution.

Pick the larger straight line at the top of the goblet.

Response: `Start angle <0>`

Type: `<RETURN>`

Response: `Included angle (+=ccw, -=cw) <Full circle>`

Type: `<RETURN>`

Now erase the axis line at the top of the goblet. **DVIEW** lets you rotate and tilt the goblet to get a view that looks like Figure 5-20.

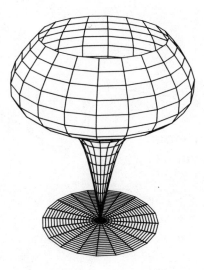

Figure 5-20: Voila!

EDGE-DEFINED SURFACE PATCHES (EDGESURF)

The last of the major 3D meshes is **EDGESURF**. This lets you draw a Coons surface patch for four adjoining edges. This means that if you have four polylines forming four adjacent edges, you can draw a 3D mesh that will find the appropriate vertices even if the polyline is complex and curved. This is particularly dramatic if you curve-fit sharp-angled polylines before using **EDGESURF**.

Draw a figure similar to Figure 5-21. Your drawing doesn't have to look exactly like the one in the book. In fact, you can make your figure look any way you want, but make sure that you use only four distinct polylines. The letters **A**, **B**, **C** and **D** show the approximate starting points of each polyline.

Once you've drawn Figure 5-21, go back and use **PEDIT** to curve-fit each polyline. This will produce an effect similar to Figure 5-22.

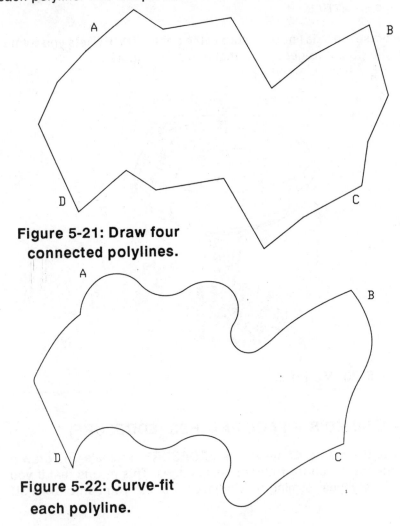

**Figure 5-21: Draw four
connected polylines.**

**Figure 5-22: Curve-fit
each polyline.**

You're now ready to apply **EDGESURF**.

> **Type:** EDGESURF <RETURN>

Response: Select edge 1.

Pick a point along the line at about point **A**. One difficulty is that once the curves have been fitted, it's hard to see where one polyline begins and the other ends. Remember: It's not important that you pick a point exactly at the end point of the polyline. It *is* important that you pick a point consistently close to the beginning of that polyline. You can get ·some very strange results if you pick one polyline at its beginning vertex and another toward its ending vertex.

Response: Select edge 2.

Pick a point at about point **B**.

Response: Select edge 3.

Pick a point at about point **C**.

Response: Select edge 4.

Pick a point at about point **D**. This should now produce the 3D mesh as in Figure 5-23.

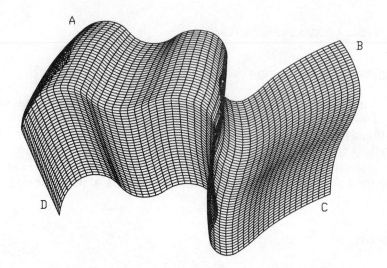

Figure 5-23: Apply EDGESURF.

You may encounter two problems using **EDGESURF**. If you have **SURFTAB1** and **SURFTAB2** set too low, your 3D mesh will not be dense enough to give you the image you need. As a result, the 3D mesh may not be accurate. The second problem occurs if you're inconsistent about where you pick each edge. Although the order in which the edges are picked doesn't matter, you must pick them all toward one end of the polyline or the other.

GENERAL POLYGON MESHES (3DMESH)

One other command produces a 3D mesh: **3DMESH**. Although the other four commands give you a wide latitude and ease of operation, **3DMESH** gives you total control of the size and density of the mesh and the placement of each vertex.

In normal AutoCAD operations **3DMESH** isn't used. Even drawing simple 3D meshes can be a time-consuming, tedious operation, so **EDGESURF, REVSURF, TABSURF** and **RULESURF** should be your usual choices. **3DMESH** is mainly used in AutoLISP programs to construct specific 3D meshes.

When you issue the **3DMESH** command, you're asked for the size of **M** and **N**. Remember that these control the density (space between the mesh lines). The total number of vertices to be specified will equal **M** x **N**. AutoCAD then asks for the 2D or 3D coordinates for each vertex.

As you can see, 3D meshes aren't hard to construct, as long as you learn the rules for the four major commands and know when to use each one. It will take a little practice, but you'll soon be able to apply a surface to any entity.

6 Putting It All Together

So far, you've learned a lot about the different commands that help orient you with 3D space and how to work with 3D objects. This chapter not only gives you the tools for drawing and editing in 3D, but shows you how each of these commands works together in 3D and 2D drafting and design problems.

Let's look now at the most important command, regardless of your discipline, for increasing your productivity in Release 10.

VIEWING YOUR DRAWING WITH WINDOWS (VPORTS)

Beginning with Release 10, you can now create up to four windows, called *viewports*, using the command **VPORTS**.

The productive application of **VPORTS** is limited only by your imagination and needs. But this invaluable tool has two distinct general uses.

First, let's look at a basic 2D application. Even if you never view a thing in 3D, this application makes Release 10 worthwhile. Next to plotting, **ZOOM** is the biggest productivity killer in AutoCAD. Unless you have a high-speed display list processing graphics board, you know what it's like to wait for a **ZOOM ALL**. When you're in the middle of your drawing and need to **ZOOM** to another part of the drawing to continue a command, you know what it's like when AutoCAD tells you you're too deep to use transparent **ZOOM**.

Now with multiple **VPORTS**, you can set one up with a **ZOOM EXTENTS** and the other three with areas of the drawing and various levels of zooms. You can begin a command in one **VPORT** and continue the command in any of the other **VPORTS**. You can restore various views to any **VPORT** and have an unlimited number of whole **VPORT** configurations, which can be saved and restored. With proper organization, you can almost eliminate **ZOOM ALL**'s.

The second major use of **VPORTS** is with 3D modeling. The last thing you want to do is continuously rotate the object as you work on it. This can be a problem as you're drawing from one side of the object to another, where the view isn't apparent. Just set up **VPORTS** for each side and **PLAN** view. Now toggle from one **VPORT** to another, even as you're working with your commands.

To illustrate how **VPORTS** work, let's put something in the windows that you've already drawn. Starting from the AutoCAD main menu, we'll edit the drawing (2) that you saved in Chapter Four as **WIDGET**.

You should now have your widget on the screen as it appeared when you saved it in Chapter Four.

From your screen menu, pick **SETTINGS**, then pick **NEXT,** then pick **VPORTS**. The subcommand options are:

```
Save/Restore/Delete/Join/SIngle/?/2/3/4
```

> **Type:** CTRL C

This will cancel the command. If you have pull-down menus, pick **SETTINGS**, then pick **VIEWPORTS**. You're now shown a picture of the possible viewport configurations in a dialogue box. Now you can pick any of the possible configurations. From the dialogue box, pick **EXIT**.

> **Type:** VPORTS <RETURN>

> **Response:** Save/Restore/Delete/Join/SIngle/?/2/3/4

To activate the viewports, choose one of the number options (**2, 3** or **4**). Note what happens with each of these options.

> **Type:** 2 <RETURN>

> **Response:** Horizontal/Vertical.

You can now split your screen into two vertical or horizontal screens of equal size.

Type: V <RETURN>

Your screen should now have two windows.

Type: VPORTS <RETURN>

Response: Save/Restore/Delete/Join/SIngle/?/2/3/4

Type: SI <RETURN>

By choosing **SI** as an option, you restore the view to a single window.

Type: VPORTS <RETURN>

Response: Save/Restore/Delete/Join/SIngle/?/2/3/4

Type: 3 <RETURN>

Response: Horizontal/Vertical/Above/Below/Left/Right

Type: H <RETURN>

By choosing either **HORIZONTAL** or **VERTICAL** after the three view-ports are selected, you divide the screen into three windows of equal size.

Type: VPORTS <RETURN>

Response: Save/Restore/Delete/Join/SIngle/?/2/3/4

Type: SI <RETURN>

This returns you to a single screen.

Type: VPORTS <RETURN>

Response: Save/Restore/Delete/Join/SIngle/?/2/3/4

Type: 3 <RETURN>

Response: Horizontal/Vertical/Above/Below/Left/Right

If you choose **ABOVE**, **BELOW**, **LEFT** or **RIGHT**, the viewports will be divided into one large and two small windows. You can place the large window above, below, to the left or to the right of the two smaller windows.

Type: R <RETURN>

You should now have one large window on the right and two smaller windows on the left.

Type: VPORTS <RETURN>

Response: Save/Restore/Delete/Join/SIngle/?/2/3/4

Type: SI <RETURN>

This returns you to a single window.

Type: VPORTS <RETURN>

Response: Save/Restore/Delete/Join/SIngle/?/2/3/4

Type: 4 <RETURN>

This creates four viewports of equal size.

Type: VPORTS <RETURN>

Response: Save/Restore/Delete/Join/SIngle/?/2/3/4

Type: S <RETURN>

Response: ?/Name for new viewport configuration.

Type: VP1 <RETURN>

SAVE lets you assign a name to the current configuration. When restored, the current view for each window is restored along with the viewport configuration. *Note*: the current view is the one that's active in a particular window when you saved the **VPORTS** configuration. As you'll see, you can have a different view for each **VPORTS** and save the whole configuration.

Type: VPORTS <RETURN>

Response: Save/Restore/Delete/Join/SIngle/?/2/3/4

Type: R <RETURN>

Type: ? <RETURN>

The I.D. numbers may differ on your screen. The following are examples.

Response: Current configuration:
id# 16
corners: 0.5000, 0.0000   1.0000, 0.5000
id# 13
corners: 0.5000, 0.5000   1.0000, 1.0000
id# 14
corners: 0.0000, 0.5000   0.5000, 1.0000
id# 15

```
corners: 0.0000, 0.0000    0.5000, ·0.5000
```

```
Configuration VP1:
0.5000, 0.0000    1.0000, 0.5000
0.5000, 0.5000    1.0000, 1.0000
0.0000, 0.5000    0.5000, 1.0000
0.0000, 0.0000    0.5000, 0.5000
?/Name of viewport configuration to restore
```

Type: VP1 <RETURN>

As you can see, whenever you ask for information about a viewport configuration, you get a lot of it. You're given the identification numbers and screen positions of the active viewports. The positions of the active viewports assume limits of **0,0** for the lower left-hand corner of the screen and an upper right-hand corner limit of **1,1** (see Figure 6-1).

Therefore screen 1 would go from **0,0** to **.5,.5**. Screen 2 would be **0,.5** to **.5,1**. Screen 3 would be **.5,0** to **1,1**. When referring to screen I.D.'s, always list the current active viewport first.

You should now have restored a viewport configuration of four viewports of equal size.

Type: VPORTS <RETURN>

Response: Save/Restore/Delete/Join/SIngle/?/2/3/4

Type: J <RETURN>

Response: Select dominant viewport.

Pick the upper left-hand screen.

Response: Select viewport to join.

Pick the lower left-hand screen.

The **JOIN** subcommand lets you join two adjacent windows into one larger window. You're first asked to choose the dominant viewport and then to select the viewport to merge. The two viewports *must* be adjacent to each other. The object will take on the **VIEW**, **SNAP**, **GRID**, etc., of the dominant viewport.

The **DELETE** subcommand lets you delete a previously saved viewport.

DIVIDING VIEWPORTS

If you create a window while in a window, then the current window will be subdivided if possible. Remember that the maximum number of viewports available to you at any one time is four.

To explore the usefulness of the **VPORTS** command, create three **VPORTS** as shown in Figure 6-1. The object is the same in all three windows. Pick window **1**. The crosshairs should indicate that it is the active window.

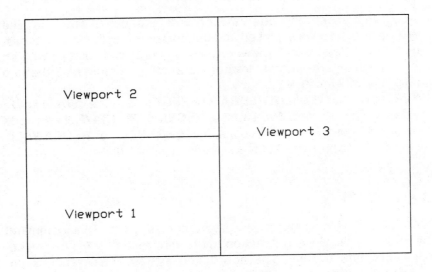

Viewport 2

Viewport 3

Viewport 1

Figure 6-1: Viewports.

Now change the view in this window. Remember that in Chapter Four you saved a view, **V1**.

Type: VIEW <RETURN>

Response: ?/Delete/Restore/Save/Window

Type: RESTORE <RETURN>

Response: View name to restore.

Type: V1 <RETURN>

A new view should now appear in window **1**. Windows **2** and **3** have the same view of the object.

REGEN AND REDRAW WITH VIEWPORTS

As you'll remember, only one viewport can be active at any time. The active viewport is always picked and the cursor is displayed with cross-hairs, while in the inactive viewport(s) the cursor is displayed with an arrow. To change from one viewport to another, simply pick the one you wish to make active.

If you issue the command **REDRAW** or **REGEN,** *only the current active viewport will be affected.* If you want to **REGEN** or **REDRAW** all viewports at once, you need to use the commands **REGENALL** or **REDRAWALL.** Try these on the current windows and see how they differ.

PLAN VIEWS

PLAN sets a plan view for any coordinate system. This command changes only the viewing direction to the viewpoint of **0,0,1** for the active coordinate system. The coordinate system itself remains unchanged. You have three options:

Type: PLAN <RETURN>

Response: Current UCS/UCS/World.

CURRENT UCS generates a plan view for the current **UCS**.

UCS asks you for the name of a previously saved **UCS**. A plan view for that **UCS** is then generated.

WORLD generates a plan view of the **WCS**. Pick and make active window 3. Now set this window to the world plan view.

Type: PLAN <RETURN>

Response: Current UCS/UCS/World.

Type: WORLD <RETURN>

Notice how the object in window **3** is now in world plan view. The important thing to remember about **VPORTS** is that each **VPORT** operates independently of the others. Remember also that **VPORTS** aren't limited to 3D. You can use them at any time to have various 2D zooms or views.

BASIC 3D DRAWING COMMANDS

3DLINE

Even though **3DLINE** is a valid command in AutoCAD, it's really a leftover from earlier versions. For all practical purposes, there's no difference between **3DLINE** and **LINE**.

In earlier versions, the regular **LINE** command wouldn't let you draw using the **Z** coordinate; **3DLINE** was the only such command available then. Beginning with Release 10, you can draw any entities with three coordinates. Therefore, **3DLINE** as a separate command serves no special purpose. Feel free to use **3DLINE** and **LINE** interchangeably.

3D POLYLINE (3DPOLY)

The **3DPOLY** command (which generates a 3D polyline) and **PLINE** are *not* one and the same, so don't confuse them with each other. **PLINE** won't accept a **Z** coordinate across planes. **PLINE**s may be drawn in 3D, but only in one plane.

3DPOLY is a general-purpose 3D polyline. This command will accept coordinates across planes. You may use **3DPOLY** only with straight line segments. Polyarcs aren't supported across planes. **PEDIT** works with both, and B-spline curves are permitted.

To fully understand the difference between **PLINE** and **3DPOLY**, let's use each one and then do a **LIST** on them.

    Type: `PLINE <RETURN>`

Draw one small segment of a polyline without terminating the command.

    Type: `.XY <RETURN>`

and continue the polyline in another direction and pick a point. Terminate the polyline by pressing **<RETURN>**. Notice that AutoCAD didn't ask you for the **Z** coordinate as it would if you'd used the **FILTER** commands.

    Type: `3DPOLY <RETURN>`

Draw one small segment similar to the first line segment previously drawn, without terminating the command.

    Type: `.XY <RETURN>`

and continue the polyline in another direction and pick a point.

Response: `(need Z)`

    Type: `4 <RETURN>`

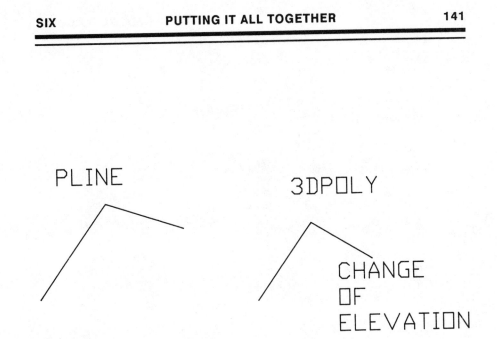

Figure 6-2: 3D Polys are coplanar.

To terminate the polyline, press <**RETURN**>. You should have a drawing similar to Figure 6-2. Now list each polyline group.

      Type: LIST <RETURN>

Response: Select Objects.

    Pick the entity drawn with **PLINE**. Then pick the entity drawn with **3DPOLY** and **CONFIRM**. You'll see that each **PLINE** section maintains a **Z** coordinate of zero. On the other hand, **3DPOLY** has a **Z** coordinate of zero for the two vertices of the first segment, but then changes to a **Z** of **4** in the second segment.

    In brief, this means that **PLINE** polylines can be drawn in 3D, but all vertices must be on the same plane. **3DPOLY** polylines are full-purpose 3D entities whose vertices may cross planes.

    A good visual example of this is Figure 6-3. Note the direction of the **UCS** icon. Remember that the polyline and the **3DPOLY** were drawn visually the same in plan view, but that the second line segment of the **3DPOLY** was drawn four units into **Z**.

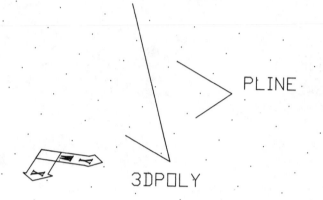

PLINE

3DPOLY

Figure 6-3: Note direction of lines.

The true **3DPOLY** will be of special interest to civil engineers. Now it's not only possible to create 3D visual topos and contours, but true coordinate, area and distance information can be extracted from the database and exact measurements taken from within the drawing.

3DFACE

You've used **3DFACE** extensively in previous chapters. **3DFACE** is used to draw objects that appear to be solid. Unlike the **SOLID** command, **3DFACE** may not be filled or shaded in AutoCAD, but both are used to pass information to AutoSHADE, which performs this function. However, you can **HATCH** a **3DFACE** as you did in Chapter One. Take care to do all hatching on a separate layer, since hatching increases the time necessary to hide lines.

Unlike the **SOLID** command, **3DFACE** is drawn from corner to corner, clockwise or counterclockwise around the object, without the need to draw a "bow tie."

However, remember that **3DFACE** is closed after four points. If you continue, it uses the previous third point as point **1** for the next four.

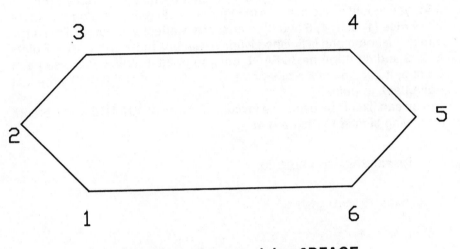

Figure 6-4: Be careful when applying 3DFACE.

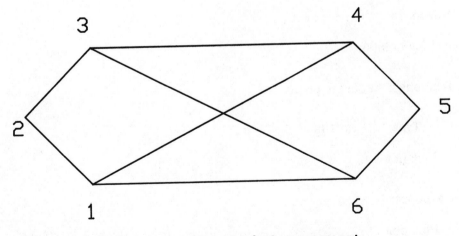

Figure 6-5: You may not get what you expect.

As long as the object is square or rectangular, there's generally no problem applying a **3DFACE**. The problem arises when the object is odd-shaped. For example, if you try to go around the six points (Figure 6-4), you would cross over, as in Figure 6-5. By going around the figure clockwise (**1, 2, 3, 4, 5** and **6**), a crisscross effect is created. That's because the command is finished when it reaches the fourth vertex. Points **1, 2, 3** and **4** return the **3DFACE** back to point **1**. When you resume at point **5**, it uses point **3** as its point **1**. Thus **3, 4, 5** and **6** return the last point back to point **3**.

You can fix this by using the invisible feature of **3DFACE**. Let's create a drawing similar to Figure 6-4.

Type: 3DFACE <RETURN>

Response: First point.

    Pick point 1.

Response: Second point.

    Pick point 2.

Response: Third point.

    Pick point 3.

Response: Fourth point.

Type: I <RETURN>

    Pick point 4.

Response: Third point.

    Pick point 5.

Response: Fourth point.

Type: I <RETURN>

Pick point 6.

Type: <RETURN>

You've now put two **3DFACE**s on the object. But at the points where the lines would have crossed over, they were prefaced with I<**RETURN**>, which stands for "invisible." The lines weren't actually drawn, even though the **3DFACE** was added. It's possible to have all edges invisible. Then the **3DFACE** wouldn't appear at all in the wire frame view, but the items would be hidden behind them. To actually finish out the **3DFACE** on the entire object, you'll still need to go around one more level back to **1**, which will complete points **4, 5, 6** and **1**.

One final thing to note about **3DFACE** is that it can't have thickness. If you assign thickness, it's ignored when a **3DFACE** is drawn.

ELEVATION

This is a predetermined setting for the default of the **Z** coordinate. Therefore, if **ELEVATION** is set to **4** when a line is drawn from **X-Y** point **0,0** to **X-Y** point **3,5**, then the actual coordinates for each point would be **0,0,4** to **3,5,4**.

ELEVATION is set with the command **ELEV**. The responses are:

```
New current elevation     New current thickness
```

Remember that once issued, **ELEVATION** remains in effect until changed.

ELEVATION isn't just the command that precedes **THICKNESS**. Once any **UCS** that redefines the **X Y** plane is set, **ELEVATION** can act as an offset above the plane, instead of resetting your **UCS**.

THICKNESS

Think of **THICKNESS** as adding height to an entity. This "height" or "thick" entity projects toward positive **Z** if **THICKNESS** is a positive number. AutoCAD calls this projection an *extrusion*. Therefore, a line drawn with a **THICKNESS** of **4** is said to *extrude* into the **Z** axis four units.

In AutoCAD's earlier versions, this extrusion was an illusion. You couldn't **OBJECT SNAP** to the extruded portion of the object. Release 10 now allows this, and it's extremely valuable. **THICKNESS** automatically forms a *solid* (surface face) object, similar to **3DFACE** in that it creates a barrier for hidden lines for the extent of the thickness. The outline of the object isn't solid, but the thickness of the *walls* is.

When **TEXT**, **ATTRIBUTES** and **DIMENSIONS** are created, they're always initially given a thickness of **0** regardless of the original settings. Except for **ASSOCIATIVE DIMENSIONING**, the thickness may later be changed through the **CHANGE** command.

THICKNESS is set through **ELEVATION**.

Type: ELEV <RETURN>

Response: New current elevation.
                New current thickness.

FILTERS

The **FILTERS** command was available in earlier versions, but is still very useful. You might call this the "Gimme a Z" concept. Before AutoCAD gave all entities the ability to have a **Z** coordinate in the database, it needed a way to produce the **Z** coordinate for the few entities that could use the coordinate. One of the methods in the earliest 3D version was **ELEVATION**. But **ELEVATION** couldn't be reset as you continued to draw a **3DLINE**. Therefore, the filtering system was used.

The way this works is simple. You start your command with a period (.) and the one or two coordinates where you'll point. For example, when pointing to an **X-Y** coordinate, you type **.XY** and pick a point on the **X-Y** plane. After selecting the **X-Y** point, AutoCAD asks you to enter the **Z** coordinate from the keyboard. If you choose a single coordinate filter (such as **.X**), then after you pick a point, it asks for **Y-Z**. Remember that the current **UCS** affects what is **X** and **Y**; that is, any change in the **UCS** redefines the **X-Y** plane.

Type: LINE <RETURN>

Response: From point.

Pick a point.

Response: To point.

Type: .XY <RETURN>

Response: Of

Pick another point.

Response: (need Z)

Type: 4 <RETURN>

<RETURN>

If you now do a listing of this line, you'll see that the **FROM** point has a **Z** coordinate of zero and the **TO** point has a **Z** coordinate of **4**.

You can also filter any one or two coordinates and supply the third coordinate from the keyboard. You might type **.YZ** and AutoCAD would respond (**NEED X**) after you pick the point.

DIMENSIONING IN 3D:
WHAT YOU SEE IS NOT WHAT YOU GET!

Be careful! There are some obvious problems with dimensioning in 3D. As you might expect with text, it can be hard to predict the exact appearance of the 3D lines and text for an object. Your first inclination might be to simply change to a **UCS VIEW** as you would with text, thus making the **X** axis parallel to the screen. You have one alternative concerning where you want the dimension lines to appear.

The problem with this approach is that the measurements won't be correct and can be off by a great deal, depending upon the angle of view to the object.

Only three available **UCS**'s will guarantee an accurate measurement: **WCS**, **UCS ENTITY** and **UCS 3POINT**, where the entity being dimensioned or measured is parallel to the **X** axis.

If you want to use the **UCS VIEW** approach, first take your measurements using the **DIST** command and write them down. Set your drawing to **UCS VIEW** and proceed to dimension the object. When the

DIMENSION command displays the dimension text, change it to the correct dimension.

There are several things wrong with this method. It can be used only for plotting a specific view of the object. The dimensions should, of course, be saved to a special layer, so that they can be frozen if necessary. If you try to rotate the object using **DVIEW**, there's no telling where the dimensions will be or what they'll look like in the other view. Finally, **ASSOCIATIVE DIMENSIONING** will be worthless to you.

A better way to dimension an object in 3D space is to set the **UCS** parallel to the object with **UCS ENTITY** or **UCS 3POINT**. **UCS ENTITY** is easier, but has its own problems. You can't control which direction is positive **X** or positive **Y**; that was controlled for each entity when it was created. As a result, you might be surprised by the direction of the dimensioning text or dimensioning lines.

The most precise method of dimensioning is to use **UCS 3POINT**. This lets you control the direction of positive **X** and positive **Y**. Remember that your dimensioning text will follow the path of positive **X**, the same as regular text. As you go around each side of the object, you'll need to change the appropriate **UCS**.

You must be very careful using dimensioning. Unless you know the exact dimensions of each side of the drawing, it's hard to be sure of the results. If you're ever in doubt, use the **DIST** command while in **WCS** to take the measurements to check against the dimensions. When you're more comfortable with the proper **UCS**, you must be more confident of your dimension's accuracy.

CAN YOU CORRECTLY DIMENSION WITH PERSPECTIVE?

Yes, if you use some tricks. It's easiest if you set your perspective *before* dimensioning. Then save your view, < **VIEW, S, name of view** >. Now change to your **UCS 3POINT** for the first dimension. It will **REGEN** without perspective. Now dimension the object and **RESTORE** the previously saved view, < **VIEW, R, name of view** >. The restored view will be with **PERSPECTIVE ON**, complete with dimensions ready to be plotted.

EDITING IN 3D

How does editing differ in 3D? Many edit commands now need to take into account the **Z** coordinate; and there are some restrictions.

Some edit commands work better in plan view, **UCS ENTITY** or **UCS VIEW**. The **CHANGE, BREAK, TRIM, EXTEND, FILLET, CHAMFER** and **OFFSET** commands can't work on entities whose extrusion directions aren't parallel to the **Z** axis of the current **UCS**. This sometimes can be corrected by changing the **UCS** to **UCS ENTITY**. Others, like **BREAK, TRIM, EXTEND, FILLET, CHAMFER** and **OFFSET** may give unpredictable results unless you're in plan view of the current **UCS** or **WCS**. For more information on how AutoCAD commands have changed with Release 10, see Chapter Seven, "New Twists to Old Commands."

3D ERROR MESSAGES WHILE EDITING

A couple of error messages can be troublesome when you use some of the above commands, such as **CHANGE** and **BREAK**.

```
Entity not parallel with UCS
```

You get this message when you try to break an entity whose extrusion direction isn't parallel to the **Z** axis of the current **UCS**. You can fix this by defining a new **UCS** using the **ENTITY** subcommand, which will force the **UCS** in the direction of the entity. The entity can be broken, and you can return to the **UCS** you were using by selecting **UCS PREVIOUS**.

```
(2 not parallel with UCS)
```

You'll get this message while trying to use the **CHANGE** command. After telling you how many objects were selected and found, this message tells you how many will *not* be affected by the **CHANGE** command. For these entities, you should probably use the **CHPROP** command, designed specifically for entities in 3D.

CHANGE PROPERTIES WITH CHPROP

The **CHPROP** command performs only four of the **CHANGE** command options: **COLOR, LAYER, LINE TYPE** and **THICKNESS**. The advantage of **CHPROP** over **CHANGE** is that it works with all entities, regardless of their extrusion direction.

HANDLES

The **HANDLES** command lets you turn handles on if they're currently off and destroy all handles in the drawing database. This command will be of primary interest to third-party software developers. The purpose of **HANDLES** is to assign a unique and permanent numeric identifier to every entity in the drawing database. You have only two choices with this command.

ON AND DESTROY

The **ON** subcommand turns **HANDLES ON** if they're not currently activated. This means that every time an entity is created, it's assigned a unique identifier in the database. You can see the **HANDLES** through **LIST** and **DBLIST** or through AutoLISP.

The **DESTROY** subcommand doesn't just turn **HANDLES OFF**; it destroys all existing **HANDLES** in the drawing database. Because this is such a powerful and permanent command, AutoCAD has gone to great lengths to keep you from doing this accidentally. In addition to presenting you with a dire warning, the confirming question isn't answered with a simple Y or N. You must enter a series of randomly selected code words.

I AGREE

UNHANDLE THAT DATABASE

MAKE MY DATA

PRETTY PLEASE

DESTROY HANDLES

GO AHEAD

For more information about entity handles, see *The AutoCAD Database Book* (Ventana Press).

HIDDEN LINES

The **HIDE** command gives you a more realistic view of your drawing. When a drawing is created and viewed in 3D using **DVIEW**, it's displayed in wire frame. If a drawing is complex, it can often be difficult to get a realistic picture of it.

HIDE can take a long time on a complex drawing. Therefore, use **HIDE** only when necessary. Once lines are hidden, they stay hidden until the next regeneration of the drawing.

Hidden lines are treated differently, depending on the type of entity. **CIRCLES**, **SOLIDS**, **TRACES** and wide **POLYLINES** have closed tops and bottoms if they're drawn with **THICKNESS**. Other entities are transparent; you can force hidden lines by adding a **3DFACE** to them.

Text is always drawn and is never hidden. This can cause problems, so text should always be put on its own layer so that it can be **FROZEN** when necessary.

In general, don't turn layers **OFF** or **ON**. Instead, use **FREEZE** and **THAW**. This is particularly true when using **HIDE**. Entities on a layer that's turned off can hide other entities even though they, themselves, are invisible. This isn't true with frozen layers.

Sometimes you'll want an entity to be visible even though it normally would be hidden from view by another entity. You can force this by creating a **HIDDENLAYER** of the same name as the target entity's layer.

For example, assume you want an entity on layer **PRT1** to never be hidden. Create a layer called **HIDDENPRT1** (the layer's name is "HIDDEN," *plus* the name of the target layer). The entities on that layer will then be drawn according to the definition of that layer during the **HIDE** command.

LET'S PULL IT ALL TOGETHER

Let's see how many concepts you can apply in a practical application by drawing a simple object. First, be sure you're starting with a single **VPORT** and a clear screen. Erase everything on your screen or start a new drawing.

Use decimal units and limits of **36,24**. Set **SNAP** and **GRID** to **1**. (Figure 6-15 at the end of this chapter shows how your final drawing should look.)

Divide your screen into two **VPORTS**.

```
<VPORTS, 2, V>
```

Pick and make active the right window. The crosshairs should be visible in the right viewport.

Type: DVIEW ‹RETURN›

Response: Select objects.

Type: ‹RETURN›

Response: CAmera/TArget/Distance/POints/PAn/Zoom/TWist/
CLip/Hide/Off/Undo/eXit

Because you didn't select any objects, the image of a house now appears in the right viewport.

Type: CAMERA ‹RETURN›

Response: Enter angle from X-Y plane.

Type: 45 ‹RETURN›

Response: Enter angle in X-Y plane from X axis.

Type: 45 ‹RETURN›

Type: ‹RETURN›   (This exits you from DVIEW.)

The purpose of splitting the screen and changing the angle of view
in one screen is to let you see the object from a different point in 3D
space as it develops. It also lets you toggle from one screen to the other
in order to construct the object using different views.

Pick the viewport on the left. The crosshairs should now be in the
viewport on the left, indicating that it's now the active screen. Draw a
5 X 8 rectangle, as illustrated in Figure 6-6.

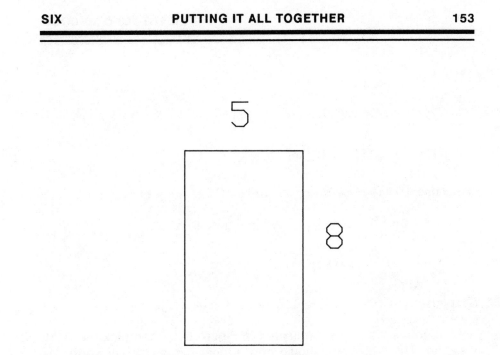

Figure 6-6: Draw rectangle.

`<ZOOM, W>`

You might want to **ZOOM** in on the object to enlarge it on your screen.

Type: `FILLET <RETURN>`

Response: `Polyline/Radius/<Select two objects>`

Type: `RADIUS <RETURN>`

Response: `Enter fillet radius.`

Type: 1.75 <RETURN>

Type: FILLET <RETURN>

Response: Polyline/Radius/<Select two objects>

Pick points **1** and **2** as indicated in Figure 6-7.

Type: FILLET <RETURN>

Response: Polyline/Radius/<Select two objects>

Pick points **3** and **4** as indicated in Figure 6-7. Then pick the right viewport. The crosshairs should now appear in the right viewport, indicating that this is the active screen.

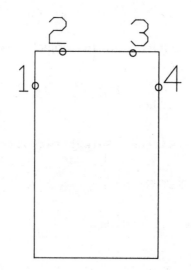

Figure 6-7: Fillet lines.

You'll now create a new **UCS** rotating **90** degrees around the **X** axis.

Type: UCS <RETURN>

Response: Origin/ZAxis/3point/Entity/View/X/Y/Z/Prev/
Restore/Save/Del/?/World

Type: X <RETURN>

Response: Rotation angle about X-axis.

Type: 90 <RETURN>

Now make a copy of the object 18 units above the current object.

Type: COPY <RETURN>

Response: Select object.

Select the entire object and **CONFIRM**.

Response: Basepoint or displacement/Multiple.

<OS-Intersection>

Pick one of the corners of the object.

Response: 2nd point of displacement.

Type: @18<90 <RETURN>

Because the **Y** axis was rotated 90 degrees around the existing **X** axis, a copy of the object was placed directly above the existing object at a distance of 18 units. Now rotate (**TWIST**) your object using **DVIEW**.

Type: DVIEW <RETURN>

Response: Select objects.
               Select both objects.

Response: CAmera/TArget/Disancnce/POints/PAn/Zoom/-
               TWist/CLip/Hide/Off/Undo/eXit

Type: TWIST <RETURN>

Response: New view twist.

Type: 125 <RETURN>

Type: <RETURN>

<ZOOM, W>

Zoom in on the objects to make them larger on the screen.
Connect intersection points **1** and **2** and points **3** and **4** with a regular line. Be sure to set your **OBJECT SNAP** to **INTERSECTION** when connecting these points (Figure 6-8).

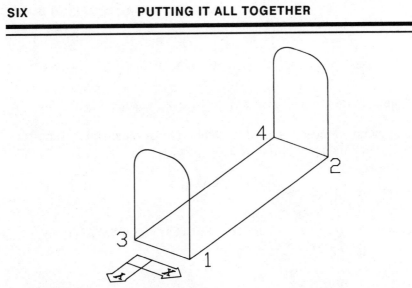

Figure 6-8: Connect objects.

The next step is to turn the five individual entities that made up the initial object (filleted top and sides) and convert them into one polyline.

Type: PEDIT <RETURN>

Response: Select polyline.

Pick a point on the line at approximately point **1** in Figure 6-9.

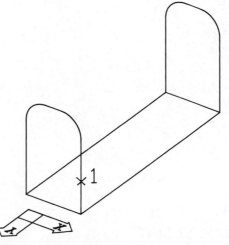

Figure 6-9: Pick object at point 1.

Response: Endpoints have different Z values.

  You have now received one of the editing error messages. To correct the error, you must change the **UCS**.

  Type: UCS ‹RETURN›

Response: Origin/ZAxis/3point/Entity/View/X/Y/Z/Prev/
             Restore/Save/Del/?/World

  Type: 3 ‹RETURN›

Response: Origin point.

‹OS-Intersection›

  Pick the intersection at point **1** in Figure 6-10.

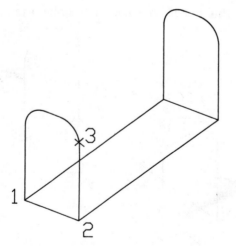

Figure 6-10: UCS 3POINT.

Response: Point on positive portion X-axis.

⟨OS-Intersection⟩

Pick the intersection at point **2** in Figure 6-10.

Response: Point on positive-Y portion of the UCS X-Y plane.

⟨OS-Endpoint⟩

Pick the end point at point **3** in Figure 6-10.

Now you can change the entities into a polyline without error.

   Type: PEDIT ⟨RETURN⟩

Response: Select polyline.

Pick a point at point **1** in Figure 6-9.

Response: Entity selected is not a polyline.
               Do you want to turn it into one?

   Type: Y ⟨RETURN⟩

Response: Close/Join/Width/Edit vertex/Fit curve/
               Spline curve/Decurve/Undo/eXit

   Type: JOIN ⟨RETURN⟩

Response: Select objects.

Pick objects at points **2**, **3**, **4** and **5** in Figure 6-11. **CONFIRM**
selections.

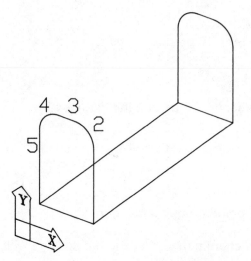

Figure 6-11: Join polyline segments.

Type: ⟨RETURN⟩ (to exit from PEDIT.)

Do the same thing with the entities that make up the object at the other end. Turn the first into a polyline, then join the other four entities so that each of the two ends is now a single polyline entity.

Now, let's put an **EDGESURF** over the object. But first be sure your system variables are correctly set.

Type: SETVAR ⟨RETURN⟩

Response: Variable name or ?

Type: SURFTAB1 ⟨RETURN⟩

Response: New value for SURFTAB1.

Type: 20 ⟨RETURN⟩

Type: SETVAR <RETURN>

Response: Variable name or ?

Type: SURFTAB2 <RETURN>

Response: New value for SURFTAB2.

Type: 20 <RETURN>

Now let's apply the **EDGESURF** mesh. As you'll remember, **EDGESURF** requires exactly four edges. The points you'll pick for each of the four edges are indicated in Figure 6-12. Don't pick the points at the intersections. Pick them on the lines approximately where the numbers are indicated.

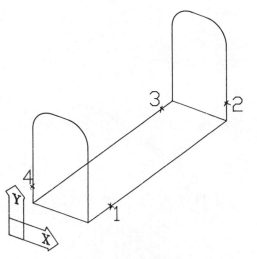

Figure 6-12: Apply EDGESURF at points 1, 2, 3 and 4.

Type: EDGESURF <RETURN>

Response: Select edge 1.

Pick point 1.

Response: Select edge 2.

Pick point 2.

Response: Select edge 3.

Pick point 3.

Response: Select edge 4.

Pick point 4.

Your drawing should now look like Figure 6-13 with hidden lines. Now turn the object so that you can add a **3DFACE** to the bottom.

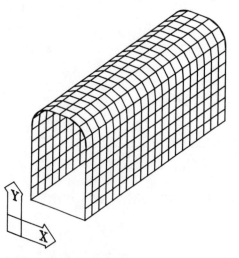

Figure 6-13: Mesh complete.

Before you change your view, save this view in order to return to it when you're finished.

```
<VIEW, S, V1>
```

Type: DVIEW <RETURN>

Response: Select objects.
                 Select the entire object.

Response: CAmera/TArget/Distance/POints/PAn/Zoom/TWist/
                 CLip/Hide/Off/Undo/eXit

Type: CAMERA <RETURN>

Response: Enter angle from X-Y plane.

Type: -30 <RETURN>

Response: Enter angle in X-Y plane from X-axis.

Type: 160 <RETURN>

You'll probably need to **PAN** two or three times to bring the object into full view.

Type: <RETURN> (in order to exit from DVIEW.)

Type: 3DFACE <RETURN>

Using < **OS-Intersection** >, pick each of the four intersections of the bottom of the object. You may need to **ZOOM** in very closely in order to pick the points; you can do this with the transparent zoom, "**ZOOM**. After you've picked your last point, < **RETURN** > one more time to exit.
Return now to your previous view, which you saved as **V1**.

‹VIEW, R, V1›

   Now it's time to add perspective to the object.

     Type: DVIEW ‹RETURN›

 Response: Select objects.
                 Select entire object.

 Response: CAmera/TArget/Distance/POints/PAn/Zoom/TWist/CLip/
                 Hide/Off/Undo/eXit

     Type: DISTANCE ‹RETURN›

 Response: New camera/target distance.

     Type: 50 ‹RETURN›

     Type: ‹RETURN› (to exit from DVIEW.)

   Save this perspective view of the object as **V2**.

‹VIEW, S, V2›

   Let's dimension two sides of the object. To do this, set the **UCS** where the **X** axis is parallel to the side of the object being dimensioned and in the positive direction you want your text.

   If you try to set your **UCS** by pointing, you'll be told that **OBJECT SNAP** isn't allowed in **PERSPECTIVE** view. Therefore, you must turn **PERSPECTIVE OFF** or work in the other **VPORT** when **PERSPECTIVE** is **OFF**. That's why you saved a view of the object, prior to turning **PERSPECTIVE OFF** and changing your **UCS**.

     Type: DVIEW ‹RETURN›

 Response: Select objects.

Type: <RETURN> (Do not select objects.)

Type: OFF <RETURN> <RETURN>

PERSPECTIVE is now **OFF** and you can change your **UCS**.

Type: UCS <RETURN>

Response: Origin/ZAxis/3point/Entity/View/X/Y/Z/Prev/
Restore/Save/del/?/World

Type: 3POINT <RETURN>

Response: Origin point.

<OS-Intersection>

Pick the intersection at point **1** in Figure 6-14.

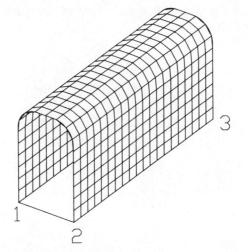

Figure 6-14: UCS 3POINT.

Response: Point on positive portion of the X axis.

`<OS-Intersection>`

Pick point **2** in Figure 6-14.

Response: Point on positive-Y portion of the UCS X-Y plane.

`<OS-Intersection>`

Pick point **3** in Figure 6-14.

At this point, **UCS** is lined up where the dimension text and lines will be, parallel to the current **X** axis. Now, dimension from points **1** to **2**, then again from points **2** to **3**.

To give your drawing a more realistic look, restore the view with the perspective that you saved.

`<VIEW, R, V2>`

Depending on how you've set your dimension variables, your figure should look like Figure 6-15.

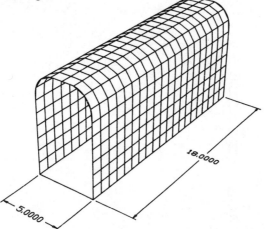

Figure 6-15: With perspective and dimensions.

MOVING ON

This simple exercise has shown you how many of the tools work together. Naturally it would be too cumbersome to design a project that would use all the concepts, but it's surprising to see just how many were necessary even with this simple design.

Each tool, each concept you've learned has a specific purpose. Go back and study this exercise at least one more time or until you're sure you know why each command was chosen to perform a specific task in constructing the model.

Remember, though, there isn't just one way to do things. See if you can find other ways to draw the object. When you're working on your own construction solutions, don't be afraid to experiment. With practice, you'll begin to see what works, and — perhaps as important — what doesn't.

7 New Twists to Old Commands

Most of AutoCAD's Release 10 features were created to support 3D. While it's true that many of these new features, such as **UCS**, **VPORTS** and **3D MESHES** can be used in 2D plan view, the major emphasis is on 3D.

But more has changed in Release 10 than the addition of features that support a 3D database. Many of the commands that you've become so comfortable with have changed. Often, these changes are so subtle you might not even consider them features. There has been a small enhancement here, a little twist there, but nothing really earth-shattering when taken individually. In whole, however, Release 10 is one of AutoCAD's biggest revisions to date.

Let's look at the changes that have occurred to many of the tried-and-true old commands. If you don't understand how they differ now, you not only will be missing out on many of the new features and enhancements of Release 10, but you'll be making assumptions that are no longer true.

In this chapter, you'll examine many changes to existing commands, and you'll be introduced to some new commands. As you've seen, many of the editing commands have changed dramatically (see Chapter Four). Those aren't discussed here unless there are additional features which we haven't presented yet.

By reading this chapter, you'll begin to understand the full benefits that Release 10 has to offer.

GENERAL CHANGES TO MOST COMMANDS

Three major changes have affected most commands. Because these changes are so universal, it's easier to consider them as a group and point out exceptions, where they might occur.

1. Almost all entities now include a **Z** coordinate in the database. Because your input device is 2D, the **Z** coordinate always defaults to the current set elevation relative to the current **UCS**. You can override it through explicit coordinate input or by using the **FILTER** commands (such as **.XY**), followed by the input of the **Z** coordinate.

   Most of the existing commands let you input a 3D or 2D point when input is requested. A few commands, such as **PAN**, use only a 2D point and simply ignore the **Z**. **ARC**, **CIRCLE**, **TEXT**, **PLINE**, **ATTRIBUTE DEFINITIONS**, **SOLIDS** and **TRACES** accept 3D points for their initial point only. The **Z** then becomes the default. This effectively prohibits you from crossing planes. However, **3DFACE**, **3DPOLY** and **3D MESHES** accept 3D coordinates for all points input.

2. Almost everything is now relative to the current **UCS**. There are a few exceptions; we'll point them out as they occur. This doesn't mean just the direction of **X** and **Y**, but angles as well. For example, **0** degrees will always be the positive direction of **X**, and **90** degrees the positive direction of **Y**, assuming a counterclockwise rotation.

3. Many of the editing commands now have major restrictions on the extrusion direction and performing these commands in plan view. See Chapter Four for a full explanation of these restrictions.

CONVERTING POINTS AND ANGLES TO WCS

As before, you can enter points from the keyboard as absolute coordinates such as **5,7,9**, or relative to the preceding point such as **@4 < 90**. If entered in this way, they're coordinates in the current **UCS**.

You can enter absolute and relative coordinates in relation to the **WCS** by preceding the input with a *. For example, ***5,7,9** would place the point at those coordinates in the **WCS**, not the **UCS**. **@*4 < 90** would cause the angular directions to be measured **90** degrees from **0** degrees (the direction of positive **X** unless changed) in the **WCS**.

INDEPENDENT SETTINGS IN EACH VIEWPORT

Each viewport is independent, which means that the settings for **GRID**, **SNAP**, **ORTHO**, **VIEWRES** for fast zooms, and **VIEWS** can be different for each one.

AXIS AND GRID

If you use **AXIS**, it may be displayed only in plan view. **AXIS** isn't available if you're using more than one viewport.

GRID will clearly show only the drawing limits if the current **UCS** is equal to the **WCS**. If the **UCS** isn't equal to the **WCS**, **GRID** encompasses the full screen or viewport.

OBJECT SNAP – THE EXCEPTION

OBJECT SNAP is one command that doesn't recognize the current **UCS**. That's because **OBJECT SNAP** finds the coordinate points of a given entity.

Remember when you drew the cube, one exercise involved drawing a line visibly over another line. By looking at the line from different angles in two viewports, you could see that unless the **UCS** was properly set, you couldn't fully depend on what you were seeing.

In order to make this mistake work, you were advised not to use **OBJECT SNAP** to the intersection. If you had, **OBJECT SNAP** would have properly picked up the coordinates of the intersection and forced you to the correct coordinates, even though your **UCS** wasn't properly set.

SPECIAL CONSIDERATIONS WITH TEXT

Text is an unusual case, and you must follow certain rules. Generally, text is created while you're using the **VIEW** suboption of **UCS** or in plan view to the current **UCS**. These will create a flat area upon which the text may be displayed; so the **UCS** is in the direction of the screen. As with dimensioning, you may also align the text with the entity using **UCS ENTITY** before the text is written.

UCS VIEW is valid only for that particular view and angle. Therefore, if you rotate the angle of view, the text may seem to disappear. *Note:* Place text on a layer of its own so that you can control its visibility. If you want text to label different views of the object, then a different layer might be set up for each group of text.

One other aspect of **TEXT** should be noted. The **HIDE** command will not hide text. If the text were ordinarily hidden, then the object would seem transparent in regard to the text only.

DISTANCE AND AREA

The performance of the **DISTANCE** command hasn't changed. It will accept 3D points and will measure the distance between those points. Instead of simply reporting **Angle**, it reports **Angle in X-Y plane** and **Angle from X-Y plane**. The **Angle in X-Y plane** is what you might normally consider to be the angle. It's relative to the **X** axis. The **Angle from X-Y plane** is the angle of the line as it extends from the **X-Y** plane. Let's say you drew a cube by drawing four lines with a thickness of **4**. If you measured the distance of any of the four original lines you drew, the **Angle in X-Y plane** would be **90** and the **Angle from X-Y plane** would be **0**. If you then measured one of the lines that creates the "height" or thickness, **Angle in X-Y plane** would be **0** and **Angle from X-Y plane** would be **90**.

In addition to giving you the delta of **X** and **Y**, the command now also displays the delta of **Z**.

The **DISTANCE** command computes the real distance in 3D without respect to the current **UCS**.

The **AREA** command works the same way as before, except that before making calculations, it projects the object onto the **X-Y** plane of the current **UCS** and then calculates area and perimeter. It doesn't make the calculations based upon which plane(s) the points may lie.

LOAD LINETYPES ENHANCED

There have been two related enhancements to loading linetypes. You can now use a wild-card specification as you do for **LAYER** in response to the name of the linetype. Also, more than one linetype can be loaded at one time from a file. To illustrate how this works:

Type: LINETYPE <RETURN>

Response: ?/Create/Load/Set

Type: L <RETURN>

Response: Linetype(s) to load.

Type: D* <RETURN>

Response: File to search.

Type: ACAD <RETURN>

Response: Linetype Dashed loaded.
                 Linetype Dot loaded.
                 Linetype Dashdot loaded
                 Linetype Divide loaded

RENAME COMMAND ENHANCED

As before, **RENAME** lets you rename blocks, layers, linetypes, styles and views. **UCS** and **VPORTS** have been added.

SMALL CHANGE IN THE PURGE COMMAND

The **PURGE** command lets you delete unreferenced blocks, layers, linetypes, shapes and styles. Previously, the **PURGE** command would work only if it were the first command you issued after entering the drawing editor. This restriction still applies, but you may now **PURGE** until you've made a change in the drawing database (such as adding or deleting entities). So, for example, you can now **PAN** or **ZOOM** and still be able to use **PURGE**.

DIVIDE AND MEASURE

DIVIDE and **MEASURE** work essentially the same way, but with one exception: The division points were placed on the current elevation; now they're placed on the entity itself.

MISCELLANEOUS CHANGES

FILL ON will do only a solid fill in plan view of the current **UCS**.

HATCH is now available for **3DFACES** and **3DPOLY**. If you do a **HATCH** on an entity that contains a **3D MESH** then the **3D MESH** is ignored. **HATCH** is always drawn at the current elevation.

PEDIT contains new suboptions to edit **3DPOLY** and **3D MESHES**.

STATUS now has information on **UCS**.

3DLINE command is now a useless command. Use the regular **LINE** command instead. The **3DLINE** command is still supported, however.

NEW SYSTEM VARIABLES

Several new system variables have been introduced with Release 10. See Appendix A.

SPECIAL CONSIDERATIONS WHEN PLOTTING

Don't change your **UCS** before plotting; you could go insane trying to position your plot precisely where you want it. When you're working in **DVIEW** and want to plot a specific 3D view, it's difficult to predict exactly where on the paper it's going to plot for anything but **FIT**.

The difficulty seems to arise because the plot sequence converts your plot origin to what it sees as the plot origin in the **WCS**. Thus, even the plot origin of **0,0** might be translated to negative coordinates and throw the drawing off the page.

Let's look at a practical application of this. Assume that you've established two viewports of the same object, viewed from different angles. You want to plot both of these objects side by side, at a given scale. You might think that it's easy to run a sample plot on the active viewport to see where it will line up on the paper. Then you might readjust the plot origin up and to the right, to position the first object correctly. You'd rerun the plot on the same paper and adjust the second object accordingly. This is where you'd run into trouble. No matter what you seem to input, AutoCAD converts this plot origin to the **WCS**. Don't despair; there's an easy fix to this problem. Before plotting, change your current **UCS** to **WCS**. Then run your sample plot to see where it will line up on the paper. You can readjust the plot origin as you've done in the past, and it will work. Because the view doesn't change when you change to **WCS**, **WCS** will plot your desired view. And because the object is already using **WCS**, no conversion is necessary.

3D views of the plots cannot be rotated 90 degrees clockwise using that option. If you need to rotate your drawing, use **DVIEW** before plotting a given view.

Remember that in any AutoCAD release, it does you no good to hide lines and not remove them before you plot. The **HIDE** command for the screen and the hidden line removal option are separate. You can plot with hidden line removal only by choosing that option when you plot. So, unless you need to see on the screen what it's going to look like before you plot, there's no need to hide the lines on the screen.

8 Tips and Tricks

The following is a collection of 3D tips and tricks that have proven to be helpful when using Release 10. It also gives some practical insights into the concepts you've just learned.

Some of these ideas have been described elsewhere in the book, but we think it's helpful to have these tips in one chapter for easy reference.

1. When using **DVIEW**, be sure **SNAP**'s **OFF**. When you choose **CAMERA** or **TARGET** while in **DVIEW**, the horizontal or vertical bar is almost impossible to control if **SNAP**'s **ON**. So press **CTRL B** a couple of times to make sure that **SNAP**'s **OFF**.

2. When you have **PERSPECTIVE ON**, you can't edit, zoom, draw or do many other things you might want to do with the drawing by pointing. Each time you try, you'll get the message, "Pointing in **PERSPECTIVE** view not allowed here." Wouldn't it be nice if you could regen, edit or draw, then return to **PERSPECTIVE ON** exactly as it was before? Well, you can.

   Before you issue any editing or drawing commands in perspective, save the view. After the view is saved, enter **DVIEW**, defaulting with < **RETURN** > when you're asked to select objects. Choose the **OFF** subcommand and exit. **PERSPECTIVE** is now **OFF** and you can draw, edit or zoom as you like.

   After you've completed the edits, restore the view. **PERSPECTIVE** will return with the view and will include any edits that have been made.

   Another way to edit and draw while **PERSPECTIVE** is **ON** is to use the multiple viewports. Have the same view of the object in one viewport with **PERSPECTIVE ON** while another viewport has

PERSPECTIVE OFF. Do your work in the viewport with **PERSPEC-TIVE OFF**. The changes that you make will show up in almost real time, in perspective, in the viewport that has **PERSPECTIVE ON**.

3. You'll find that commands sometimes operate a little differently when **PERSPECTIVE** is **ON** than when it's **OFF**. The **POINTS** sub-command of **DVIEW** is a prime example.

   When changing the position of your **TARGET** and **CAMERA** through the **POINTS** subcommand, you can get some frustrating results. If you expect to be able to position the **CAMERA** at a specific point in relation to the **TARGET**, you might be surprised to find yourself somewhere in 3D outer space. At other times, it may seem to work perfectly well.

   To understand this, be aware that the distance of the **CAMERA** to the **TARGET** is set mainly by the **DISTANCE** subcommand. Therefore, when you issue the **POINTS** command, AutoCAD draws an imaginary line of sight from the **TARGET** to the **CAMERA**, but it doesn't change the distance. Rather, it extends that straight line of sight to the distance already set. This changes your viewing angle to the **TARGET**, but also places you somewhere unexpected.

   Here's the solution. If **PERSPECTIVE** is **ON** when the **POINTS** command is chosen, the distance from the **CAMERA** to the **TAR-GET** is changed to the new point of the **CAMERA**. Therefore, you get the results you probably expected. So, if you want to reposition the **TARGET** and **CAMERA** exactly to the points chosen, be sure that **PERSPECTIVE** is **ON** before you issue the **POINTS** command.

4. Never use **DVIEW DISTANCE** instead of **ZOOM**, or confuse the two. Naturally the **DISTANCE** option of **DVIEW** lets you set the **CAMERA** to **TARGET** distance in order to add **PESPECTIVE**. This may seem a convenient way to **ZOOM** in on the detail, but if you're not careful, you can distort the **PERSPECTIVE** tremendously. If you need to work in detail, use **ZOOM**, not **DISTANCE**.

5. As you know, the **HIDE** command can eat up considerable time, depending on the complexity of your drawing. You'll often need to **HIDE** some lines in order to find out where you are in 3D space; but you usually don't need all the lines hidden. Unfortunately, there's no **HIDE WINDOW** command, but there *are* a couple of tricks that can speed up the process.

First, you need not include the entire object or drawing when you use the **DVIEW** command. You can put a window around only that portion you want to hide. Then use the **HIDE** command, which works as a subcommand of **DVIEW**, rather than the general-purpose **HIDE** command.

Another way is to **ZOOM** in tightly on the object, then issue **HIDE**. Only those lines visible within the **ZOOM** area will be hidden. Of course, you should **FREEZE** any hatching or meshes, since they may take too much time to **HIDE**.

6. Always use **FREEZE** and **THAW** instead of **OFF** and **ON** (which is the normal practice). You *must* observe this when hiding lines. If you use **OFF**, the lines won't be visible but they'll continue to hide anything they normally would have hidden. This can make your drawing look strange as well as eat up a lot of processing time. **FREEZE,** on the other hand, will act as though the layer doesn't exist.

7. You don't need a **UCS** when snapping to real points. The purpose of changing your **UCS** is to give AutoCAD the third coordinate as a default, because your input device, mouse or digitizer can supply only the **X** and **Y** coordinates. Therefore, changing the **UCS** redefines the **X**, **Y** and/or **Z** planes.

If you use **OBJECT SNAP** on a real object in 3D space, AutoCAD knows all three of the coordinates and will use them no matter how you set the **UCS**. You can save time by using **OBJECT SNAP** as much as possible.

8. You can save your **UCS** definition under the name of your choice. Unfortunately, you can't tell AutoCAD to save the angle of view as well. Therefore, when you restore a **UCS** or **UCS PREVIOUS**, it restores only the **UCS**, not the view. And when you restore the view, it doesn't restore the **UCS** that was active with that view.

One way around this is to save the view and the **UCS** at the same time, which requires two operations. You might want to save **UCS** and **VIEW** under the same name, but use the prefix **V** for **VIEW** and **U** for **UCS**. When you restore the view, you're then able to restore the **UCS** that was in effect at the same time.

9. Often, you'll use a subcommand of **DVIEW** but you won't need to actually see the object to execute the command. This might be a

tighter **ZOOM**, turning **PERSPECTIVE ON**, **PAN**ning slightly to the right or keying in the two **CAMERA** or **TARGET** angles.

When this is the case, and you're prompted to select objects in your drawing, don't. Instead, simply **<RETURN>**. AutoCAD will then substitute its simple little house (or whatever drawing you've chosen) in its place. The command will be executed and your drawing will be updated on the screen with the new parameters at the end of the **DVIEW** command.

10. In many cases your drawing can get so crowded with hatching, **3DFACES** and extruded lines that it becomes difficult to **OBJECT SNAP** to an endpoint or intersection. There are two reasons for this. The **VIEW** direction might be close to looking "edge-on" at the object in relation to the current **UCS**. Pointing to locations on the screen can be difficult or impossible. When this occurs, the **UCS** icon changes to a broken pencil.

The solution to the broken pencil is to use **DVIEW CAMERA** and change your vertical inclination by as little as one degree. But another problem may arise with picking with **OBJECT SNAP** if the area is too crowded. There are three possible solutions if that happens. First, try choosing endpoint, but don't put your box directly over the intersection or endpoint itself. Simply touch the entity close to the endpoint. Then AutoCAD isn't confused as to which entity you want.

If that doesn't work, try a transparent zoom (**ZOOM** to get in a little closer to a crowded area). If the above two don't work, **FREEZE** some layers so that the area isn't as crowded.

11. Sometimes, you might want to capture a 3D-view angle of an object and combine it on the same drawing with other 3D-view angles of the same object or of different objects.

First, using **DVIEW**, create the desired view of the object. Next, change **UCS** to **UCS VIEW**, which makes the **X-Y** plane parallel to the screen. Third, **BLOCK** and **WBLOCK** the object. Do this with each of the objects you want to place on the single sheet.

Now start with the sheet on which you want to compile the objects. Insert and place each of the objects where you want it to go. They can be rescaled as you bring them in, or later, using the **SCALE** command.

Note: If you don't change to **UCS VIEW** before the object is blocked, it will be inserted parallel to the current **UCS** of the new sheet and at the correct rotated **DVIEW** viewing angle.

12. If you're not careful, you can run into some serious trouble while dimensioning an object from a 3D view. If you set the **UCS** arbitrarily, then the measurement taken for the dimension may not be correct.

    If you want the dimension to be displayed as the correct distance, align your **UCS** with the entity before dimensioning, using the **UCS ENTITY** or the **UCS 3POINT** command. **UCS ENTITY** might cause a minor problem by adding an extra step, because you can't be sure of the direction of positive **X**. Therefore, you might have to rotate an additional time around **Y**.

    If you use **3POINT**, set positive **X** and the top of the text will run in the direction of positive **Y**.

13. **DVIEW CAMERA** and **TARGET** can be quite unpredictable when using a **UCS**, since the angle of inclination is above the **X Y** plane of the current **UCS**. That may be different from your current view of the object. Remember that the **VIEW** and the **UCS** aren't tied together, so it's entirely possible to look down on the object with a negative inclination.

    The solution to this is simple. Change your **UCS** to **WORLD** before using **DVIEW**. When you exit **DVIEW**, change the UCS back to **UCS PREVIOUS**.

    This is so important that Release 10 comes shipped with a system variable called **WORLDVIEW** set to **1**. This automatically sets you to **UCS WORLD** every time you enter **DVIEW**. When you exit **DVIEW**, you're automatically returned to your previous **UCS**. If **DVIEW** starts acting really strange, check **WORLDVIEW** to make sure it's set to **1**, not **0**. Otherwise, **DVIEW** can drive you absolutely crazy.

    You might want **WORLDVIEW** set to **0** if you want to maintain the point of origin in your current **UCS** during **DVIEW**, to enter absolute coordinates for **CAMERA** and **TARGET** positions as in the **POINTS** subcommand. Otherwise, the point of origin will be changed back to **WORLD** during the **DVIEW** session, with absolute coordinates based on the original **WORLD** point of origin.

14. Sometimes when using the **DVIEW DISTANCE** command, you can move your cursor all the way in both directions of the horizontal bar and not much seems to happen. That means you're too close to the object. Therefore, the distance factor doesn't make much difference.

   The solution is simple. Move your cursor to the far right and pick. Now repeat the **DISTANCE** subcommand. Again, move the cursor to the right and pick. You may have to do this two or three times until you gain control over the object. Each time you move the cursor to the right and pick, you're increasing the distance from the **CAMERA** to the **TARGET** by the indicated factor. After two or three times, the factor is great enough to move in and out with better control.

15. If you've set a **UCS** when you enter the **PLOT** command, you can go mad trying to position your drawing on the page. A simple fix is to set **UCS WORLD** before beginning the **PLOT**. Then change to **UCS PREVIOUS** when you leave the plot.

   You might even want to set up a script file that changes to **UCS WORLD**, plots, and then changes you back to **UCS PREVIOUS**. (An AutoLISP program might be more elegant, but you can't invoke **PLOT** from AutoLISP.)

   To create the script file, use EDLIN or a text editor in the non-document mode:

   Type: EDIT <RETURN>

   Response: File to edit:

   Type: PLOTW.SCR <RETURN>

   Response: New file

   Type: I <RETURN>

   Then type in the following text. Don't type the numbers (they're the EDLIN line numbers).

1. UCS
2. World
3. Plot
4. (Blank line)
5. (Blank line)
6. (Blank line)
7. (Blank line)
8. UCS
9. Previous
10. Control C

Response: *

    Type: E <RETURN>

Don't write on lines 4, 5, 6 and 7. They should be left blank. On line 10, press **CTRL C**. This will break you out of **INSERT** mode and return you to the * prompt.

You've now created the script file. To run it,

    Type: SCRIPT PLOTW <RETURN>

The script file will now change you to **UCS WORLD**, plot, then change you back to **UCS PREVIOUS**.

You can create many useful variations of this routine.

16. There are two basic ways to place **TEXT** in your drawing. Many times, the purpose of **TEXT** is simply to label the drawing from a specific view. If you want the **TEXT** to appear flat against the screen or paper, not at the same angle as the drawing, then change your **UCS** to **UCS VIEW**. Be sure to put the **TEXT** on a separate layer so that it can be frozen.

If you want your **TEXT** to be aligned with some entity in the drawing, use the same technique used with dimensioning in Tip 12.

17. When working with **UCS 3POINT**, you needn't choose the direction of positive **Y** exactly at **90** degrees from the point of origin. You may pick a point for the direction of positive **Y** above the point you picked positive **X** or anywhere in your drawing, even though your rubberband is still from the point of origin. You may even **<RETURN>** and AutoCAD will default positive **Y** as the current plane. It's looking for a coordinate to define the **Y** plane. As a result, you may **OBJECT SNAP** to any object on the desired plane.

18. At times, **EDGESURF** is the appropriate surface mesh to use; but it doesn't have four edges. Use **PEDIT** and turn the line into a **POLYLINE**, if it's not already one. Then **JOIN** or **BREAK** the **POLYLINES** as necessary so you have exactly four edges.

19. Drawing with **THICKNESS** is often fast and convenient. But you'll often want separate entities without extrusions. Drawing these separate lines from scratch in 3D can be a real chore. Instead, draw using **THICKNESS** on a separate layer. Then change layers. Rotate the object using **DVIEW** and begin to trace over the extruded object using **OBJECT SNAP** on the endpoints and intersections.

    Once the object has been replicated, **FREEZE** your current layer and **ERASE** the old extruded entities. Then **THAW** your current layer. What you'll be left with are the separate entities without extrusions, easily drawn in 3D, upon which you can now build.

20. Remember that **TEXT** is never hidden with the **HIDE** command. This can be good and bad. If you want to hide **TEXT**, then you must manipulate the layers to **FREEZE** it. AutoCAD needs a system variable that gives you text hiding choices.

MOVING ON

You've now completed the 3D tutorial section of this book. But as you can imagine, you've only just begun. Now that you know the tools, it's up to you to use them and practice what you've learned. Your reward will be increased efficiency, productivity and creativity.

Section II

RENDERING, AUTOSHADE AND THIRD-PARTY APPLICATIONS

9 CAD Photography Using AutoSHADE

Your journey into three-dimensional design has led you through the wire frame model, which shows corners, edges and surface approximations. This may seem like the ultimate in computer-aided design, but to many of us, 2D CAD was the final stop not too long ago.

When you realize that your documents are created to convey as much information as possible to help construct, manufacture or assemble what you're designing, the wire frame — even with hidden lines removed — isn't a true representation of your design at all.

Yes, we do live in a 3D world, but one with opaque surfaces. The wire frame model has led you to one more stepping stone — and a realism you never thought possible.

In brief, rendering your 3D design involves applying illumination to your drawing, bringing out color shade, shadow detail, texture and pattern. As you might guess, a rendered wire frame design comes to life so that presentations become a true view of what the design will look like when it becomes an object.

Is the rendering process necessary or worth the time? If you want to convey information as accurately as possible, a wire frame might be enough for CAM, FEA or a bill-of-materials software package to provide further engineering or manufacturing information. However, if you want accurate *visualization*, you'll want to explore rendering and modeling.

AUTOSHADE ILLUMINATED

AutoSHADE is produced by Autodesk, Inc., as a separate software package, with hooks within AutoCAD to prepare your wire frame for shading. Once the preparation is completed, you leave AutoCAD and enter AutoSHADE, where the rendering occurs.

AutoSHADE helps you and others to see objects better. Using AutoSHADE is roughly like taking a photograph of an object or group of objects. You'll often want to use AutoSHADE to present your design to someone who might not understand a wire frame. AutoSHADE is great for prospective clients, proposals, shows, marketing and documentation.

It's important to realize that AutoSHADE is a surface modeling program that deals with the activity of light on a surface. It's *not* a solids modeling program that provides information on the mass, inertial properties or rotational properties of an object. AutoSHADE is a visualization tool that reveals nothing about the internal or physical properties of an object. Such tasks are handled by highly complex solids modeling software, such as Autodesk's AutoSOLID, discussed in Chapters Ten and Eleven.

GETTING STARTED

In the following pages, you'll use AutoCAD and AutoSHADE to create a three-dimensional wire frame model that can be shaded and manipulated in a number of ways. You'll learn how to create a variety of visual effects using the commands provided in the AutoSHADE package.

AutoSHADE is a complex program that employs dozens of commands, many of which require a knowledge of light behavior and physical law to fully appreciate. The purpose of the following exercise is to get you using AutoSHADE quickly so that you can begin to experiment with it. You'll soon discover a tantalizingly powerful tool that can place endless variations on your wire frame.

Finally, remember that shading and solids modeling are in their infancy, just as microcomputer-based CAD was five years ago. Autodesk will no doubt make great strides in the near future in adding power and performance to their rendering and modeling packages.

INSTALLING AUTOSHADE

AutoSHADE can be installed in two ways. You can copy the contents of your three AutoSHADE disks into your current drawing subdirectory, or make a subdirectory called **SHADE** and, as the manual suggests, copy AutoLISP routines and special blocks from diskette to your **ACAD** subdirectory, then copy all other files to the **SHADE** subdirectory.

Either way, it's important that 1) blocks such as **CAMERA**, **DIRECT**, **OVERHEAD**, **SHOT** and **CLAPPER** are easily available in your ACAD library search path (i.e., your **ACAD** subdirectory, **SET ACAD** subdirectory or current subdirectory), and 2) the AutoLISP routines, such as **ASHADE.LSP,** are loaded easily at the keyboard or from a menu pick for **ASHADE.**

Your AutoCAD **lispheap** and **lispstack** environment settings should be set in your **AUTOEXEC.BAT** or your **ACAD.BAT** file to **39000** and **6000** respectively. You'll probably also need a batch file to set the environment and execute AutoSHADE from your **c** prompt. An example of such a batch file might be:

```
1    CD\SHADE
2    Mouse
3    SET shadefaceDir = E:\  (optional)
4    SET shadepageDir = E:\  (optional)
5    SET shadefile = 640,480,1,1,256,255,32   (optional)
6    Shade
```

This batch file changes to the **SHADE** subdirectory (line 1), installs your mouse driver (line 2), tells AutoSHADE to use your RAM disk drive **E:** for holding surface faces and triangles during the rendering process for performance considerations (lines 3 and 4), lets you produce a portable hard-copy render file that can be tailored to any device (line 5), then finally runs AutoSHADE (line 6).

You can create this batch file (call it **ASHADE.BAT**) with any text editor (see your AutoSHADE manual for details).

When you configure AutoSHADE, video considerations will be critical. Read the directions in the AutoSHADE manual carefully and make sure you're using your video display card to its fullest.

The drawings you create should be in your current subdirectory when in AutoCAD. Be certain that AutoSHADE is installed as the manual describes in a directory called **SHADE**, with the block drawings, and that **.LSP** files are in your **\ACAD** subdirectory.

CREATING A SHADABLE WIRE FRAME

Let's begin by creating a wire frame that can be shaded easily. This drawing should take 12 to 15 minutes to create. Get into AutoCAD and start a new drawing called **SHADEIT.** Change the **LIMITS** to a value of **UPPER RIGHT 34,22** and **LOWER LEFT 0,0.**

Type: LIMITS

Response: On/Off/<Lower left corner> <.000, 0.000>

   Type: <RETURN>

Response: <Upper right corner> <12,000, 9.000>

   Type: 34,22

Set the **SNAP** to **.25** and **GRID** to **1.0**, then **ZOOM ALL**:

   Type: SNAP .25

   Type: GRID 1.0

   Type: ZOOM A

Now let's draw a small table with objects on it. Turn **FILL OFF**.

   Type: FILL OFF

Let's start by making two short round pillars:

   Type: ELEV

Response: New current elevation <000>.

   Type: <RETURN>

Response: New current thickness 12.

Draw a **CIRCLE** with radius **1.5** and its center at **7,14**.

Type: CIRCLE

Response: 3p/2p/TTR <center point>.

Pick **7,14** and type **1.5**.

COPY the circle to point **7,6**.

Type: COPY

Response: Select objects.

Type: L

<RETURN>

Pick a base point that's the center of the circle, using **OSNAP**. **CENTER** and **DRAG** to point **7,6**. Now change the elevation to **12** and **THICKNESS** to **1.0**.

Type: ELEV

Response: New current elevation <0.000>.

Type: 12.0

Response: New current thickness <12.000>.

Type: 1.0

Now use a **3D SOLID** to create a surface.

Type: SOLID

Type: 2,17

Response: Second point.

Type: 2,2

Response: Third point.

Type: 12,17

Response: Fourth point.

Type: 12,2

Type: < RETURN >.

Response:

Now let's change the table to the color red.

Type: CHPROP

Response: Select objects.

WINDOW your table and press < **RETURN** >.

Type: CO

Response: New Color <Bylayer>.

Type: RED

Type: COLOR BLUE

Now let's draw in the color blue. Change your **ELEVATION** to **13** and **THICKNESS** to **0**.

Type: ELEV 13 0

Pull down your **DRAW** menu and select **3D CONSTRUCTION**. From the icon menu, pick the **CONE**.
Note: If you don't have pull-downs, type **(LOAD "3D")**, then type in the individual names of the entities you need (e.g., **CONE**), or use your screen menu.

Response: Base center point.

Type: 7,10

Response: <Base Radius>/Diameter.

Type: 1.0

Response: <Top Radius>/Diameter <0>.

Type: <RETURN>.

Response: Height of cone.

Type: 2

Response: Number of segments <16>.

Type: 32

Let's put a pyramid on the surface. Pick **PYRAMID** from your icon menu or type in **PYRAMID**. You'll be presented with a first, second and third base point, which you should pick at 4,16; 5,16; 5,15; and 4,15.

Response: Height of Pyramid.

Type: 1.0

Response: Apex point.

Type: 4.5,15.5

Type: COLOR GREEN

Type: WEDGE

Response: Starting point of wedge.

Type: 10,6

Response: Length.

Type: 2.0

Response: Width.

Type: 1.0

Response: Height.

Type: 1.5

Response: Rotation about the Z axis ⟨0⟩.

Type: ⟨RETURN⟩

Now's a good time to experiment with **DVIEW** and **HIDE** to view your table from different perspectives (see Figure 9-1). Next, you'll take a photograph of this model using the AutoSHADE features within AutoCAD.

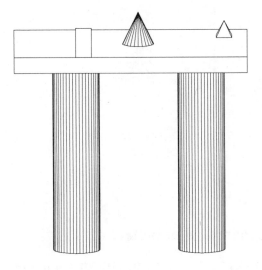

Figure 9-1: AutoCAD drawing of a 3D table.

If you were taking a photograph of this table and the objects on it in real life, you'd be concerned with the placement of your camera and the light sources illuminating your subjects. You'd adjust the intensity and type of lights as well as the object's position. Exposure time and aperture aren't as big a concern, because AutoSHADE's camera is a lot like your eye (in that it doesn't accumulate light on a film).

Now back to AutoCAD and our model. For simplicity, take your photograph **WCS** in plan view. Be careful about the current **UCS** view when placing your lights and camera (see Figure 9-2).

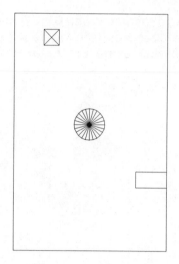

Figure 9-2: Plan view of table.

Make sure **ELEVATION** and **THICKNESS** are **0**. From your pop-up menus, pick **OPTIONS**, then **AUTOSHADE**. An AutoLISP routine will load and report no errors, then an icon menu will appear. If you don't have pop-ups, you can load **AUTOSHADE** from the keyboard by typing **(load "ashade")**. Pick the **CAMERA** from the icon or screen menu, or type in **CAMERA**.

Response: Enter camera name.

Type: CAMRA1

Response: Enter target point.

Pick the **.XY** filter from the screen menu, or type **.XY**.

Response: .XY of

Type: 8,10

Response: (Need Z).

Type: 13.5

This should put you right at the face of the pyramid.

Response: Enter camera location.

Type: 33,10,13.5

Note the camera icon that appears on the right side of the drawing. From the icon menu pick the point light source, or type **LIGHT**.

Response: Enter light name:

Type: LITE1

Response: Point source or directed<P>.

Type: P

Response: Enter light location.

Type or pick **.XY** and then pick point **12,17**.

Response: Of (need Z).

Type: 35

A **LIGHT** icon is inserted into the drawing at the corner of the table at point **12,17** and **35** inches off the **X,Y** plane. From your icon menu,

Pick: Scene (Type **SCENE** or pick **ACTION**, then **SCENE**
from the screen menu.)

Response: Enter scene name.

Type: SCENE1

Response: Select the camera.

Pick the camera.

Response: Select a light.

Pick the light icon.

Response: Select a light.

Type: <RETURN>

Response: Enter scene location.

Type: 29,21

A **CLAPPER** icon appears with pertinent information on it (see Figure
9-3). If you want to get a view of what the camera is seeing, select
CAMVIEW from your icon menu and a **DVIEW** camera shot of the table
in perspective will appear. Type or select **FILMROLL** from your screen
menu and accept the default name of **SHADEIT** by pressing **RETURN**.
A file is created named **SHADEIT.FLM**. End your drawing, saving it
under the name **SHADEIT**. For convenience, place the **FILMROLL** file
in the same subdirectory in which AutoSHADE is installed. Exit
AutoCAD to your DOS prompt.

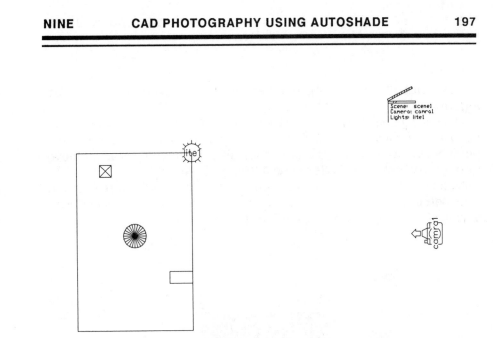

Figure 9-3: Scene 1 plan view.

The **FILMROLL** file you created represents one of a series of photographs or scenes taken in AutoCAD. You can move **CAMERA** and **TARGET** positions around in AutoSHADE, but the **LIGHTS** are fixed. You can also create scenes in AutoCAD that have different **LIGHTS** and **CAMERA** combinations.

SHADING YOUR DRAWING

Depending on how you installed AutoSHADE, you now execute it by typing **SHADE**. If you created a batch file as described earlier, execute it.

When entering AutoSHADE, notice that pop-ups and dialogue boxes are the rule, with several function keys available as shortcuts (see Figure 9-4). The filled **TIME** and **%** memory are displayed across the top of the menu bar. Pick **FILE** from the menu bar, then pick **OPEN**, or just press **F10**. A dialogue box appears that looks like AutoCAD's dialogue boxes. Your **CURRENT** subdirectory is displayed and you can page through other subdirectories and **FILMROLL** files by picking **UP** or **PAGE UP**. Find **SHADEIT** in the list and pick the box to the left (see Figure 9-5). Then choose **OK**. As you can see, you could have created a **FILMROLL** file in AutoCAD that had several scenes defined in it (see Figure 9-6).

Now bring up a perspective wire frame of **SHADEIT** by either pressing **F2** or pulling down **DISPLAY** and picking **WIRE FRAME**. This perspective wire frame is very much like what you could achieve through **DVIEW** at **POSITION** and **TARGET** in AutoCAD.

Notice that you're at eye level with the table top, and a wire frame in true perspective is shown. By pressing **F7** or using the pull-down, select **SETTINGS** and pick **CAMERA** position.

Figure 9-4: File pull-down in AutoSHADE.

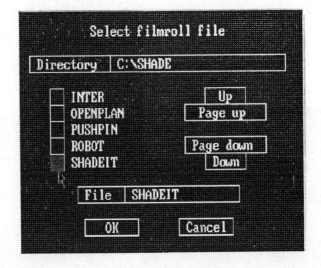

Figure 9-5: File selection dialogue box in AutoSHADE.

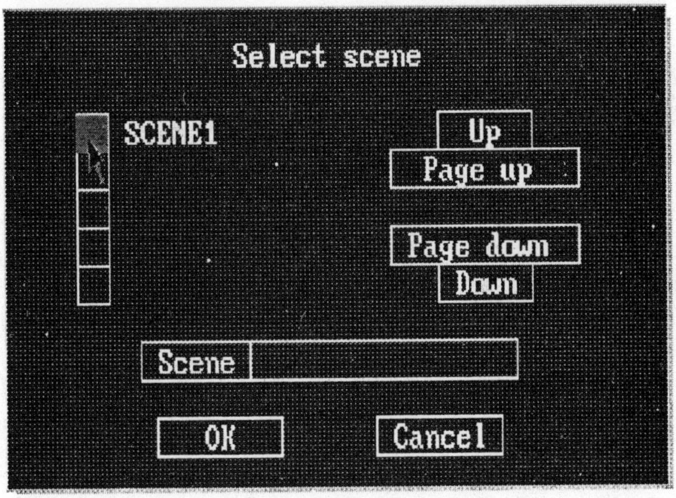

Figure 9-6: Select scene dialogue box.

From this dialogue box, change **DEGREES RIGHT** to **0** if needed and **DEGREES UP** to **5**. Then pick **OK** (see Figure 9-7). Hit **F2** for a wire frame again. You now can see more of the tabletop and you're right where you placed your camera in AutoCAD.

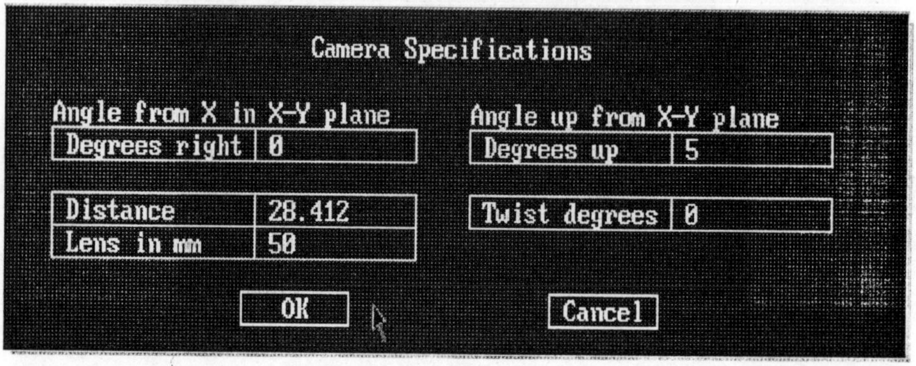

```
                    Camera Specifications

Angle from X in X-Y plane        Angle up from X-Y plane
 ┌─────────────────┬─────┐        ┌────────────────┬─────┐
 │ Degrees right   │ 0   │        │ Degrees up     │ 5   │
 └─────────────────┴─────┘        └────────────────┴─────┘

 ┌─────────────────┬───────┐      ┌────────────────┬─────┐
 │ Distance        │ 28.412│      │ Twist degrees  │ 0   │
 │ Lens in mm      │ 50    │      └────────────────┴─────┘
 └─────────────────┴───────┘

            ┌──────────┐              ┌──────────┐
            │    OK    │              │  Cancel  │
            └──────────┘              └──────────┘
```

Figure 9-7: Camera specification dialogue box.

To get a visual representation of where your **LIGHTS** and current **CAMERA** position are at this point, hit **F5** for a plan view. When ready to shade, hit **F4** or pick **DISPLAY**, then **FULL SHADE**.

Here's where the real crunching occurs. AutoSHADE now computes distance, angles and reflective properties for surfaces. Each surface is made up of two triangles, and you're updated on what's happening at the bottom of your screen as approximately 150 triangles are compared.

Isn't that beautiful? (see Figure 9-8). You've rendered your first drawing. Press **F1** and pull down **SETTINGS**, pick **CAMERA POSITION** or just hit **F7** and then change **DEGREES RIGHT** to **85**. Pick **OK** and press **F4** for a **FULL SHADE** again. Take the time to experiment with **CAMERA POSITION** and make changes to **DEGREES RIGHT** and **DEGREES UP**.

Figure 9-8: Full shade of a table.

WORKING WITH LIGHT

To see how AutoSHADE deals with light's interaction with your model, pick **SETTINGS**, then pick **SHADING MODEL**.

The brightness of your light source is a distance we'll call *intensity*. In general, we'll deal with two types of lights: 1) *point sources,* of negligible size and with light beams or rays emanating in all directions; and 2) *directed sources,* which have a definite direction. Both sources are considered to have light beams traveling parallel. A real-life example of an ideal point source is a distant star, and a directed light might be a spotlight used in stage lighting.

Normally in nature, the intensity of a point source of light falls off as the inverse square of its distance (see Figure 9-9).

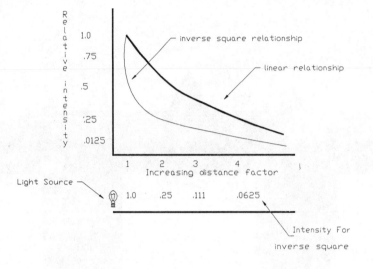

Figure 9-9: Graph of inverse square law vs. linear relationship.

This means that as the distance between a light source and a surface increases, the light's intensity decreases rapidly. The inverse square relationship describes the light intensity of a point source at a distance and implies that as the distance between a source and a surface doubles, the light intensity reaching the surface drops to one-half or one-quarter of its original value. AutoSHADE provides a setting for the inverse square law for your light sources.

Since you often deal with large light sources, such as fluorescent lights relatively close to reflecting surfaces, the inverse square relationship is often inaccurate. AutoSHADE provides a linear lighting relationship along with a linear constant to take care of situations that aren't inverse squares. In this case, as the distance between a light source and a surface doubles, for example, the intensity of light reaching that surface decreases to one-half its original value plus a constant value. This relationship is helpful when you want to simulate situations where the light source is large, as with fluorescents.

The colors of your light sources in AutoSHADE are considered white but the colors of the shaded surfaces are determined by the entity's color. If you have only 16 colors, AutoSHADE will use a dither effect to show shades of a color when the rendering process takes place.

Dithering is a process in which AutoSHADE achieves a particular color shade by using a pattern of different available colors. If you have 256 colors available, of course AutoSHADE will have many more colors to work with in rendering.

A white light source is considered to be emanating all colors of the visual spectrum, red through violet, in roughly equal proportions. Your light sources in AutoSHADE are white, simple and considered ideal.

AMBIENT LIGHT AND REFLECTION

In the AutoSHADE rendering process, there's a light source that we can call background light, originating from reflected beams off nearby objects. This background light is also called ambient light and you set its intensity with the ambient light factor, a number between 0, as minimum, and 1 as maximum.

When light strikes a surface, depending on the nature of the surface, it bounces off. Reflection is critical to the rendering process. When light strikes a surface (see Figure 9-10), the angle of incidence **i** equals the angle of reflection **r**. Angles are measured from the beam to the normal, the normal being an imaginary line perpendicular to the surface.

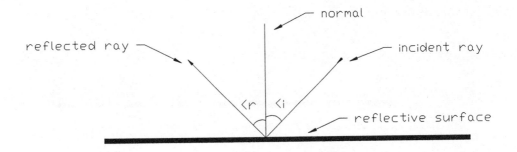

Figure 9-10: The law of specular reflection.

This type of reflection is called "specular reflection," and is characteristic of flat, shiny surfaces. Specular reflection sometimes causes images to be created as in a mirror. AutoSHADE has a specular reflection factor, represented as a number between 0 and 1. The closer the factor is to 1, the shinier the surface.

In AutoSHADE, specular reflection is described even more completely with the *specular exponent*, which defines the width of the cone of light that reflects off a shiny surface to the observer's eye or camera. The specular exponent, as with most described shading factors, is expressed numerically—the higher the number, the more the gloss on the surface, and subsequently the more chance of fewer surfaces reflecting light toward the eye of the camera. The numeric value of the specular exponent ranges from 2 to 400.

Another type of reflection where the angle of incidence doesn't equal the angle of reflection (see Figure 9-11) is *diffuse reflection*. This is the result of light striking a matte surface and bouncing off at many different angles. AutoSHADE's diffuse factor describes the reflective coefficient of all objects in view. This, combined with the angle between the source and the normal (perpendicular) to the surface, will contribute to the shading factor for that surface.

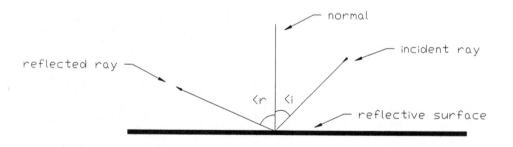

Figure 9-11: Diffuse reflection.

The diffuse factor is expressed in AutoSHADE as a number between 0 and 1. The closer to 1 the factor is, the higher the reflective property of the surfaces.

When light reflects off a surface, a combination of diffuse and specular reflection occurs. This, along with the angle of incidence (see Figure 9-12), helps to determine a shading factor.

Colors of reflective surfaces occur in nature when white light consisting of all colors strikes a surface of one color. All colors are absorbed except for the surface color, which is reflected. If the light source has a hue to it, only surfaces able to reflect those colors making up the hue will be seen; otherwise, the surface appears dark or even black. The colors of your AutoSHADE surfaces are determined by the color of the entity in AutoCAD.

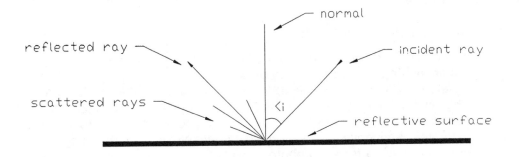

Figure 9-12: Diffuse and specular reflection.

AutoSHADE does take into account how the intensity of light decreases after reflection through the user's choice of two mathematical shading models: Z shading and stretch contrast. In the case of Z shading, a form of the inverse square law is used on reflected light from a surface and only the ambient light factor is used in the calculation. Z shading can show depth perception and a phenomenon known as *diminution* for objects of the same color. This effect in AutoSHADE could be used experimentally to achieve a desired effect. It would be useful if you could assign it to only certain entities in your model, but like most settings in AutoSHADE, it has a global effect.

The stretch contrast model is like automatic exposure on a camera. It uses all factors in its calculation. Relative reflective intensities are computed from a minimum value represented by the ambient light setting to a maximum value represented by the brightest surface. All other shade calculations are relative to those extremes. With this model, no absolute numeric value for the brightness of any face can be determined — the dimmest object is zero, and relative brightnesses are determined from that value.

Usually you'll want to leave your shading model at stretch contrast, but as in photography, how light reacts and how the picture should be taken, developed and printed present infinite choices, so experiment!

You can describe surfaces quite accurately by assigning **AMBIENT**, **DIFFUSE** and **SPECULAR** factors that sum to 1.0. The specular exponent will be numerically assigned separately, along with a shading model and light source characteristics, to further control shading for the 3D model.

FINE-TUNING YOUR WORK

Now pick **OK** from your shading model dialogue box and return to your camera settings dialogue box by pressing **F7**.

Return to a view of **DEGREES RIGHT = 0** and **DEGREES UP = 5**. While in the **CAMERA SPECIFICATIONS** dialogue box, change **LENS** in millimeters from **50** to **70**. This will reduce your field of view to about 35 degrees and move you in about 40 percent closer, like changing the lens on a camera for a telephoto or wide angle effect. The larger the focal length of the lens, the closer in the picture is, and the tighter the field of view.

Now choose **OK** from the dialogue box. Before you shade, a setting needs to be made so you can see exactly what the camera sees.

Press **F8** or choose **SETTINGS**, then **EXPERT** (see Figure 9-13). Change screen percent to **-1** to see a bird's-eye camera view, then pick **OK**. Now hit **F4** for a full shade.

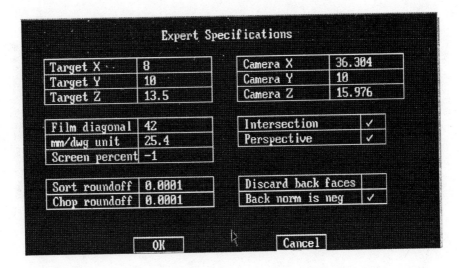

Figure 9-13: Expert specifications dialogue box.

Note that you're closer and can see shading on the cone quite well. Note also that AutoSHADE didn't cast shadows, because shadow-casting is not yet supported. Remember that a point source of light in AutoSHADE emanates light in all directions.

This particular rendering might be worth recording, so let's turn **RECORD ON** and create an **.RND** file. Press **F1** and choose **DISPLAY**, then **RECORD** (after pressing **F1**, **ALT-F3** would also turn **RECORD ON**). Hit **F4** to render again. This time a dialogue box appears to show the path and name of the render (**.RND**) file to be created (see Figure 9-14). Accept the default (**SHADEIT.RND**) by picking **OK**, and the rendering begins. An **.RND** file is created and the results displayed on the screen. You can play back this **.RND** file by choosing **REPLAY** from your **DISPLAY** pull-down.

Figure 9-14: Rendering replay file dialogue box.

When you choose **REPLAY** or execute an **ALT-F1**, a dialogue box appears and you can pick that .RND file to **REPLAY**. Pick **SHADEIT**, and your rendering appears quickly. These **.RND** files are used in AutoFLIX animation sequences and can be displayed in AutoSHADE at any time by choosing **REPLAY**. **REPLAY ALL** from the **DISPLAY** pull-down would show all **.RND** files in a particular subdirectory.

From your pull-downs, choose **SETTINGS**, then **LIGHTS** (see Figure 9-15). The **SET LIGHT INTENSITIES** dialogue box appears and the **NAME**, **TYPE** and **INTENSITY** of your lights in the scene are displayed. You have one light, **LITE1**, which was a point source, showing an intensity of **1**. This number normally is relative to any other lights you may have in the scene. Because you have only one light, it means nothing to change it here. Choose **OK** to get out of this dialogue box.

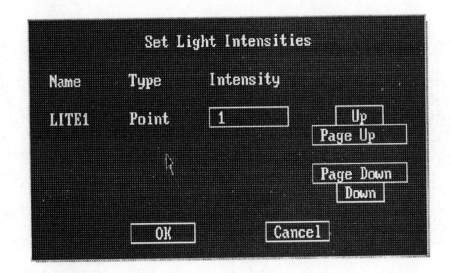

Figure 9-15: Light intensities dialogue box.

From your pull-downs, choose **SETTINGS**, then **SHADING MODEL** or press **ALT-F5**. The **SHADING MODEL** dialogue box appears (see Figure 9-16). This dialogue box will let you tweak AutoSHADE's shading for more realism. The setting that needs to be changed here is an inverse square that needs a setting of **1**. This applies the inverse square law to your light source so that it behaves as a true point source. Choose **OK** and reshade with an **F4**. If you like, you can turn **RECORD MODE OFF** so as not to create an **.RND** file for each shade you do.

The shaded model appears dimmer and actually more realistic. If you turn off **INVERSE SQUARE** by giving it a value of **0** and turning on **LINEAR LIGHTING** with **LINEAR CONSTANT**, you can simulate a fluorescent light source. Press **F1**.

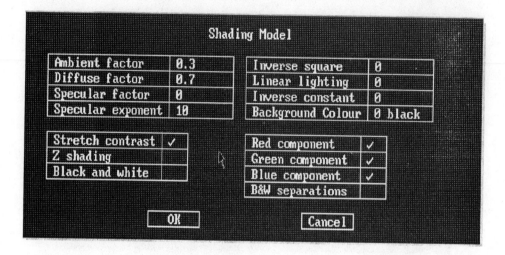

Shading Model			
Ambient factor	0.3	Inverse square	0
Diffuse factor	0.7	Linear lighting	0
Specular factor	0	Inverse constant	0
Specular exponent	10	Background Colour	0 black
Stretch contrast	✓	Red component	✓
Z shading		Green component	✓
Black and white		Blue component	✓
		B&W separations	
	OK	Cancel	

Figure 9-16: Shading model dialogue box.

The full effect of making minor changes to the AutoSHADE settings depends on your rendering device's resolution and color capability. You can achieve desirable effects by putting both **POINT** and **DIRECTED** lights in a scene to achieve an indoor or outdoor effect.

For example, if you were an architect shading a room with a back-lit ceiling, you'd find it difficult to place lights behind the ceiling grid to shine through, as in real life. As a solution, you'd have to place directed lights on the floor, shining up at the ceiling. A separate light would be needed for each tile, to produce the effect of being lit from behind.

You may have noticed that there's a choice in your **DISPLAY** pull-down menu for a **FAST SHADE**. **F3** also does a **FAST SHADE**. Try it — when the rendering is complete, you may notice some imperfections. That's because **FAST SHADE** doesn't take intersecting objects into account. If a circular rod intersected your wedge, AutoSHADE would need extra time to calculate how those objects intersected and how they should be rendered.

In the **FULL SHADE** process, AutoSHADE *does* look at all faces to see if one obscures another. If faces intersect one another and one face is closer to the camera than another, AutoSHADE starts to chop intersecting faces into smaller pieces. If you have intersecting faces in any of your **FILMROLL** files, always do a **FULLSHADE** (with **F4** or menu pick) and make sure that **INTERSECTION** is checked in your **EXPERT SPECIFICATIONS** dialogue box. This ensures that AutoSHADE handles your intersecting objects properly. The shading process will take longer, but will be much more accurate. You may also want to investigate speed-up procedures such as virtual disks.

MOVING ON

You certainly have a lot to experiment with up to this point. By now, you should have an idea of what AutoSHADE can do and how it can be of benefit in your work. In the next chapter, you'll do more fine-tuning and explore some customization ideas.

10 More Rendering and Solids

AutoSHADE is proving to be an excellent companion to AutoCAD in making your designs more realistic. In this chapter, you'll concentrate on the details of how light reacts with a surface and the shading model. You'll also begin to customize AutoSHADE to make your work go faster.

In this chapter, you'll be exposed to a number of commands that may seem confusing; consult the AutoSHADE manual for details on individual commands.

BACK TO THE WIRE FRAME

Let's start by getting into AutoCAD and bringing up your drawing, **SHADEIT**. Your table with the objects on it should come up in plan view in **WCS**. If not,

> **Type:** UCS

> **Response:** Origin/ZAxis/3point/Entity/View/X/Y/X/Prev/
> Restore/Save/Del/?/<world>.

> **Type:** <RETURN>

This restores the **WCS**; then

> **Type:** PLAN W

This gets you into plan view **WCS** (see Figure 10-1). Now create a new scene, called **SCENE2**, with one **DIRECTED LIGHT** and a **CAMERA** pointed directly at the blue pyramid. The apex of your blue pyramid is 14 units above the **X,Y** plane. Load AutoSHADE by picking **OPTIONS** from your pull-downs or **ASHADE** from your screen menu, or type **(Load "ASHADE")** at the keyboard. From your menu, pick **DIRECTED LIGHT** or type **LIGHT**.

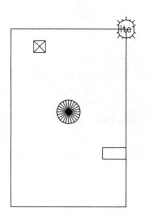

Figure 10-1: Scene 1 plan view.

Response: Enter light name:

Type: LITE2

Response: Point source or directed.

Type: D

Response: Enter light AIM point.

Type: .XY

Response: of

Pick the point 4.5, 15.500.

Response: (Need Z)

Type: 14

Response: Enter light location:

Type: 26,4,25

Note the appearance of your directed light source. Now pick or type **CAMERA**.

Response: Enter camera name:

Type: CAMRA2

Response: Enter target point.

Type: 4.5,15.5,13.5

This aims the camera at the center of your pyramid.

Response: Enter camera location:

Type: 14,21,13

Pick or type scene.

Response: Enter scene name.

Type: SCENE2

Response: Select the camera.

   Pick **CAMERA2**.

Response: Select a light.

   Pick **LITE2**.

Response: Select a light.

   Type: <RETURN>

Response: Enter scene location.

   Pick point 29,18 (so that **SCENE2** clapper is under **SCENE1** clapper; see Figure 10-2).

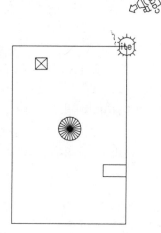

Figure 10-2: Scene 2 plan view.

Now type or pick **FILMROLL**.

Response: Enter filmroll name.

   Type: SHADEIT   (or place the FLM file in your AutoSHADE
                                    subdirectory for convenience.)

End your drawing and go to DOS.

Get right into AutoSHADE and pick **FILE PULLDOWN**, then **OPEN**.
Select **SHADEIT2** from the dialogue box, then **SCENE2** from the
SELECT SCENE dialogue box, then **OK**.
Use your **F7** key to pull up **CAMERA SETTINGS**, then adjust
DEGREES RIGHT to **30** and **DEGREES UP** to **5** (see Figure 10-3).
Change the lens to 60mm, then pick **OK**. Using **F8**, bring up the **EX-
PERT** dialogue box and change **SCREEN PERCENT** to **-1**. Also check
the **INTERSECTION** box, then pick **OK**. Hit **F4** to produce a **FULL
SHADE**.

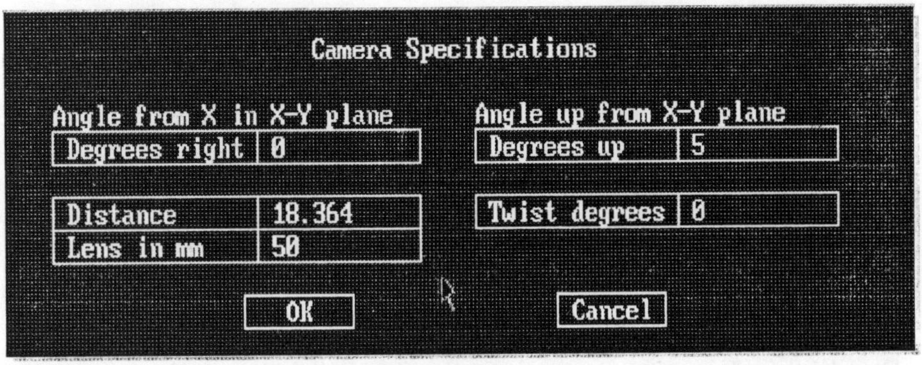

**Figure 10-3: Camera specifications dialogue box from
Scene 2.**

Now let's change our camera position slightly by flipscreen, using **F1** and **F7** for camera position. Change **DEGREES RIGHT** to **20**, pick **OK**, then press **F4** for a **FULL SHADE** (see Figure 10-4).

Figure 10-4: Full shade of Scene 2.

CREATING SHINY SURFACES

Try to imagine where the light source is, and how it affects what the camera is "seeing." Let's change the shading model slightly. Flip screen with an **F1** and select **SETTINGS** and then **SHADING** model (or simply hit **ALT-F5**).

The inverse square and linear lighting factors apply only to point sources of light, so we won't experiment with them here. However, suppose your pyramid was made of shiny plastic. How could you show that effect? The **AMBIENT** + **DIFFUSE** + **SPECULAR** factors must add up to 1.0. So by reducing background — or ambient light as well as the **DIFFUSE** factor — you can increase the **SPECULAR** factor to describe a shinier surface.

Adjust the **AMBIENT** factor to **.2**, the **DIFFUSE** factor to **.5** and the **SPECULAR** factor to **.3**. Raising the **SPECULAR EXPONENT** also provides a glassy effect. Choose **OK**, then press **F4** for a **FULL SHADE**.

Depending on your display, the rendering should be very different (see Figure 10-5).

Feel free to experiment with the **SHADING MODEL** dialogue box. You might want to try the Z-shading model and re-render with **F4**. Remember that this model uses only ambient light factors and distances to the camera in a surface calculation, so a poor rendering will result. Also note that in the **SHADING MODEL** dialogue box, you have the opportunity to make background color changes, color separations and a black-and-white-only rendering.

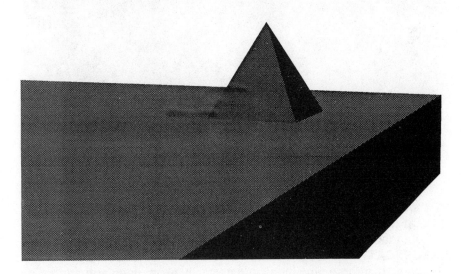

Figure 10-5: Reshade of Scene 2 with modified settings.

Now readjust the **SHADING MODEL** dialogue box so that **AMBIENT** = .2, **DIFFUSE** = .5, **SPECULAR** = .3 and **SPECULAR EXPONENT** = 30. Also make sure **STRETCH CONTRAST** is chosen (not Z-shading). Choose **OK**.

By pressing **F8**, you can bring up the **EXPERT** dialogue box and experiment. First, move the **TARGET Y** position to **12.0** (between the **PYRAMID** and **CONE**). Choose **OK**, then re-render with **F4**. Your screen should display an attractive rendering of the **CONE** and **PYRAMID** on the table (see Figure 10-6).

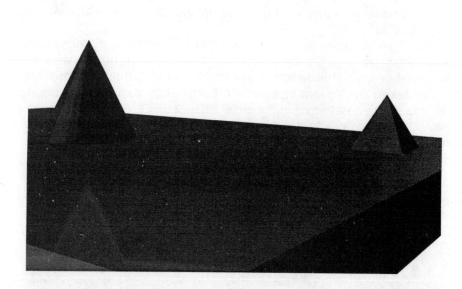

Figure 10-6: Reshade of Scene 2 at a different camera and target.

If you'd like to see a wider field of view, adjust your **FOCAL LENGTH** to a smaller value. Press **F1** for a flipscreen, then **F8** for an **EXPERT SPECIFICATION** dialogue box.

Note that your **CAMERA** and **TARGET** positions are in the **EXPERT SPECIFICATION** dialogue box. **SORT** and **CHOP ROUNDOFF** affect accuracy on intersecting faces and normally never need adjusting. You can increase performance of **SORT** and **CHOP ROUNDOFF** calculations if you minimize hard-disk activity and use a virtual disk (see "Installing AutoSHADE" in Chapter Nine). Note that you can ignore the backfaces on your model; this speeds rendering, but it often produces undesirable effects.

The checkbox called **BACK NORM IS NEG** lets you specify which faces are considered backfaces. You should usually leave this checkbox undisturbed; choose **OK**.

CLIPPING PLANES

From your **SETTINGS** pull-down, select **CLIPPINGS** and refer to the diagram below of the **CLIPPING** dialogue box (Figure 10-7).

From the dialogue box, pick **OK**, then **DISPLAY**, then **PLAN** view.

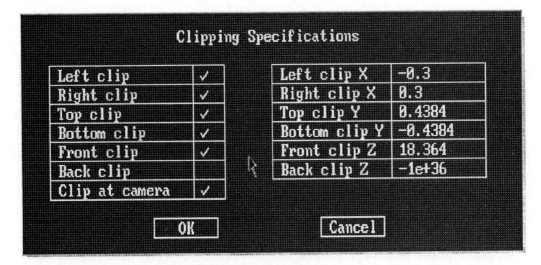

Figure 10-7: Clipping dialogue box.

Here we can see a good representation of **CAMERA, LIGHTS, TAR-GET** and **FIELD OF VIEW**. The arrowhead's tip represents the **TARGET**. In Figure 10-7A, notice a similar situation. The front **CLIP Z** plane is at a positive **Z** distance and perpendicular to the line of sight. The **FRONT CLIP DISTANCE** is measured from the **TARGET** (arrowhead) to the **CAMERA** in drawing units. If you set **CLIP** at **CAMERA ON** in the **CLIP-PINGS** dialogue box, then the front **CLIP** distance equals the distance from **CAMERA** to **TARGET**.

The **BACK CLIP DISTANCE** is measured from the **TARGET** position away from the **CAMERA** (negative **Z**). A **BACK CLIP DISTANCE** of **0** is clipped at the **TARGET**. Back clipping is usually used to section objects.

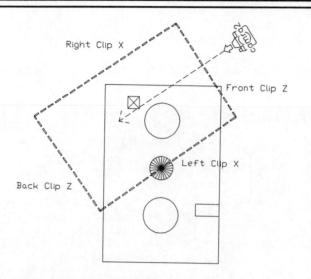

Figure 10-7A: Clipping planes.

LEFT CLIP and **RIGHT CLIP** are automatically computed from the *film diagonal size*. Not shown in Figure 10-7A is a top and bottom clip plane in the positive **Y** and negative **Y** direction. So all the clipping planes do form a "box of view" of sorts. In Figure 10-7B, note the definition of the film diagonal. This plane is perpendicular to the line of sight and is at a distance equal to the **FOCAL LENGTH** from the **CAMERA**. The default size of the diagonal of the film plane is 42 mm. Details about the film diagonal are in the **EXPERT SPECIFICATION** dialogue box.

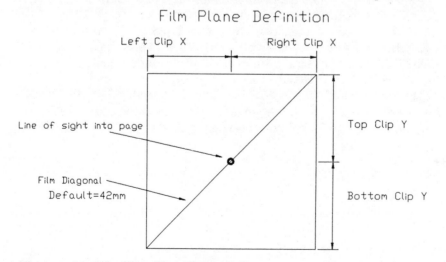

Figure 10-7B: The film diagonal.

When experimenting with clipping planes in AutoSHADE, take care to follow the rules regarding positive and negative directions. The **CLIPPING SPECIFICATION** dialogue box has checkboxes to the left to determine whether you want the clip value to the right to be honored. Notice that the back clip is vertically set to a large negative number. To clip off a left and right portion of your view, adjust the left clip value to a smaller negative value (e.g., **-.40**), and your right clip value to a smaller positive value (e.g., **+.40**).

Remember the target has a clip value of **0**. After changing these values, choose **OK** and re-render with an **F4**. See what clipping does! After experimenting with clip values, quit AutoSHADE.

SPEEDING YOUR WORK WITH SCRIPT FILES

An elementary feature of AutoCAD's open architecture is the script file—an ASCII text file created with a text editor that batches AutoCAD commands in single execution, in much the same way a **DOS.BAT** file does. AutoSHADE has its own batch files, which let it run on automatic pilot. Why would you need script files? Suppose you need to create a series of sequential **.RND** files for a walk-through designed in AutoFLIX. This project could take hours of work: moving the **CAMERA**, **FULL SHADE** with **RECORD ON**, moving the **CAMERA** again, **FULL SHADE** again with **RECORD ON** again.

Running an AutoSHADE batch file could create dozens of **.RND** files overnight. AutoSHADE scripts are created with a text editor and can be executed within AutoSHADE in the **SCRIPT FILE** dialogue box or at the DOS prompt, very much like AutoCAD script files. At the DOS prompt you would type in **SHADE -S** <name of script> where <name of script> is the name of a script file with an **.SCR** extension. Script files may contain the following commands:

CAMERA <**X, Y, Z**>	Set camera location.
DELAY <# of seconds>	Hold everything for a time specified.
DISTANCE <distance>	Set camera target distance.
DXB <filename>	Create a **DXB** file.
FASTSHADE <filename>	Cause a fast shade and create a filename, used if **RECORD** is **ON**.
FULLSHADE <filename>	Cause a full shade and create a filename used if **RECORD** is **ON**.

HARDCOPY < on/off >	Use hard-copy device instead of screen.
INTERSECTION < on/off >	Check intersecting faces.
LENS < in mm >	Set lens **FOCAL LENGTH**.
OPEN < flm file >	Open a **FILMROLL** file.
PERSPECTIVE < on/off >	Turn **PERSPECTIVE ON** or **OFF**.
QUIT	Quit AutoSHADE.
RECORD < on/off >	Create **.RND** file when shading.
REPLAY < filename >	Replay an **.RND** file.
REWIND	Repeat script over again.
SCENE < name >	Select a scene.
SLIDE < filename >	Create a slide file.
SPERCENT < number >	Set screen percent.
TARGET < X, Y, Z >	Set a camera target.
TWIST < angle >	Used for comments in the script file.

Below is an example of a script file created with a text editor like DOS's EDLIN. To execute it, type **SHADE -S TEST** at the DOS command prompt. This file gets you into AutoSHADE and brings up the **FILMROLL** file **SHADEIT2**, then selects **SCENE2** and creates a series of **.RND** files as the camera changes position. Then all render files are replayed with a delay of five seconds between each rendering. This automates a lengthy series of operations, freeing you from your computer.

```
OPEN SHADEIT2
SCENE SCENE2
CAMERA 22.8,15.5,13.5
RECORD ON
FULLSHADE RENDER1
CAMERA 22.5,18.68,13.5
FULLSHADE RENDER2
CAMERA 21.76,21.78,13.5
FULLSHADE RENDER3
```

CAMERA 20.4,24.68,13.5

FULLSHADE RENDER4

REPLAY RENDER1

DELAY 5

REPLAY RENDER2

DELAY 5

REPLAY RENDER3

DELAY 5

REPLAY RENDER4

DELAY 5

QUIT

This assumes the script file is named **TEST.SCR**. A script file like this can save you hours of work! If you want to minimize the echoed messages and run AutoSHADE in batch mode with a script file, you can include the **-b** option at the DOS command prompt (for example, **SHADE -b -S TEST**).

The **-b** option instructs AutoSHADE to use a null display driver. This executes the batch file quickly and no AutoSHADE dialogue flashes at you. To try it with your script file at the **C:** prompt while logged into your AutoSHADE subdirectory, type **SHADE-B -S TEST**.

DRAWBACKS TO AUTOSHADE

Because the interaction of light with objects is extremely complex, AutoSHADE has its limitations. Below are a few phenomena and circumstances that AutoSHADE presently has trouble dealing with.

The phenomenon of refraction occurs when light strikes a surface and all or part of that light passes through, or is transmitted through, that material (see Figure 10-8). The light beam bends when passing into the optically denser medium, and part of the light is reflected off the surface and never makes it through the medium. The amount that reflects off the surface increases with the angle of incidence. AutoSHADE doesn't support refractive properties of objects. However, you can control reflection off the transparent surface through the specular factor and specular exponent.

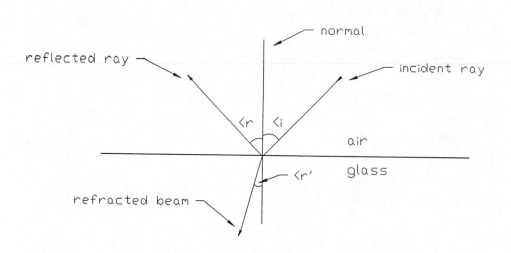

Figure 10-8: Refraction with partial reflection.

When a light source shines obliquely on an opaque object, a shadow is cast. If the light source is assumed to have parallel beams (as in AutoSHADE), the shadow is very sharp. If the light source is relatively large and close to the object, or if there's more than one light source, the shadows become fuzzy around the edges. The angles at which shadows fall and the appearance of shadows are quite difficult to predict—a good job for an AutoLISP routine!

AutoSHADE doesn't handle shadows, not to mention other complex phenomena such as diffraction where light waves bend around corners and edges. AutoSHADE does a fine job of dealing with objects that are in the shade. AutoSHADE's ambient light factor will, along with the **Z SHADING** or **STRETCH CONTRAST** models, take care of illuminating surfaces that aren't lit directly in a realistic fashion.

AutoCAD provides AutoSHADE with an accurate wire frame in perspective. You depend on AutoSHADE to depict your model as you apply **LIGHTS** and a **CAMERA**. However, AutoSHADE cannot handle some of nature's reaction with light on surfaces such as refraction, diffraction and shadows.

There are a few other optical phenomena found in nature that AutoSHADE can't handle directly. However, by adjusting several parameters and by experimenting, we can often simulate their effects.

For example, look at the picket fence in Figure 10-9. Vertical pickets in the fence seem to become smaller with increasing distance from the eye, a phenomenon known as foreshortening. The rails on the fence appear to be converging at a point in the distance known as the vanishing point. Both foreshortening and vanishing point will be taken care of as side effects to working with true perspective.

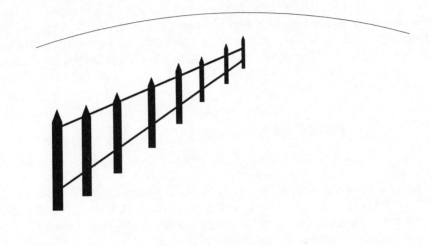

Figure 10-9: Vanishing point, foreshortening and diminution.

To create the feeling of objects fading into the distance *(diminution)*, causing detail to get fuzzier, tones to get more neutral, and colors to appear grayer, you need to adjust the shading model as well as the inverse square or linear relationship. Phenomena such as diminution are best handled directly by software that allows paint capabilities, using much more sophisticated rendering algorithms than AutoSHADE uses.

OTHER SHADING ALGORITHMS

AutoSHADE's rendering algorithm, *Lambert shading*, represents a first step toward realism. Its limitations include allowing only ideal light sources with one color represented per surface. Other shading algorithms, such as *Gouraud* and *Phong*, deal with light in a much more facets, are dealt with according to the way light reacts with their edges as well as their centers. This provides more colors per surface, much more realism—and much more computing time!

AutoSHADE has quite a job ahead of it. It must be able to deal with light intensity, angles, surface characteristics and colors in your drawings, not to mention camera settings when you create your scene. The renderings produced will be quite accurate and realistic if parameters have been set properly, your wire frame is shadable and you have the hardware to create video and/or hard-copy output. You won't be able to paint surfaces or set surface characteristics for individual surfaces in the wire frame. This basic way of dealing with rendering may seem somewhat limited, but you'll soon see that your creativity can still run wild as you experiment.

SHADING VERSUS MODELING

In the past two chapters, you've taken wire frames created in AutoCAD and rendered some very realistic models. But again you've reached an impasse. Even if AutoSHADE used a more sophisticated shading model than Lambert, this would only make your rendered model *look* more realistic. However, in terms of a mathematical physical description, how much more valuable would it be?

If you had produced an assembly drawing, could you fit the pieces together and look for part interference? Could you cut away a cross-section of a model and study its internal structure? Does the material that your model is made of have an effect? Could mass, inertia, torque, dynamic and static stress studies be conducted? Could surface properties of the model be studied?

The answer to all of these questions is no, and from an engineering standpoint, this can be frustrating. Remember that shading is primarily for presentation; solids modeling represents true objects—free from some of the restrictions and restraints we experienced in shading—where mass, internal structure and surface properties are all vital parts of the computations.

The origins of solids modeling began in the early 1970s, with a series of algorithms that described an object both inside and out. This series of algorithms, called PADL-2, was started by Herbert B. Voelcker at the University of Rochester. PADL-2 is based on both CSG (Constructive Solid Geometry) and B-rep (Boundary representation). With CSG, an object is considered to be made up of basic solid objects such as cubes, cones and spheres. These shapes are fused together to make a model or, more likely, a portion of one. The number crunching is based on the fact that two or more of these shapes cannot occupy the same place at the same time. The mathematics involve some of the same basic Boolean concepts as in set theory of union, intersection and interference.

As you might guess, calculations on a complex solid model are complex — and very taxing on any computer system, let alone a PC. B-rep involves accurate representation of surface information. This involves calculating not only creases and edges but also surface characteristics — much like what AutoSHADE does, but more accurately.

Together, CSG and B-rep describe an object inside and out. Because materials making up the model are taken into account, the object has mass. Compare this to a hollow wire frame with a shaded skin stretched around it, and you can readily see the difference between shading a wire frame and creating a solid model.

Atlanta-based Cadetron (now owned by Autodesk) was responsible for exporting PADL-2 capabilities to the PC. The code was changed from FORTRAN to C and a user interface was created. Because this software was originally designed for mainframe applications, some limitations were inevitable; mostly in the form of interior descriptions and cutaways. Surface descriptions were accurate, however, so visual representation was good.

Through Autodesk's acquisition of Cadetron, and after a few false starts, this software eventually became AutoSOLID. Now when you think of your 3D wire frame, you can express further design needs at two levels: one at the presentation level and one at the engineering/manufacturing level.

AutoSOLID lets you design a part through assembly in much the same way as a hobbyist glues together the pieces of a model airplane. You can design the pieces in 3D using entities such as cubes, cylinders and spheres as if they were physical objects. Shading and rendering are done, but the internal structure as well as the mass properties of the object are also defined. Since the modeling is done with such precision, an engineer/designer can allow for and measure interference checking, tolerances, rotational dynamics and inertial properties. In the case of a plastic part, a designer can even allow for shrinkage when the molten plastic cools during manufacturing. In AutoSOLID, a designer works with the closest thing to the object itself — a mathematically complete, simulated model of the object. For some designers, this dramatically reduce the need for building prototypes: the AutoSOLID design *is* the prototype.

The next chapter explores the future and how some of the excellent third-party software available for AutoCAD will take advantage of Release 10's 3D database and capabilities.

11 Third-party Software and the Future

As you've explored AutoCAD and 3D, you've learned about several new tools that help you step into the third dimension. Some of them are elementary: 3DLINEs, for example. Some are quite complex, such as many of the AutoLISP routines found in Section Three of this book.

By using these tools, you now have a foundation for 3D capabilities in your work that you might never have thought possible before. Working in 3D presents yet another learning curve, but it will flatten rapidly with practice and some help.

AutoCAD grew from a generic 2D CAD package that offered wide-open architecture, and that tradition has been kept alive and well in Release 10. However, this brings up several points regarding your continued use of the software. AutoCAD's open-architecture concept lets you modify and enhance the software to increase productivity, and lends itself well to particular applications. Open architecture is represented by several levels, as in the pyramid shown in Figure 11-1.

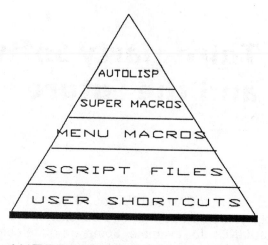

Figure 11-1: The customization pyramid.

This pyramid of customization has changed over the years with the growing maturity of AutoLISP. AutoCAD's customization package—in 2D or 3D—will continue to be popular and successful. However, because of a lack of time or expertise, most AutoCAD users have decided to waive serious modifications. Consequently, hundreds of third-party developers have written a variety of software programs that use AutoCAD as a graphics front end for drafting and design.

As AutoCAD becomes more complex and established in the CAD world, third-party development tools are becoming highly productive, cost-effective tools for streamlining work. Many of these third-party developers have grown literally from their basements, so check their products and reputations carefully.

Because Release 10 represents a quantum leap into true 3D, enhancements will certainly be incorporated into these third-party packages in response to users' needs. Nearly every AutoCAD user needs 3D, but its applications may not be immediately obvious. Third-party developers may well provide the catalyst that sparks your need for 3D capabilities. A few examples:

CIRCUIT BOARD DESIGN

The uses of 3D in circuit board design are far less obvious than in mechanical engineering. Circuit board design today involves more than highly complex designs of objects that have themselves become more complex. Circuit boards are smaller, denser, sometimes flexible, and often odd-shaped and molded to fit a particular space. When board designers look at the 2D drawing of their circuit board, they see a flat representation of the outline of the board and where each part (capacitor, resistor, etc.) is placed.

In design, these parts are 3D objects and the board itself is more than an outline. With Release 10, designers can now lay out the parts in 3D and end up with a shadable wire frame that can represent exactly what the board will look like after manufacturing. This can greatly help in documenting, analyzing and marketing the product.

The most established third-party developer is Great Softwestern Company in Denton, Texas, which produces AutoBoard, an add-on to AutoCAD that helps you design circuit boards.

SURVEYING

In civil survey applications, third-party packages like DCA (DCA Engineering in Henniker, New Hampshire) have a very clear path on how to use 3D in their design software. 3DFACES have been used before Release 10 to generate triangulated meshes representing earth surface terrain models. In road design, where a plan view and a profile view are on the same plot, the user can visualize changes in elevation of the road while simultaneously following the profile and plan. However, this isn't easy.

With 3D capabilities, a civil engineer can design so that cross-sections can be viewed at any angle, and "movement" along the road is possible. Improvements in earthwork calculations are another obvious application.

LANDSCAPE ARCHITECTURE

Landscape architects who use LandCADD from LandCADD, Inc., in Boulder, Colorado, can look forward to more of the same. 3D capabilities now allow rendering, painting and walk-throughs in presentations that would wow any client. Tree and shrub growth simulation are dramatic in 3D. Imagine providing a client with a videotape presentation instead of a stack of drawings!

FINITE ELEMENT ANALYSIS

Finite element analysis involves stress, vibration, temperature, magnetic and other testing on a design model. This computer application dates back to before AutoCAD existed. The intense number crunching and 3D requirements restricted this application to only the largest systems. A leader in this field, Los Angeles-based McNeal-Schwendler Corporation has a PC product that has worked reasonably well with AutoCAD in versions before Release 10. However, AutoCAD's lack of 3D features meant that a number of intermediary steps were needed before designs could be analyzed. MSC/pal2 will now take in AutoCAD's 3D information, and with the help of a deluxe 386 PC, finite element modeling and analysis will be routine.

MANUFACTURING

AutoCAD users in the world of manufacturing have a tremendous amount to gain from the new 3D database their design software now offers. ENCODE Technologies (Nashua, New Hampshire) is a relative old-timer in the world of CAM. Because five-axis numerical control applications demand a 3D representation of the part to be created, its third-party package, AutoCAM, takes full advantage of AutoCAD's 3D features. Describing tool paths in milling applications to create surfaces is now a routine step in the design process. With 3D, a mechanical designer/draftsman has a new world of options that describe and manufacture a product much more easily.

A LOOK AT THE FUTURE

Who needs 3D? Every AutoCAD user. Once its benefits are fully realized, the demand for 3D will undoubtedly result in more enhancements from Autodesk and third-party developers. What's next? Integration, user interfaces and connectivity.

In the early days of the PC software revolution, some users working with spreadsheets, word processing and database management began to demand at least partial integration — one package that tied all applications or environments together in an integrated bundle.

Many AutoCAD users have bought or created software that runs with AutoCAD. Some of this software is produced by Autodesk, such as AutoSHADE, AutoSOLID, and AEC Mechanical and Architectural. Some comes from third-party developers. Integration lets you perform tasks simultaneously that were once done separately in CAD/CAE or CAM sessions.

The beginnings of integration can be seen in Autodesk's products today. For example, the **FILMROLL** command foreshadows a tight link between AutoCAD and Shade software; the software will be right within AutoCAD.

Integration of third-party products will demand that developers cooperate to tie their products tightly into the AutoCAD environment.

The immediate future holds many enhancements and innovations. With the acceptance of a new operating system that allows multi-tasking, more conventional memory and easier connectivity, you'll begin to see AutoCAD users doing analysis, plotting, rendering, editing numerical code and sharing resources and files within a smooth user interface.

This user interface will manage operations inside and outside the AutoCAD drawing editor and will behave and think much as you do. Tablet menus will appear on your LCD digitizing tablet as you need them, you'll be able to type English sentences at the keyboard, and you'll become used to seeing your work in 3D every day.

MOVING ON

Until you live in a tidy world of totally integrated, self-customizing CAD systems, you'll need to take on the task of revising your Release 10 program. The AutoLISP programs in the next section are written exclusively for 3D, and can save you hours in creating special programs to enhance your application.

Section III

THE AUTOCAD 3D LIBRARY

The AutoCAD 3D Library

As good as AutoCAD is, and with all the tools for 3D you've learned so far, more is still needed. AutoCAD by its very nature tries to be everything to everybody. As a result, it's a large, cumbersome program. These complications often get in the way of even some of the simplest tasks.

The purpose of the AutoCAD 3D Library is to give you some examples and programs that show how to make AutoCAD simpler and more useful for the tasks you do over and over again. The programs also let you do things in AutoCAD that can't easily be done any other way. These programs are only the beginning of your customized 3D library. Your needs and imagination are the only limits to what you can do with AutoLISP.

The programs were designed to be as simple and understandable as possible. As a result, extensive error-checking every step of the way hasn't been included. Therefore, run the programs exactly as they're described in the library. Otherwise, you might crash the program if it doesn't receive the data it's expecting. Don't worry, you can't hurt anything. Feel free to experiment, alter the programs and customize them for your needs.

It's not the purpose of this book to teach you AutoLISP. For a beginning and easy-to-understand tutorial on AutoLISP, please read George Head's *AutoLISP In Plain English* (published by Ventana Press).

However, to use the programs in this book, you'll need to know a few fundamentals on how to create, load and run AutoLISP programs.

CREATING AN AUTOLISP PROGRAM

An AutoLISP program is created as an ordinary text file. If you don't have the optional disk, you must create the file yourself.

In BASIC programming, files and programs are the same. This isn't so with an AutoLISP program; it's called a *function*. Each function begins with (**defun** and ends with a closing parenthesis. You type functions into a text file. The name of the text file is up to you, but it must end with the extension .LSP. You may have more than one function in a single file. In fact, it's possible to put all the functions into one file.

Before you can use a program (function), the file containing it must be loaded. One file, called **ACAD.LSP**, is loaded automatically. If each function is included in **ACAD.LSP**, they'll all be loaded and ready at the beginning of each drawing. When you're ready to run the program, type in the name of the program, and it will begin executing.

You'll need to make some preparations before you can use the programs. First, you must reserve some memory for AutoLISP to run. Issue the following **SET** commands from the DOS C: prompt or place these commands in the **AUTOEXEC.BAT** file:

```
SET LISPHEAP = 39000
SET LISPSTACK = 5000
```

If you don't issue these commands before going into AutoCAD, you'll quickly get an error message indicating you're out of node (memory) space.

Another thing that will help you with memory management is the **(vmon)** command. If you're working with AutoLISP programs you should always have an **ACAD.LSP** file, even if all of the programs aren't located in that file. Be sure that **(vmon)** is the first line in the **ACAD.LSP** file. This is necessary so that **(vmon)** is the first command issued as you go into a drawing. **(vmon)** means Virtual Memory On, and lets you run very large AutoLISP programs in a small memory environment.

As we've mentioned, programs are typed into an ordinary DOS text file whose name has the extension .LSP. You can create a text file in several ways. The easiest way is with the DOS program EDLIN.COM. If this program is in the ACAD directory or you're pathed to a directory containing EDLIN, you can access it directly from inside AutoCAD. All you need to do is type **EDIT** from the AutoCAD command line. You'll then be asked for the file to edit. When you give it the file name, you can begin editing the file using EDLIN.

Now let's try the first program and see how it works.

Type: EDIT <RETURN>

Response: File to edit.

Type: MACRO1.LSP <RETURN>

Response: New file.

Now you're ready to begin typing in the first program.

Type: I <RETURN>

This begins an insert function for the first line. Now each line will increment by one line number.

Response: 1:*

Now type in the program, ending each line with **<RETURN>.**

Type:
```
(defun C:PON ()
(command "DVIEW" "" "D" "" "")
)
^C
```

When you finish typing in the program, you must break out of Insert mode with a **CTRL-C**.

Response: *

Type: E <RETURN>

This will end the EDLIN program and return you to the AutoCAD command line.

Now that the AutoLISP file has been created, you must load the file.

Type: (load "macrol") <RETURN>

Notice that the **load** command is in parentheses. This indicates to AutoCAD that the command is an AutoLISP command, not the AutoCAD **LOAD** command. The name of the file that's being loaded is enclosed in quotation marks.

Now that the file is loaded, you can run the program simply by typing its name.

Type: PON <RETURN>

The program will now turn **PERSPECTIVE ON**.

If you have the optional disk, then each of the macro .LSP files is already created and typed in for you. You should then begin with the **(load)** command to try each program.

We hope you'll enjoy these programs and that they'll prove useful to you by themselves and in the examples they provide.

Perspective On

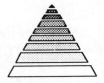

PURPOSE: The **DVIEW** command includes the prompt **DVIEW OFF** but not **DVIEW ON**. This simple routine will turn **PERSPECTIVE ON** from the current viewpoint, target and camera-to-target distance.

TO CREATE:

```
(defun C:PON ()
(command "DVIEW" "" "D" "" "")
)
```

TO INVOKE: Save this macro as an AutoLISP file (**.lsp**).

LET'S TRY IT: Get into a drawing and load **MACRO1** (**Load "MACRO1"**). Select a view by using the **DVIEW** command and either setting **CAMERA** and **TARGET** angles or using **DVIEW PO**ints and specifying **CAMERA** and **TARGET** points. Exit the **DVIEW** command. Type **PON**. You'll see the current view, with **PERSPECTIVE ON**.

TIPS: To use this as a menu macro, add the following line to your menu:

```
^C^C(if(null C:PON)(load "PON"));PON
```

This macro is equivalent to the non-AutoLISP macro:

```
^C^CDVIEW;;D;;;
```

   We're giving you the AutoLISP version because it provides a new command, **PON**, which you can invoke from the keyboard or a menu; it's more flexible. Throughout this section, we'll present several variations for macros and suggest possible applications.

NOTE: This macro uses the current **TARGET** point, **CAMERA** point and **DISTANCE**. If you use **PON** after a **VPOINT** command, you may not see anything at all on your screen! This is because **VPOINT** uses points such as **1,1,1** for orientation, and is always looking at the origin, **0,0,0**. **VPOINT** actually presents a view along a line through the point **1,1,1** and zoomed out automatically. If you just turn **PERSPECTIVE ON**, you may be inside the model and only one unit distant from the origin, and this "auto zoom" won't be performed for you. If you want to use **VPOINT** to move to new views, use **MACRO2** and **MACRO3**; **MACRO2** will use the correct **VPOINT** target and viewpoint, and **MACRO3** will provide a useful zoom option to move in and out of this extreme close-up.

Macro **2** **Perspective On for VPOINTS**

PURPOSE: Turns **PERSPECTIVE ON** from the current viewpoint, when selected by the **VPOINT** command. This macro automatically supplies its own **CAMERA** and **TARGET** points. This will correct the orientation of the line of sight, but you may be zoomed in too close to the model. Correct this with the **DVIEW ZOOM** command or **MACRO3**.

TO CREATE:

```
(defun C:PONV (/ VPT)
(setq VPT(list(getvar "VPOINTX")(getvar "VPOINTY")
  (getvar "VPOINTZ")))
(command "DVIEW" "" "PO" "0,0,0" VPT "D" "" "")
)
```

TO INVOKE: Save this macro as an AutoLISP file (**.lsp**).

LET'S TRY IT: Get into a drawing and load **MACRO2** (**Load "MACRO2"**). Select a view by using the **VPOINT** command. Type **PONV**. You'll see the current view, with **PERSPECTIVE ON**.

TIPS: To use this as a menu macro, add the following line to your menu:

```
^C^C(if(null C:PONV)(load "PONV"));PONV
```

Macro

3 Zoom Perspective

PURPOSE: The **DVIEW** command has a **ZOOM** option that lets you use current **TARGET** and **CAMERA** points and zoom in and out. To get controlled zooms, you must read off the current zoom distance and multiply or divide to get your new zoom distance. The onscreen graphic interface lets you zoom by approximation. This macro lets you choose the ratio to your current zoom, and does the math for you. A larger ratio will move you farther away from the current target, and a smaller ratio will move you closer—like a telephoto lens. This is useful in combination with **MACRO1** or **MACRO2**, which turn **PERSPECTIVE ON** but cannot set the proper view distance.

TO CREATE:

```
(defun C:ZP (/ RAT DI)
(setq RAT(getreal"\nWhat is ratio of current view distance?"))
(setq VPT(list(getvar "VPOINTX")(getvar "VPOINTY")
  (getvar "VPOINTZ")))
(setq TARG(getvar "TARGET"))
(setq DIS(* RAT(distance TARG VPT)))
(command "DVIEW" "" "D" DIS "")
)
```

TO INVOKE: Save this macro as an AutoLISP file (**.lsp**).

LET'S TRY IT: Get into a drawing and load **MACRO3** (**Load "MACRO3"**). Select a view by using the **DVIEW** command. Turn **PERSPECTIVE ON** using **PON**. You'll see the current view with **PERSPECTIVE ON**. Type **ZP**. When prompted, provide a ratio such as **2** for zooming out twice as far or **.5** for zooming in twice as far.

TIPS: To use this as a menu macro, add the following line to your menu:

```
^C^C(if(null C:ZP)(load "ZP"));ZP
```

Macro
4
Snap to Top
Z Value

PURPOSE: Provides a new, 3D object snap that will supply the top **Z** value from a set of objects. This is useful in such applications as architectural modeling, in which you may want to place a typewriter on a desktop, a roof assembly on a house or construct any element "exactly" on top of another without referring to the **LIST** command.

TO CREATE:
```
(defun TOP (/ ENTS BIG COUNT ENT DESCR TH NUM ELEV A AS)
(setq ENTS(ssget) BIG 0.0 COUNT 0 NUM 0.0)
(while(< COUNT(sslength ENTS))
(setq ENT(ssname ENTS COUNT))
(setq DESCR(entget ENT))
(setq TH(assoc 39 DESCR))
(if TH
(progn
  (setq NUM(cdr TH))
  (setq ELEV(nth 3(assoc 10 DESCR)))
  (if(>(+ ELEV NUM) BIG)(setq BIG(+ ELEV NUM)))
)
)
(foreach A '(10 11 12 13)
(setq AS(assoc A DESCR))
```

```
(if AS(setq NUM(nth 3 AS)))
(if(> NUM BIG)(setq BIG NUM))
)
(setq COUNT(1+ COUNT))
)
(setq TOPZ(rtos BIG(getvar "lunits")(getvar "luprec")))
)
```

TO INVOKE: Save this macro as an AutoLISP file (**.lsp**).

LET'S TRY IT: Get into a new drawing and load **MACRO4 (Load "MACRO4")**. Create a series of objects of different elevations and thicknesses. To create a new object at the topmost elevation, type **ELEV !(TOP)**, select the group for determining the highest Z value, then type the thickness to end the **ELEV** command. Succeeding objects will have their baselines at the top Z value in the selection set.

TIPS: You can insert this macro in a menu as a transparent object snap. Copy the following to your menu: **!(TOP)**. You may then use **TOP** in conjunction with the **.XY** filters. For instance, type **LINE .XY** (choose X-Y position) **!(TOP)** (select objects for finding top Z value), and the highest Z in the group will become the Z value for the first line's endpoint.

WARNING: This macro works on all the "simple" AutoCAD entities, since it grabs the insertion point or endpoint and also elevation and thickness of objects in the selection set. However, when used with polylines, 3D polylines (including meshes) or blocks, it evaluates the Z value of only the insertion point, not the true top of the complex object. Use **EXPLODE** on these compound objects if you want to use the **TOP** snap.

Snap to Bottom
Z Value

PURPOSE: Provides a new 3D object snap that will supply the bottom Z value from a set of objects. This has the opposite effect of **MACRO4**, and may be useful when you want to move one object exactly on top of another. This macro would supply the bottom Z value of the object to be placed, rather than depending on the **LIST** command.

TO CREATE:

```
(defun BOT (/ ENTS LIL COUNT ENT DESCR TH NUM ELEV A AS)
(setq ENTS(ssget) LIL 0.0 COUNT 0 NUM 0.0)
(while(< COUNT(sslength ENTS))
(setq ENT(ssname ENTS COUNT))
(setq DESCR(entget ENT))
(setq TH(assoc 39 DESCR))
(if TH
(progn
  (setq NUM(cdr TH))
  (setq ELEV(nth 3(assoc 10 DESCR)))
  (if(<(+ ELEV NUM) LIL)(setq LIL(+ ELEV NUM)))
)
)
(foreach A '(10 11 12 13)
(setq AS(assoc A DESCR))
(if AS(setq NUM(nth 3 AS)))
```

```
(if(< NUM LIL)(setq LIL NUM))
)
(setq COUNT(1+ COUNT))
)
(setq BOTZ (rtos LIL(getvar"lunits")(getvar"luprec")))
)
```

TO INVOKE: Save this macro as an AutoLISP file (**.lsp**).

LET'S TRY IT: Get into a new drawing and load **MACRO5** (**Load "MACRO5"**). Create a series of objects of different elevations and thicknesses. To create a new object at the bottom-most elevation, type **ELEV, !(TOP)**, select the group for determining the lowest Z value, then type the thickness to end the **ELEV** command. Succeeding objects will have their baselines at the bottom Z value in the selection set.

TIPS: You can insert this macro in a menu as a transparent object snap. Copy the following to your menu: **!(BOT)**. You can then use **BOT** with the **.XY** filters. For instance, type **LINE .XY** (choose X-Y position) **!(BOT)** (select objects for finding bottom Z value), and the lowest Z in the group will become the Z value for the first line's endpoint.

WARNING: This macro works on all the "simple" AutoCAD entities, since it grabs the insertion point or endpoint and also elevation and thickness of objects in the selection set. However, when used with polylines, 3D polylines (including meshes) or blocks, it will evaluate the Z value of only the insertion point, not the true bottom of the complex object. Use **EXPLODE** on these compound objects if you want to use the **BOT** snap.

Macro 6   Capture Thickness of Object ❓

PURPOSE: Used in creating extruded objects at different levels but with the same thickness. If you're modeling large arrays, as in city planning, building exteriors or mechanical assemblies, it's often useful to check the extrusion thickness of an already created standard object, or "grab" it for creating the next similar object. For example, let's say you're setting thickness for chimneys on rooftops: you may want a set of chimneys to be the same height, but at different elevations. With this macro, you can "grab" the thickness of one, set your thickness, and using **ELEV** and perhaps **MACRO4**, **MACRO5** or **MACRO7** for **TOP**, **BOT** or **MIDFACE** snaps, begin drawing them in place.

TO CREATE:

```
(defun THI (/ ENT DESCR AS)
(setq ENT(car(entsel)))
(setq DESCR(entget ENT))
(setq AS(assoc 39 DESCR))
(if AS
(setq THIK(rtos(cdr AS)(getvar"lunits")(getvar"luprec")))
(setq THIK(rtos(getvar "thickness")(getvar"lunits")(getvar"
  luprec")))
)
)
```

TO INVOKE: Save this macro as an AutoLISP file (**.lsp**).

LET'S TRY IT: Get into a new drawing and create an extruded object. For instance, type **ELEV 0 3 CIRCLE 0,0,0 5** to create a circular cylinder with center at **0,0,0**, radius of **5** units, and thickness of **3** units. To create an "equal thickness" circle elsewhere in the drawing, type **ELEV 4 !(THI)** (touch edge of first circle) and draw a second circle. It will have an elevation of **4** units and the same thickness as the first circle, **3** units.

TIPS: You can inset this macro in a menu as a transparent object snap. Copy the following to your menu: **!(THI)**. You can then use **THI** with the **ELEV** command to match the thickness of an existing extruded entity. You can also use it with other object snaps. For instance, **ELEV !(TOP)** (select entities) **!(THI)** (select entities) would produce succeeding objects at the topmost Z value and with a given thickness.

Macro **7** # Capture Middle of an Entity ⊙

PURPOSE: A general-purpose object snap that finds the center of a **3DFACE** at any angle and with 1,2,3 or 4 unique vertices. It will also snap to the center of a circle or arc, the midpoint of a line, a node of a point, the middle of a solid of 1-4 vertices, etc. In extruded objects, the snap is to the middle X, Y and Z positions (i.e., midface and halfway up an object). This macro began as an attempt to snap to the middle of a **3DFACE**, but it can find the middle of any simple entity (excluding **PLINES**).

TO CREATE:
```
(defun MIDF (/ ENT DESCR THA TH ELEV MIDZ AS10 A AS VLIST VN)
(defun MID3D (PTNUM PTLIST / XDELT YDELT ZDELT
   COUNT PT1 X1 Y1 Z1 PT2 X2 Y2 Z2 XNEW YNEW ZNEW)
(setq XDELT 0.0 YDELT 0.0 ZDELT 0.0 COUNT 0
    PT1(car PTLIST)
    X1(car PT1)
    Y1(cadr PT1)
    Z1(caddr PT1))
(while(< COUNT(length PTLIST))
```

```
(setq PT2(nth COUNT PTLIST)
    X2(car PT2)
    Y2(cadr PT2)
    Z2(caddr PT2)
    XDELT(+ XDELT(- X2 X1))
    YDELT(+ YDELT(- Y2 Y1))
    ZDELT(+ ZDELT(- Z2 Z1))
COUNT(1+ COUNT))
)
(setq XNEW(+ X1(/ XDELT COUNT))
    YNEW(+ Y1(/ YDELT COUNT))
    ZNEW(+ Z1(/ ZDELT COUNT))
    MPT(list XNEW YNEW ZNEW))
)
;
; MAIN PROGRAM
;
(setq ENT(car(entsel)))
(if ENT
(progn
(setq DESCR(entget ENT)
    THA(assoc 39 DESCR))
(if THA(setq TH(cdr THA) ELEV (cadddr(assoc 10 DESCR))
  MIDZ(+ ELEV(/ TH 2.0))))
(setq AS10(cdr(assoc 10 DESCR)))
(if MIDZ(setq AS10(list(car AS10)(cadr AS10)MIDZ)))
(setq VLIST(cons AS10 VLIST))
(foreach A '(11 12 13)
(setq AS(cdr(assoc A DESCR)))
(if MIDZ(setq AS(list(car AS)(cadr AS)MIDZ)))
(if(and AS(car AS)(null(member AS VLIST)))(SETQ VLIST
  (CONS AS VLIST)))
)
(setq VN(length VLIST))
(MID3D VN VLIST)
```

```
)
(progn
(princ"\nOBJECT NOT FOUND...PICK AGAIN...")
(setq MPT nil)
)
)
)
```

TO INVOKE: Save this macro as an AutoLISP file (**.lsp**).

LET'S TRY IT: Get into a new drawing and create a series of objects: a circle, line, point, and solids and 3DFACES with 1, 2, 3 and 4 unique endpoints. Extrude several of the 2D entities using the **CHANGE** command. Now, load **MACRO7** (**Load "MACRO7"**). Type **LINE !(MIDF)** and touch an entity on its edge. The line will be snapped to the geometric center of the object. Try viewing in isometric by typing **VPOINT 1,1,1**. Type **LINE !(MIDF)** and touch an extruded entity, **3DFACE** or **3DLINE**. The line will snap to the three-dimensional center of the entity.

TIPS: You can insert this macro in a menu as a transparent object snap. Copy the following to your menu: **!(MIDF)**. You can then use **MIDF** with an entity creation command to snap to an entity's center of mass. You can also trap the X, Y or Z values of the centerpoint by combining 3D filters with the **MIDF** snap. For instance, **.XY !(MIDF)** (select entity) **!(BOT)** (select entities) would produce a point in the middle of a chosen face and at the bottom elevation of a set of entities.

Macro
8 Automatic Entity Extrusion

PURPOSE: Automatically extrudes 2D entities into 2 1/2 D (and back). You can accomplish this by using a series of **CHANGE** or **CHPROP**

commands on selected entities; but for large drawings — for instance, entire interior space plans for architects — the use of **CHANGE** or **CHPROP** is rather tedious. Once your office standards are set up, determining the typical heights of such linear elements as interior walls, exterior walls or window mullions, this macro provides a lightning-fast way to extrude and unextrude large plans.

To use this macro, you'll need both the AutoLISP routine and the data file it will scan. The "TO CREATE" section below lists the AutoLISP code; now let's create the data file.

This file uses a space-delimited data file. Using any ASCII editor, create the file **XTRULIST.DTA** that contains the necessary information. The following is a sample of the file included on the optional AutoCAD 3D diskette:

```
0
0
54
TEST1
0
108
TEST2
28.5
1.5
TEST3
96
2
```

Create this file in exactly the same format as the example above. The first line of an entry is the layer name, such as **0**, **TEST1**, **TEST2**, etc. The second line of an entry is the elevation or bottom Z value for extruding entities on that layer. The third line is the thickness for extruding entities on that layer. The names of the layers and their heights will depend on your system of 2D drafting. In a typical architectural application, layer **0** might contain low interior walls 54" high, while **TEST2** might contain workspace surfaces 28.5" high and 1.5" thick.

TO CREATE:

```
(defun C:XTRU (/ S FIL RM CM LAYER ELEV THIK BLOX)
(defun *ERROR* (s)
(close FIL)
(setvar "REGENMODE" RM)
(setvar "CMDECHO" CM)
(setvar "EXPERT" 0)
(princ s)
(setq *ERROR* nil)
(terpri)
)
(graphscr)
(setq RM (getvar "REGENMODE") CM (getvar "CMDECHO"))
(setvar "REGENMODE" 0)
(setvar "EXPERT" 3)
(setvar "CMDECHO" 0)
(if(null XTRUDIR)(setq XTRUDIR "2D-3D"))
(princ(strcat "\nEXTRUSION DIRECTION BEGINS: " XTRUDIR "\n"))
(setq FIL(open "XTRULIST.DTA" "r"))
(while(setq LAYER(read-line FIL))
(setq ELEV(read-line FIL))
(setq THIK(read-line FIL))
(setq BLOX(ssget "X" '((0 . "INSERT"))))
(if(and(equal XTRUDIR "2D-3D")(tblsearch "layer" LAYER))
(progn
(command "change" (ssget "X"(list(cons 8 LAYER))))
(if BLOX(command  "r" BLOX))
(command "" "p" "e" ELEV "t" THIK "")
)
)
(if(and(equal XTRUDIR "3D-2D")(tblsearch "layer" LAYER))
(progn
(command "change" (ssget "X" (list(cons 8 LAYER))))
(if BLOX(command "r" BLOX))
(command "" "p" "e" "0" "t" "0" "")
```

```
)
)
)
(close FIL)
(command "REGEN")
(setvar "REGENMODE" 1)
(setvar "CMDECHO" 1)
(setvar "EXPERT" 0)
(if(equal XTRUDIR "2D-3D")(setq XTRUDIR "3D-2D")
  (setq XTRUDIR "2D-3D"))
(princ(strcat "\nEXTRUSION DIRECTION IS NOW: "XTRUDIR))
(terpri)
)
```

TO INVOKE: Create this macro as an AutoLISP file (**.lsp**).

LET'S TRY IT: Get into a new drawing and load **MACRO8** (Load "MACRO8"). Create objects on various layers. If you wish, use layers **0, TEST1, TEST2** and **TEST3**. Type **XTRU**. If it finds the file **XTRULIST.DTA**, it will begin. It will change the elevation and thickness of all 2D entities that aren't blocked — lines, arcs, solids, traces, etc. — to the appropriate extruded or "2 1/2 D" values. If the macro is run a second time, entities will be "unextruded" back to an elevation and thickness of 0. This macro will affect an entity regardless of whether its layer is on, off, frozen or thawed!

You can insert this macro into a menu by including the line:

```
^C^C(if(null C:XTRU)(load "MACRO8"));XTRU
```

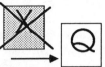

Macro **9** # Symbol Replacement

PURPOSE: Redefines blocks in your drawing. This macro will perform three useful functions: "refresh" a block definition, replacing the current block with its definition as found on hard disk; replace a block definition with the definition of a different block on hard disk; or replace a 2D symbol with its 3D counterpart from hard disk, or vice versa.

While you might use the **INSERT** command and a library of 3D symbols to create a 3D model from scratch, it's sometimes better to create a complete 2D diagram and replace each 2D symbol with its 3D counterpart. This macro shows how to use such a technique.

TO CREATE: The basic routine for symbol replacement is to use the "insert equals" command (i.e., **INSERT blockname** =, which replaces the current block definition with that of a **.DWG** file on disk, if available). At the end of the command, it will ask for a new insertion point. By pressing < CTRL C > you can redefine a symbol without inserting an extra instance.

An interesting feature lets you provide a **.DWG** filename on the right side of the equals sign. All instances of the first block in the drawing will be redefined using the **.DWG** file definition. For instance, if you type **INSERT CH1 = CH2**, all instances of **CH1**, perhaps a symbol for a secretarial chair, will be replaced by **CH2**, perhaps a symbol for an executive chair. If the second symbol is actually a 3D or "2 1/2 D" block, you can use this technique to perform an automatic 2D to 3D conversion. The results can help a great deal in creating complex 3D models.

TO INVOKE: Use this technique in an existing drawing by typing at the **Command:** prompt.

LET'S TRY IT: Get into an AutoCAD drawing and insert a typical symbol. Type the command **INSERT sym1 = sym2**, where **sym1** is the current block name and **sym2** is the replacement symbol name. The system will respond "Block (sym1) redefined:" and request an insertion point. Press < CTRL C > if you don't want to insert another instance.

You may use a symbol from another subdirectory or disk. Simply include the proper path in its name; for instance: **INSERT CH1 = C:\SYM3D\CH13D.**

If you list the symbol, it will still have its original name even though it's now represented by the new symbol data. To change its name, type **RENAME BLOCKS oldname newname**, where **oldname** is the name of the original symbol and **newname** is the name of its replacement symbol. This macro will work whether the symbols' layers are on, off, frozen or thawed.

Macro
10 Automatic 2D/3D Symbol Replacement

PURPOSE: Replaces 2D symbols in your drawing with the appropriate 3D or "2 1/2 D" symbol. You could accomplish this by manually invoking the **INSERT=** command as in **MACRO9**, over and over. But once set up, **MACRO10** provides a repeatable and much faster exchange. It scans the current drawing for all "standard" symbols and replaces them as described in a data file you'll create. The macro eliminates the listing and fumbling of a manual technique, and if you use it with **MACRO8** and **MACRO11**, you can convert 2D plans to 3D models in moments.

This macro requires that both 2D and 3D symbols exist and reside on the current subdirectory. It also requires both the AutoLISP routine and the data file it will scan. The "TO CREATE" section below lists the AutoLISP code; now let's create the data file.

This file uses a space-delimited data file. Using any ASCII editor, create the file **SWAPLIST.DTA** that contains the necessary information. The following is a sample of the file included on the optional AutoCAD 3D diskette:

SYM1

SYM13D

SYM2

SYM23D

SYM3

SYM33D

　　Create this file in exactly the same format as the example above. The first line of an entry is the name of the 2D block, such as **SYM1**, **SYM2** or **SYM3**. The second line is the name of the 3D replacement block, such as **SYM13D**, **SYM23D** or **SYM33D**. The names of the 2D and 3D blocks will depend on your system of 2D drafting. In a typical architectural application, **SYM1** might be a 2D chair, while **SYM13D** would be the 3D model to replace it.

TO CREATE:

```
(defun C:SWAP (/ S FIL RM CM SYM2D SYM3D)
(defun *ERROR* (s)
(close FIL)
(setvar "REGENMODE" RM)
(setvar "CMDECHO" CM)
(setvar "EXPERT" 0)
(princ s)
(setq *ERROR* nil)
(terpri)
)
(graphscr)
(setq RM (getvar "REGENMODE") CM (getvar "CMDECHO"))
(setvar "REGENMODE" 0)
(setvar "CMDECHO" 0)
(setvar "EXPERT" 3)
(if(null SWAPDIR)(setq SWAPDIR "2D-3D"))
(princ(strcat "\nSWAP DIRECTION BEGINS: " SWAPDIR "\n"))
(setq FIL(open "SWAPLIST.DTA" "r"))
```

```
(while(setq SYM2D(read-line FIL))
(setq SYM3D(read-line FIL))
(if(and(equal SWAPDIR "2D-3D")(tblsearch "block" SYM2D))
(progn
(command "rename" "block" SYM2D SYM3D)
(command "insert" (strcat SYM3D "=") \c)
)
)
(if(and(equal SWAPDIR "3D-2D")(tblsearch "block" SYM3D))
(progn
(command "rename" "block" SYM3D SYM2D)
(command "insert" (strcat SYM2D "=") \c)
)
)
)
(close FIL)
(command "REGEN")
(setvar "REGENMODE" 1)
(setvar "CMDECHO" 1)
(setvar "EXPERT" 0)
(if(equal SWAPDIR "2D-3D")(setq SWAPDIR "3D-2D")
  (setq SWAPDIR "2D-3D"))
(princ(strcat "\nSWAP DIRECTION IS NOW: " SWAPDIR))
(terpri)
)
```

TO INVOKE: Create this macro as an AutoLISP file (**.lsp**).

LET'S TRY IT: Get into a new drawing and load **MACRO10** (**Load "MACRO10"**). If you don't have both a 2D symbol and a 3D counterpart, do the following:

Type **SOLID 0,0 1,0 0,1 1,1**. End the **SOLID** command with an extra < **RETURN** >. Now create a block. Type **BLOCK SYM1 0,0**. Select the solid and press an extra < **RETURN** > to end the **BLOCK** command. Type **OOPS** to bring it back. Type **CHANGE L** followed by a < **RETURN** > and **P E 0 T 1**. This will change the solid into a cube with its bottom Z elevation at **0** and a thickness of one unit. To prove this, type **VPOINT 1,1,1** and you'll see the cube from another angle. Type **BLOCK SYM13D 0,0**. Select the solid and press an extra <**RETURN**> to end the **BLOCK** command. There will now be no solids visible in the drawing. Insert several of the 2D blocks using **INSERT SYM1**.

Now **WBLOCK** the two blocks, 2D and 3D cubes, out to disk. Type **WBLOCK SYM1 SYM1**, then **WBLOCK SYM13D SYM13D**. Assuming you use the sample data file, you may now type **SWAP**. Each instance of **SYM1** will be replaced from disk by **SYM13D**, and the 2D cube will become 3D. Type **LIST** and select a few of the 3D cubes. Their names should be **SYM13D** now. Type **SWAP** again, and they'll become 2D again, and will list as **SYM1** insertions.

TIPS: In addition to 2D/3D swaps, this routine could show space plans with alternative sets of furniture, or replace one manufacturer's components with another's. Insert this macro into a menu by including the line:

```
^C^C(if(null C:SWAP)(load "MACRO10"));SWAP
```

Macro 11   Nonstandard Block Extrusion

PURPOSE: If a block isn't "standard" (i.e., it isn't listed in the **SWAPLIST.DTA** file or doesn't have a ready-made 3D counterpart), you can still redefine it by inserting it, exploding, extruding its subentities and reblocking it. This macro will redefine nonstandard blocks by selection (as long as they are nested only one level deep).

This routine uses the same **XTRULIST.DTA** file as **MACRO8**. If this file doesn't already exist, create it using any ASCII editor, following the instructions in **MACRO8**.

TO CREATE:
```
(defun C:REDEF (/ S NAMLIST BLKS COUNTER NAM LAST ENT ENTS
LAY LAY3D FIL ELEV THIK)
```

```
(defun *ERROR* (s)
(close FIL)
(setvar "HIGHLIGHT" 1)
(setvar "BLIPMODE" 1)
(setvar "REGENMODE" 1)
(setvar "CMDECHO" 1)
(setvar "EXPERT" 0)
(setq *ERROR* nil)
(terpri)
)
(setq NAMLIST nil)
(if(null RDIR)(setq RDIR "2D-3D"))
(princ"\nINDICATE BLOCKS TO REDEFINE BY EXTRUSION: ")
(setq BLKS(ssget))
(princ(strcat"\nREDEFINING DIRECTION BEGINS: " RDIR))
(initget 1 "Y N")
(setq ANS(getword"\nREVERSE REDEFINING DIRECTION? (Y N) "))
(if(and(equal ANS "Y")(equal RDIR "2D-3D"))
(setq RDIR "3D-2D" ANS nil))
(if(and(equal ANS "Y")(equal RDIR "3D-2D"))
(setq RDIR "2D-3D"))
(princ(strcat"\nREDEFINING DIRECTION IS NOW: " RDIR))
(princ"\nABOUT TO REDEFINE ALL BLOCKS SELECTED...PLEASE WAIT!")
(setvar "HIGHLIGHT" 0)
(setvar "BLIPMODE" 0)
(setvar "REGENMODE" 0)
(setvar "CMDECHO" 0)
(setvar "EXPERT" 3)
(setq COUNTER 0)
(while(< COUNTER(sslength BLKS))
  (if(equal(cdr(assoc 0(entget(ssname BLKS COUNTER)))))"INSERT")
  (progn
  (setq NAM(cdr(assoc 2(entget(ssname BLKS COUNTER)))))
  (if(null(member NAM NAMLIST))
  (setq NAMLIST(cons NAM NAMLIST)))
```

```
)
)
(setq COUNTER(1+ COUNTER))
)
(setq LAST(entlast))
(setq COUNTER 0)
(while(< COUNTER(length NAMLIST))
  (princ(strcat"\nEXTRUDING BLOCK: " (nth COUNTER NAMLIST)

  "...WAIT!"))
  (command "insert" (strcat "*" (nth COUNTER NAMLIST))
  "0,0" "1" "0")
  (setq ENTS(ssadd))
  (setq ENT(entnext LAST))
  (while ENT
    (setq ENTS(ssadd ENT ENTS))
    (if(equal RDIR "2D-3D")
    (progn
    (setq LAY(cdr(assoc 8(entget ENT))))
    (setq FIL(open "XTRULIST.DTA" "r"))
    (setq LAY3D nil)
    (while(and(not(equal LAY LAY3D))
    (setq LAY3D(read-line FIL)))
      (setq ELEV(read-line FIL))
      (setq THIK(read-line FIL))
      (if(equal LAY LAY3D)
      (command "change" ENT "" "p" "e" ELEV "t" THIK ""))
    )
    (close FIL)
    )
    )
    (setq ENT(entnext ENT))
  )
  (if(equal RDIR "3D-2D")
  (command "change" ENTS "" "p" "e" "0" "t" "0" ""))
```

```
    (command "block" (nth COUNTER NAMLIST) "0,0" ENTS "")
    (princ(strcat"\nBLOCK: " (nth COUNTER NAMLIST)
    " REDEFINED!"))
    (setq COUNTER(1+ COUNTER))
)
(command "REGEN")
(setvar "HIGHLIGHT" 1)
(setvar "BLIPMODE" 1)
(setvar "REGENMODE" 1)
(setvar "CMDECHO" 1)
(setvar "EXPERT" 0)
(princ "\nFINISHED!")
(terpri)
)
```

TO INVOKE: Create this macro as an AutoLISP file (**.lsp**).

LET'S TRY IT: If you're using the **XTRULIST.DTA** file listed in **MACRO8**, you've defined elevation and thickness of extrusion for layers **0**, **TEST1**, **TEST2** and **TEST3**. Type **LAYER S 0** and press an extra <**RETURN**> to exit the **LAYER** command. Draw several 2D entities, such as lines. Type **BLOCK ONE** and select an insertion point. When prompted, select each entity and press an extra <**RETURN**> to exit the **BLOCK** command. Repeat this procedure for another layer, creating **BLOCK TWO**.

Type **INSERT ONE**, and select an insertion point, X scale, Y scale and rotation angle. Create several insertions of **BLOCK ONE** at different locations and scales. Do the same for **BLOCK TWO**.

Make sure **MACRO11** is loaded, or load it now (**Load "MACRO11"**). Type **REDEF**. You'll be prompted to select blocks for redefinition. Select at least one insertion of **BLOCK ONE** and one insertion of **BLOCK TWO**. The macro will tell you which direction you're currently extruding in, 2D-3D or 3D-2D, and you'll be asked if you want to change the current direction. Assuming this is your first run, objects will be extruded from their current elevation and thickness to their **XTRULIST.DTA** heights, so you'll be told that "Redefining direction begins: 2D-3D." When prompted for reversing direction, type **N**.

The macro will build a list of each block in your selection set. If you accidentally select lines or nonblocked entities, they won't be affected.

Also, a block will be redefined only once; a list of names is constructed and checked so no block is redefined twice.

From the selection set, each block will be inserted, exploded, extruded and redefined for you. At the end of the macro, the drawing will **REGEN** once to display the new 3D blocks.

If you wish, you can run the macro several different times on different nonstandard blocks in the drawing without accidentally "unextruding" your previous work. By watching the "Redefining direction" prompts and responding to the "Reverse ...direction?" prompts, you'll be in total control of the process.

TIPS: If you're converting an entire large drawing, you could thaw all layers, **ZOOM** to **EXTENTS**, and select all entities for conversion with this macro. Because the insertion points and insertion elevation of blocks aren't affected (only their subentities), this process won't interfere with symbol substitution (**MACRO10**), or with entity extrusion (**MACRO8**). After redefining all blocks, you can run **MACRO8** and **MACRO10**. The resulting drawing will have all standard, nonblocked entities extruded, standard blocks replaced and nonstandard blocks redefined. For most applications, you'd have a successful, automatic 3D conversion of your 2D drawing. By combining these routines into a "supermacro," including other levels of object revision, you could have a "one-button" 2D/3D converter.

Macro

12 3D Helix

PURPOSE: Creates a three-dimensional helix or "spring" using the **3DPOLY** command. It lets you control the number of revolutions, starting angle, radius and other characteristics of the spring.

TO CREATE:

```
(defun C:HELIX (/ REVS DIVS CEN RAD RINC STA HT HINC
   REVCNT R X Y A Z)
;
; function to create a 3D spiral
; in the form of a 3DPOLY (a zero-width wire spring)
;
(graphscr)
(setq REVS(getreal"\nNUMBER OF REVOLUTIONS? ")
    DIVS(getint"\nNUMBER OF DIVISIONS PER REVOLUTION? ")
    CEN(getpoint"\nCENTER OF BOTTOM LOOP? ")
    RAD(getdist"\nBEGINNING RADIUS ?" CEN)
    RINC(getdist"\nRADIUS INCREMENT ? ")
    STA(getangle"\nSTARTING ANGLE? " CEN)
    HT(getdist"\nBEGINNING HEIGHT BETWEEN LOOPS? ")
    HINC(getdist"\nHEIGHT INCREMENT ? ")
    STA (/(* STA PI)180.0) A STA Z (caddr CEN) R 0
    REVCNT 0)
(command "3dpoly")
(while(< R REVS)
(setq X(+(car CEN)(* RAD(cos A)))
    Y(+(cadr CEN)(* RAD(sin A))))
(command (list X Y Z))
(setq A(+ A(/(* 2.0 PI)DIVS))
    Z(+ Z(/ HT DIVS))
    R(+ R(/ 1.0 DIVS))
    REVCNT(1+ REVCNT)
    RAD(+ RAD(/ RINC DIVS)))
(if(equal REVCNT DIVS)
(setq HT(+ HT HINC) REVCNT 0))
)
(command "")
)
```

TO INVOKE: Create this macro as an AutoLISP file (**.lsp**).

LET'S TRY IT: Get into a new drawing and load **MACRO12** (**Load "MACRO12"**). Type **HELIX**. You'll be prompted for "Number of revolutions." Type **3**. The next prompt is for "Number of divisions per revolution." This number determines the smoothness of the X Y cross-section of the spring. For instance, **3** would create a triangular cross-section, **4** would be square, and larger numbers would divide a circle into smoother and smoother paths. Type **15**. The resulting spring will be roughly circular when viewed from above.

Next, set the "Center of bottom loop." Type **0,0,0**. "Beginning radius" is the initial radius of the spring when viewed from above. Type **4**. "Radius increment" will let you create a spring that gets gradually wider or narrower with each revolution, depending on the value and sign of the increment. The increment represents the distance that the radius will increase (or decrease, if negative) with each revolution. Type **0**. "Beginning angle" determines the starting angle, which will correspond to the first end of the spring's "wire." Type **0**. "Beginning height between loops" is the initial distance between loops **1** and **2** of the spring. If positive, the spring will "go up" as it's created; if negative it will "go down"; if **0**, the spring will be a 2D spiral. Type **2.0**. "Height increment" is the amount of change in loop-to-loop height with each revolution. If positive, loops will get farther apart; if negative, they'll get closer together; if **0**, they'll stay a constant distance apart. Type **0**.

The macro will now build a spring centered about the **X-Y** point **0,0**, with its base at **Z=0**. It will have three revolutions, beginning at **0** degrees. Each revolution will be two units apart, a constant radius of four and fifteen sections per revolution. If viewed from above, it will be roughly circular, and if you use **VPOINT** or **DVIEW**, you can see various 3D views of the spring. If you type **LIST** and select the helix, you'll see that it's a single **3DPOLY** that "goes up" from **4,0,0**.

TIPS: You can indicate point, angular and distance variables, using your cursor. By experimenting with different values at the prompts, you can create a variety of different 2D spirals and 3D springs. The **PEDIT** command will smooth the resulting helix. Type **PEDIT**, select the helix, then type **SPLINE** and a **<RETURN>** to end the command.

Macro
13 # 3D to 2D – An Important Trick

PURPOSE: Lets you take a "photograph" of a particular 3D view. That is, you can take the 3D view of your choice, squash it flat into an identical 2D image, and insert the resulting image into drawings containing multiple 2D or 3D images.

TO CREATE: The AutoCAD configuration process lets you specify your plotter as an ADI device. If you choose this option, you'll be asked for the output format, one of which is **DXB**. If you plot to a **DXB** file, the displayed 3D image will be traced and the resulting strokes saved in a **DXB** file. If you use the **DXBIN** command, these 2D strokes will be inserted into your drawing as standard lines.

TO INVOKE: From the main menu, choose item **5** (Configure AutoCAD). From the next menu, choose item **5** (Configure plotter). You'll be prompted with the current plotter and asked if you want to select a different one; type **Y**. If the plotter drivers aren't in the current directory, you'll be prompted for the name of their directory. If necessary, insert the driver diskette in your disk drive, then type the appropriate drive and path, as in **A:**.

You'll be presented with a list of possible plotters, one of which is ADI. Type its number. Next, you'll be asked to choose the output format for your "imaginary plotter"; type **2** for the AutoCAD **DXB** file. The remaining questions were designed to control the output resolution, size and orientation of an actual plotter. Since we're using a **DXB** plot file as an intermediary step or "imaginary plotter," your responses to these questions will affect the resulting 2D image.

"Maximum horizontal...." and "...vertical plot size in drawing units" will determine the size of the final 2D image. If you choose a maximum horizontal (**X**) plot size of **11.0** and a maximum vertical (**Y**) plot size of **8.5**, the 2D "photograph" of the 3D view will be no larger than 8.5 x 11.0

inches, regardless of actual dimensions of the 3D model. You may need to rescale the image if you're dimensioning it.

"Plotter steps per drawing unit...." controls the fineness of pen movement. In our case, this technique converts all parts of an image, whether arc, circle, text or line, into linear strokes, or lines. This number will affect the resulting resolution of arcs and circles after squashing, although simple lines are not affected by this factor. A high number such as 1,000 will result in very smooth curves after translation, but may slow down the creation of the file. We suggest an intermediate value of 256, 128 or even 64 plot units per inch.

The prompt "Do you want to change pens while plotting?" has no bearing on this technique. The resulting **DXBIN** image will be all one color, and the lines will be colored **BYLAYER** and assigned to the current layer. "Pens" don't exist in an imaginary plotter! The remaining questions determine rotation, placement in the frame, and scale of the drawing within the imaginary page. Select a plot to **Fit**. You should usually use this technique to create hidden-line images.

LET'S TRY IT: Assuming you've configured for an ADI plotter with **DXB** output as outlined, get into a new drawing. Type **SOLID 0,0 1,0 0,1 1,1**. Then type **CHANGE L** and press an extra < **RETURN** > to end object selection. Next, type **E 0 1.0**. This will extrude the solid into a one-unit cube. Type **VPOINT 1,1,1** and you'll see a typical isometric projection of the cube. Type **PLOT D** (for display) **N** and the name you want to give the **DXB** plot file; for example, **3DPLOT**. After plotting is completed, erase the cube by typing **ERASE L** and two extra < **RETURNs** >.

Now, return to a "normal" view by typing **VPOINT 0,0,1**. Next, type **DXBIN 3DPLOT** (or the name of the **DXB** file you've chosen). Type **ZOOM E** to see the entire image. You should see the hidden-line, 2D image of the cube. To prove it's a 2D "photograph," type **LIST** and choose one of the edges of the cube. It should list as a line, rather than as a solid.

TIPS: You can create multiple 3D views from within a model or from the main menu, then **DXBIN** each one into a new image sheet. By blocking each image as you **DXBIN** it and moving the blocks around, you can create a complete storyboard or visual library for the object.

Because this technique turns anything displayed into a 2D linear drawing, you may use it with **DVIEW**, perspectives, or for exploding text into vectors. If you display a piece of text, plot it and reinsert it, it'll

be broken into line segments. This solves the problem of hatching outline text, or altering a font for signage.

EXTENSION: Multiple configurations are possible, so you can plot a
DXB file or anything else whenever you want. First, make a separate
directory called **DXB**. Enter AutoCAD and configure for ADI and **DXB**.
Quit AutoCAD. At the DOS prompt, copy **ACAD.CFG** to the **DXB** directory. Enter AutoCAD and reconfigure to your usual plot setup.

   To run AutoCAD with the standard configuration, type **SET
ACADCFG = C:\ACAD** at the DOS prompt and enter AutoCAD. To run
with the **DXB** configuration, type **SET ACADCFG = C:\DXB** at the DOS
prompt and enter AutoCAD. You can insert these statements into batch
files for faster reconfiguration.

Macro
14
Plotting Multiple Views

PURPOSE: Lets you plot all the views in the current drawing, or a select
group of views, automatically. It's useful when you want to plot each
view in an animation. (See *the AutoCAD 3D Diskette* for further help on
animation programs.) If you're configuring to plot to a **.PLT** file, the
resulting images can be plotted to paper using your specifications. If
you configure to plot to a **.DXB** file as in **MACRO13**, each 3D view can
be squashed to 2D and reinserted in a storyboard (**MACRO16**), or
saved in a new drawing (**MACRO15**).

TO CREATE:

```
(defun C:VPLOT (/ FIL TYP VPREF VW VNAM)
(initget 1 "A S")
(setq FIL(open "VPLOT.SCR" "w"))
(setq TYP(getkword"\nPlot all views or a set (A S) ? "))
(if(equal TYP "S")
(setq VPREF(strcase(getstring"\nWhat is prefix for views? "))))
```

```
(princ"\nABOUT TO PROCESS VIEWS...PLEASE WAIT!")
(setq ARROWS(ssget "X" '((2 . "ARR"))))
(if ARROWS(command "erase" ARROWS ""))
(setq VW(tblnext "view" T))
(while VW
(setq VNAM(cdr(assoc 2 VW)))
(if(or(equal TYP "A")
   (equal(substr VNAM 1(strlen VPREF))VPREF))
(progn
(princ(strcat"\nVIEW: " VNAM " WILL BE PLOTTED..."))
(write-line(strcat"PLOT V " VNAM " N") FIL)
(write-line VNAM FIL)
(write-line "" FIL)
)
)
(setq VW(tblnext "view"))
)
(close FIL)
(command "script" "VPLOT")
)
```

TO INVOKE: Create this macro as an AutoLISP file (**.lsp**).

LET'S TRY IT: Get into a new drawing. Create a series of views, naming and saving the views as **CIR1** through **CIR12**, using the same prefix for each. Now load **MACRO 14 (Load "MACRO 14")** and type **VPLOT**. At the prompt "Plot all views or a set (A S)?" type **S**. At the prompt "What is prefix of views?" type **CIR**. Before using this macro, you must create a one-unit cube and create a script file **VPLOT.SCR**, which will do the actual plotting. At the end of the macro, **VPLOT.SCR** is called, and **CIR1** through **CIR12** are plotted to **.PLT** or **.DXB** files according to your configuration.

If you're configured for **.PLT** files, you may now use a plot-file spooling program to plot each drawing to paper. If you're configured for **.DXB** files as described in **MACRO 13**, you may now use these output files in **MACRO15** or **MACRO16**.

Before using the macros, you must create a block called **ARR** and save it to your disk. It should be directional or arrow-shaped, because its position will determine the camera point and its rotation angle will determine the viewpoint. It must be pointed to the right, since insertion with **MEASURE** or **DIVIDE** will place **ARR** blocks with their rotation along the line of movement.

Create **ARR** by entering a new drawing. Type **LINE 0,0 1,0 0.5,0.5** and press **RETURN**. Then type **LINE 1,0 0.5,-0.5**. This will create an arrow one unit long, facing to the right. Type **BLOCK ARR 0,0** and select the three lines. This will create a block called **ARR**, which inserts from the tail of the arrow. Type **WBLOCK ARR ARR**. This will save the block description to disk.

TO CREATE:

```
(defun C:WTC (/ S CM HL EX VPREF SPREF VW SLD SCRFIL HID FIL
   CONTARG TARGHGT CAMHGT ARROWS FRAMCNT COUNTER THISARR VIEWPT
   INSANG SLDNAM VLIST)
(defun *ERROR* (s)
(if FIL(close FIL))
(setq *ERROR* nil)
(setvar "CMDECHO" CM)
(setvar "HIGHLIGHT" HL)
(setvar "EXPERT" EX)
(terpri)
)
;
(setq CM(getvar "CMDECHO") HL(getvar "HIGHLIGHT") EX(getvar "EXPERT"))
(setvar "CMDECHO" 0)
(setvar "HIGHLIGHT" 0)
(setvar "EXPERT" 3)
(setq ARROWS(ssget "X" '((2 . "ARR"))))
(if ARROWS
(progn
(command "VPOINT" "0,0,1")
(initget 1 "Y N")
(setq VW(getkword"\nDO YOU WISH TO SAVE VIEWS (Y N) ? "))
(if(equal VW "Y")(setq VPREF(getstring"\nWHAT IS PREFIX
  FOR VIEWS? ")))
```

```
(initget 1 "Y N")
(setq SLD(getkword"\nDO YOU WISH TO SAVE SLIDES (Y N) ? "))
(if(equal SLD "Y")
(progn
(setq SPREF(getstring"\nWHAT IS PREFIX FOR SLIDES? ")
     SCRFIL(getstring"\nWHAT IS NAME OF SCRIPT FILE
     (omit extension) ? ")
     FIL(open(strcat SCRFIL ".SCR") "w"))
(initget 1 "Y N")
(setq HID(getkword"\n'HIDE'EACH SLIDE (Y N) ? "))
)
)
(initget 1 "C V")
(setq CONTARG(getpoint"\nPLEASE INDICATE CONSTANT TARGET POINT: "))
(initget 1)
(setq TARGHGT(getdist"\nPLEASE INDICATE TARGET HEIGHT: "))
(setq CONTARG(list(car CONTARG)(cadr CONTARG)TARGHGT))
(initget 1)
(setq CAMHGT(getdist"\nPLEASE INDICATE CAMERA HEIGHT: ")
     FRAMCNT 1 COUNTER(sslength ARROWS))
(prompt"\nABOUT TO CREATE VIEW AND TARGET LISTS...PLEASE WAIT...")
(while(> = COUNTER 1)
(setq THISARR(ssname ARROWS(1- COUNTER))
     VIEWPT(cdr(assoc 10(entget THISARR)))
     VIEWPT(list(car VIEWPT)(cadr VIEWPT) CAMHGT)
     INSANG(cdr(assoc 50(entget THISARR)))
     VLIST(cons VIEWPT VLIST))
(setq COUNTER(1- COUNTER))
)
(setq COUNTER(sslength ARROWS))
(command "erase" ARROWS "")
(while(> = COUNTER 1)
(princ(strcat"\nABOUT TO CREATE FRAME: " (itoa FRAMCNT) " OF "
  (itoa(sslength ARROWS)) "\n"))
```

```
(setq VIEWPT(nth(1- COUNTER)VLIST))
(command "DVIEW" "" "D" "" "PO" CONTARG VIEWPT "")
(if(equal VW "Y")(command "VIEW" "S" (strcat VPREF(itoa FRAMCNT))))

(if(equal SLD "Y")
(progn
(if(equal HID "Y")(command "HIDE"))
(command "MSLIDE" (strcat SPREF(itoa FRAMCNT)))
(write-line (strcat"VSLIDE " SPREF (itoa FRAMCNT)) FIL)
)
)
(setq FRAMCNT(1+ FRAMCNT) COUNTER(1- COUNTER))
)
(if FIL(close FIL))
(command "oops" "vpoint" "0,0,1")
)
(princ"\n\7NO INSERTS OF BLOCK 'ARR' IN THIS DRAWING...")
)
(setvar "CMDECHO" CM)
(setvar "HIGHLIGHT" HL)
(setvar "EXPERT" EX)
(princ"\nFINISHED!")
(if(equal SLD "Y")
(princ(strcat" TYPE 'SCRIPT " (strcase SCRFIL) "' TO ANIMATE\n"))

(terpri)
)
)
```

TO INVOKE: Create this macro as an AutoLISP file (**.lsp**).

LET'S TRY IT: Get into a new drawing. Let's create a cube. Type **SOLID 0,0 1,0 0,1 1, 1** and press **<RETURN>** to end the command. Type **CHANGE L, <RETURN>, E 0 1**. This will create a cube with length, width and height of 1. To create a circular "walk-around" path, type **CIRCLE 0.5 0.5 5.0**. This will create a circle centered around the cube and with a radius of five units. Type **INSERT ARR 0,0 1 1 0**. This will insert **ARR** in the drawing, so it will be a defined block. Erase the **ARR** block.

Now type **DIVIDE**, choose the circle, and type **B ARR Y 12**. This will divide the circle into 12 sections, each marked by the block **ARR**. The **ARR** blocks should be aligned along the line of movement. In this macro, with a constant viewpoint, only their position is important.

Type **WTC**. When prompted "...wish to save views?" type **Y**. In response to "What is prefix for views?" type **CIR**. When prompted "...wish to save slides?" type **Y**. Choose **CIR** for the slide prefix, **CIRCLE** for the script filename and **Y** in response to "'HIDE' each slide...." When prompted for a constant target point, type **0.5,0.5** or touch the center of the cube. When prompted for target height, type **0**. When prompted for camera height, type **3**.

The macro will make a list of viewing positions from the insertion points of the **ARR** blocks. It will prompt you, "About to create frame: 1," "About to create frame: 2," etc. For each view, it will use **DVIEW** and move the camera point to the **X,Y** position of the arrow and Z position of your chosen camera height of three units, and pointed at the constant point **0.5,0.5,0**. At the end of the macro you'll be prompted, "Finished! Type 'Script circle' to animate."

If you type **VIEW ?**, you'll see a list of saved views, **CIR1** through **CIR12**. You can bring up a view by typing **VIEW R** and its name. In addition, the files **CIR1.SLD** through **CIR12.SLD** and **CIR.SCR** will be saved to disk.

TIPS: Although the target point is constant, you can use any path you choose. For instance, you can approach a building, circle it, etc., by drawing an initial **PLINE** and using **MEASURE** or **DIVIDE** to place the **ARR** blocks. Because the viewing point is constant, this macro is most useful for making exterior surveys of a model.

Automatic Conversion of .DXB Files to Drawings

Macro 15

PURPOSE: After using **MACRO14**, this macro loads each **.DXB** file or squashed 3D, and saves the image as a separate drawing.

TO CREATE:

```
(defun C:DXB2DWG (/ FIL TYP VPREF VW VNAM ANS)
(setvar "EXPERT" 0)
(initget 1 "A S")
(setq FIL(open "DXB2DWG.SCR" "w"))
(write-line"QUIT Y 1 DXB2DWG=" FIL)
(setq TYP(getkword"\nImport all views or a set (A S) ? "))
(if(equal TYP "S")
(setq VPREF(strcase(getstring"\nWhat is prefix for views? "))))
(princ"\nABOUT TO PROCESS VIEWS...PLEASE WAIT!")
(setq VW(tblnext "view" T))
(while VW
(setq VNAM(cdr(assoc 2 VW)))
(if(and(findfile(strcat VNAM ".DXB"))
    (or(equal TYP "A")
    (equal(substr VNAM 1(strlen VPREF))VPREF)))
(progn
(princ(strcat"\nVIEW: " VNAM " WILL BE IMPORTED AND SAVED AS
    DRAWING...\n"))
(write-line(strcat"DXBIN " VNAM)FIL)
(write-line "ZOOM E" FIL)
(if(findfile(strcat VNAM ".DWG"))
```

```
(progn
(initget 1 "Y N")
(setq ANS(getkword(strcat"\nA DRAWING NAMED " VNAM "
  ALREADY EXISTS..." "DO YOU WANT TO REPLACE IT? ")))
(if(equal ANS "Y")(write-line(strcat "WBLOCK " VNAM " Y
  *")FIL))
)
(write-line(strcat"WBLOCK " VNAM " *")FIL)
)
(write-line(strcat"ERASE (ssget" (chr 34) "X" (chr 34) ")")FIL)
(write-line "" FIL)
)
)
(setq VW(tblnext "view"))
)
(initget 1 "Y N")
(setq ANS(getkword"\nERASE ALL SOURCE .DXB FILES ? "))
(if(equal ANS "Y")
(write-line(strcat"SHELL DEL " VPREF "*.DXB")FIL)
)
(close FIL)
(command "script" "DXB2DWG")
)
```

TO INVOKE: Create this macro as an AutoLISP file (**.lsp**).

LET'S TRY IT: Stay in the drawing with views **CIR1** through **CIR12**, as outlined in **MACRO14**. With your system configured for **.DXB** plot files, load and execute **MACRO14**, plotting the files **CIR1.DXB** through **CIR12.DXB**.

Now load **MACRO15** (**Load "MACRO15"**). Type **DXB2DWG**. At the prompt, "Import all views or a set (A S)?" type **S**. At the prompt, "What is prefix for views?" type **CIR**. The macro will create a script file, **DXB2DWG.SCR**, which will actually load and save the drawings **CIR1.DWG** through **CIR12.DWG**. If a drawing already exists with one of these names, you'll be asked whether it should be replaced.

At the end of this macro, the drawings **CIR1** through **CIR12** will be saved to disk. The **.DXB** files are actually imported from within a temporary drawing, **DXB2DWG.DWG**, so that the original "model" file isn't changed in any way. When the process is finished, you can leave **DXB2DWG** by typing **QUIT Y**.

TIPS: If you've already created multiple **.DXB** files in another session but didn't save the original "model" drawing with the views, you can still use this macro. Create a new drawing. For each **.DXB** view you want to import, type **VIEW S** followed by the view name. Only the view names must appear in the current drawing to use this macro; the actual construction of the model and views aren't important now if the **.DXB** files already exist.

Macro
16 Storyboard from .DXBs or .DWGs

PURPOSE: Creates a storyboard from existing **.DXB** images (as made by **MACRO13** or **MACRO14**), or from existing **.DWG** files. A storyboard is a drawing in which multiple images are arranged like a comic strip, showing the development of the action in animation.

This macro places the images in proper top-to-bottom, left-to-right order for you. In addition, it has two nice features: The board will always be framed as a 4 x 4, 5 x 5 or other square format; also, the frames surrounding each image and the outer frame will be automatically sized and positioned so the largest of the images can fit.

TO CREATE:

```
(defun C:SB (/ TYP FTYP VPREF VLIST VW VNAM LL UR WID HGT
FWID FHGT ROWS COLS C XPOS YPOS V XOFFSET YOFFSET ANS ALL)
(defun *ERROR* (s)
(princ s)
(setvar "EXPERT" 0)
(setvar "HIGHLIGHT" 1)
```

```
(setvar "CMDECHO" 1)
(setq *ERROR* nil)
(terpri)
)
(setvar "EXPERT" 3)
(setvar "HIGHLIGHT" 0)
(setvar "CMDECHO" 0)
(command "elev" "0" "0")
(setq ALL(ssget "X"))
(if ALL(command "erase" ALL ""))
(initget 1 "A S")
(setq TYP(getkword"\nImport all views or a set (A S) ? "))
(if(equal TYP "S")
(setq VPREF(strcase(getstring"\nWhat is prefix for views? "))))
(initget 1 "DXB DWG")
(setq FTYP(getkword"\nImport from .DXB or .DWG files (DXB DWG) ? "))
(princ"\nABOUT TO PROCESS VIEWS...PLEASE WAIT!")
(setq VLIST nil VW(tblnext "view" T) FWID 0.0 FHGT 0.0)
(while VW
(setq VNAM(cdr(assoc 2 VW)))
(if(and(findfile(strcat VNAM "." FTYP))
    (or(equal TYP "A")
      (equal(substr VNAM 1(strlen VPREF))VPREF)))
(progn
(princ(strcat"\nVIEW: " VNAM " ABOUT TO BE INSERTED AS FRAME
  IN STORYBOARD\n"))
(princ)
(if(equal FTYP "DXB")
(command "dxbin" VNAM "zoom" "e")
(command "insert" (strcat "*" VNAM) "0,0" "1" "0" "zoom" "e")
)
(setq VLIST(cons VNAM VLIST))
(setq LL(getvar "EXTMIN")
    UR(getvar "EXTMAX")
    WID(abs(-(car UR)(car LL)))
```

```
        HGT(abs(-(cadr UR)(cadr LL)))
        )
(if(> WID FWID)(setq FWID WID))
(if(> HGT FHGT)(setq FHGT HGT))
(command "block" VNAM LL (ssget "X") "")
)
)
(setq VW(tblnext "view"))
)
(setq WID(max WID FWID) HGT(max WID FWID)
        ROWS(fix(sqrt(length VLIST)))
        COLS(fix(+ 0.5(/(length VLIST)ROWS)))
        C 0 XPOS 0.0 YPOS 0.0 V 1
        XOFFSET(* 0.1 FWID)
YOFFSET(* 0.1 FHGT)
VLIST(reverse VLIST))
(while(<= V(length VLIST))
(command "insert" (nth(1- V)VLIST)
  (list XPOS YPOS)
  "1" "1" "0" "line" (list(- XPOS XOFFSET)(- YPOS YOFFSET))
  (list(+ XPOS FWID XOFFSET)(- YPOS YOFFSET))
  (list(+ XPOS FWID XOFFSET)(+ YPOS FHGT YOFFSET))
  (list(- XPOS XOFFSET)(+ YPOS FHGT YOFFSET))
  "c")
(setq XPOS(+ XPOS FWID(* 3.0 XOFFSET))
    C(1+ C) V(1+ V))
(if(equal C COLS)
  (setq XPOS 0.0 C 0 YPOS(- YPOS FHGT(* 3 YOFFSET))))
)
)
(command "zoom" "e")
(setq LL(getvar "EXTMIN") UR(getvar "EXTMAX"))
(command "line" (list(-(car LL)XOFFSET)(-(cadr LL)YOFFSET))
  (list(+(car UR)XOFFSET)(-(cadr LL)YOFFSET))
  (list(+(car UR)XOFFSET)(+(cadr UR)YOFFSET))
```

```
  (list(-(car LL)XOFFSET)(+(cadr UR)YOFFSET))
"c" "zoom" "e")
(initget 1 "Y N")
(setq ANS(getkword(strcat"\nERASE ALL SOURCE ." FTYP "
  FILES? ")))
(if(equal ANS "Y")
(command "shell" (strcat "DEL " VPREF "*." FTYP))
)
(setvar "EXPERT" 0)
(setvar "HIGHLIGHT" 1)
(setvar "CMDECHO" 1)
(princ"\nFINISHED!")
(terpri)
)
```

TO INVOKE: Create this macro as an AutoLISP file (**.lsp**).

LET'S TRY IT: Stay in the drawing with views **CIR1** through **CIR12** as outlined in **MACRO14**. Make your views and get the plots. Then create the **.DXB** files **CIR1.DXB** through **CIR12.DXB** as described in **MACRO14**. If you've already imported them to drawing files using **MACRO15**, use the drawing files **CIR1.DWG** through **CIR12.DWG**.

Now load **MACRO16 (Load "MACRO16")**. Type **SB**. When prompted "Import all views or a set (A S) ?" type **S**. When prompted "What is prefix for views ?" type **CIR**. When prompted "Import from .DXB or .DWG files (DXB DWG) ?" respond accordingly; if you've run **VPLOT** but not **DXB2DWG**, type **DXB**. If you've run **DXB2DWG**, type **DWG**. The appropriate file type will be imported.

The macro will now import each image, perform a **ZOOM E** on it, and block it. After blocking imported views **CIR1** through **CIR12**, it will insert each into a storyboard, in this case a 3 x 4 block sheet. Each image will be outlined, the final sheet will be outlined and a final **ZOOM E** will be performed.

TIPS: If you've created **.DXB** files but not individual **.DWG** files, you can create this storyboard, then use the following extraction macro, **MACRO17**, to **WBLOCK** the individual images out as separate **.DWG** files.

The storyboard is a useful way to show animation to clients when you don't have an onscreen slide show. For this reason, you should save views while running the animation macros. You may then perform **VPLOT**, **DXB2DWG** or **SB** at a later session.

Macro **Automated**
17 WBLOCKing

PURPOSE: Will **WBLOCK**, or create individual drawing files (**.DWG**) from blocks in the current drawing. You can use it with the storyboard macro, **MACRO16**, to export individual frames to disk, or to export symbols from any drawing you wish. This can be useful in moving blocks from the current drawing into a standard symbol library.

TO CREATE:
```
(defun C:WB (/ S TYP BPREF BL BNAM ANS)
(defun *ERROR* (s)
(setvar "EXPERT" 0)
(setvar "CMDECHO" 1)
(princ s)
(terpri)
)
(setvar "EXPERT" 3)
(setvar "CMDECHO" 0)
(initget 1 "A S")
(setq TYP(getkword"\nWblock all blocks or a set (A S) ? "))
(if(equal TYP "S")
(setq BPREF(strcase(getstring"\nWhat is prefix for blocks? "))))
```

```
(princ"\nABOUT TO PROCESS BLOCKS...PLEASE WAIT!")
(setq BL(tblnext "block" T))
(while BL
(setq BNAM(cdr(assoc 2 BL)))
(if(or(equal TYP "A")
  (equal(substr BNAM 1(strlen BPREF))BPREF))
(progn
(princ(strcat"\nWBLOCKING BLOCK: " BNAM))
(if(findfile(strcat BNAM ".DWG"))
(progn
(initget 1 "Y N")
(setq ANS(getkword(strcat"\n" BNAM ".DWG ALREADY EXISTS...
  REPLACE IT? ")))
(if(equal ANS "Y")(command "WBLOCK" BNAM BNAM))
)
(command "WBLOCK" BNAM BNAM)
)
)
)
(setq BL(tblnext "block"))
)
(setvar "EXPERT" 0)
(setvar "CMDECHO" 1)
(princ"\nFINISHED!")
(terpri)
)
```

TO INVOKE: Create this macro as an AutoLISP file (**.lsp**).

LET'S TRY IT: Get into an existing storyboard drawing, with images **CIR1** through **CIR12**. Load **MACRO17 (Load** "MACRO17").
    Type **WB**. At the prompt, "Wblock all blocks or a set (A S) ?" type **S**. At the prompt "What is prefix for blocks ?" type **CIR**.
    The macro will now **WBLOCK**, or export, each block to disk in the current directory. If the drawing already exists, you'll be prompted, "Block CIR1.DWG already exists...replace it?" etc. If you wish to do so, type **Y**.

TIPS: Use this macro when creating symbol libraries, both 2D and 3D. Because it will **WBLOCK** 2D or 3D symbols, you can modify symbols in the current drawing and update a standard library on disk. The resulting 2D and 3D symbols can be useful in macros such as **SWAP**.

When used in sequence, 3D/2D "squash," **VPLOT**, storyboard and **WB** macros give you an animation toolbox for creating complete client presentations. You can present details, multi-view drawings, animations, storyboards and fully rendered images of architectural spaces or mechanical details. Of course, when used with more esoteric models, these tools have many applications.

Macro 18 Parametric 3D Windows

PURPOSE: Demonstrates the power of parametric programming when applied to AutoCAD's 3D and 2 1/2 D components. It lets you create a complex 3D window frame with variable frame width, rows and columns of mullions. Because it automatically spaces vertical and horizontal mullions, correcting for the width of the frame and mullions, a nearly infinite range of 3D windows is possible. An architect will find this helpful in constructing details for 3D models, but you can extend the principle to other applications. This and the following variation may whet your appetite for more 3D construction tools.

TO CREATE:
```
(defun C:WIN1 (/ S PT1 PT2 LIN ROWS COLS FT FT2 MT MT2
BOT TOP LEN HT ANG COUNT MID VPTS MDIS SS STPT)
(defun *ERROR* (s)
(if LIN(command "erase" LIN ""))
(setvar "HIGHLIGHT" 1)
(setvar "CMDECHO" 1)
```

```
(setvar "BLIPMODE" 1)
(princ s)
(setq *ERROR* nil)
(terpri)
)
(setvar "HIGHLIGHT" 0)
(setvar "CMDECHO" 0)
(setvar "BLIPMODE" 1)
(graphscr)
(setq PT1(getpoint "\nINDICATE 1st END OF GLASS LINE: ")
PT2(getpoint PT1 "\nINDICATE 2nd END OF GLASS LINE:"))
(setvar "BLIPMODE" 0)
(command "line" PT1 PT2 "")
(setq LIN(entlast))
(initget 7)
(setq ROWS(getint "\nHOW MANY PANES IN DIRECTION OF GLASS
   LINE (ROWS) ?"))
(initget 7)
(setq COLS(getint "\nHOW MANY PANES IN Z DIR. (COLS) ?")
FT(getdist "\nINDICATE FRAME THICKNESS: ")
FT2(/ FT 2.0)
MT(getdist "\nINDICATE MULLION THICKNESS: ")
MT2(/ MT 2.0)
BOT(getdist "\nWHAT IS BOTTOM (SILL) HEIGHT OF WINDOW? ")
TOP(getdist "\nWHAT IS TOP HEIGHT OF WINDOW? ")
LEN(distance PT1 PT2) HT(abs(- TOP BOT (* 2.0 FT)))
ANG(angle PT1 PT2))
(command "erase" LIN "")
(princ"\nBUILDING 3D WINDOW...PLEASE WAIT!")
;
; build bottom rail and top rail
;
(princ"\nBUILDING BOTTOM AND TOP RAILS:")
(command "solid"
(polar PT1(- ANG(/ PI 2.0))FT2)
```

```
(polar PT1(+ ANG(/ PI 2.0))FT2)
(polar PT2(- ANG(/ PI 2.0))FT2)
(polar PT2(+ ANG(/ PI 2.0))FT2) "" "change" (entlast)
"" "p" "elev" BOT "t" FT "" "copy" (entlast) ""
  "0,0" "0,0" "change" (entlast) "" "p" "elev"
  (- TOP FT) "t" FT "")
;
; build end verticals
;
(princ"\BUILDING END VERTICALS:")
(command "solid"
(polar PT1(- ANG(/ PI 2.0))FT2)
(polar PT1(+ ANG(/ PI 2.0))FT2)
(polar PT1(- ANG(atan 0.5))
(sqrt(+(expt FT 2.0)(expt FT2 2.0))))
(polar PT1(+ ANG(atan 0.5))
(sqrt(+(expt FT 2.0)(expt FT2 2.0))))
"" "change" (entlast) "" "p" "elev" (+ BOT FT)
"t" HT "" "solid"
(polar PT2(- ANG PI (atan 0.5))
(sqrt(+(expt FT 2.0)(expt FT2 2.0))))
(polar PT2(+ ANG PI (atan 0.5))
(sqrt(+(expt FT 2.0)(expt FT2 2.0))))
(polar PT2(+ ANG(/ PI 2.0))FT2)
(polar PT2(- ANG(/ PI 2.0))FT2) ""
"change" (entlast) "" "p" "elev" (+ BOT FT) "t" HT "")
;
; build middle verticals
;
(princ"\nBUILDING MIDDLE VERTICALS:")
(setq COUNT 1 MDIS(/ LEN ROWS) STPT PT1 VPTS nil)
(while(< COUNT ROWS)
(setq MID(polar PT1 ANG (* MDIS COUNT))
VPTS(cons MID VPTS))
(command "solid" (polar MID(- ANG(* 0.75 PI))
```

```
(sqrt(* 2(expt MT2 2.0))))
(polar MID(+ ANG(* 0.75 PI))(sqrt(* 2(expt MT2 2.0))))
(polar MID(- ANG(/ PI 4.0))(sqrt(* 2(expt MT2 2.0))))
(polar MID(+ ANG(/ PI 4.0))(sqrt(* 2(expt MT2 2.0)))) ""
"change" (entlast) "" "p" "elev" (+ BOT FT) "t" HT "")
(setq COUNT(1+ COUNT))
)
;
; build horizontals
;
(princ"\nBUILDING HORIZONTALS:")
(setq VPTS(cons(polar PT2(- ANG PI)(- FT MT2))VPTS)
VPTS(reverse VPTS) MDIS(/ HT COLS)
STPT(polar PT1 ANG(- FT MT2)) SS(ssadd) COUNT 0)
(while(< COUNT ROWS)
(command "solid"
(polar STPT(+ ANG(/ PI 4.0))
(sqrt(* 2(expt MT2 2.0))))
(polar STPT(- ANG(/ PI 4.0))(sqrt(* 2(expt MT2 2.0))))
(polar (nth COUNT VPTS) (+ ANG(* 0.75 PI))
(sqrt(* 2(expt MT2 2.0))))
(polar (nth COUNT VPTS) (- ANG(* 0.75 PI))
(sqrt(* 2(expt MT2 2.0)))) ""
"change" (entlast) "" "p" "elev" (+ BOT MT2 MDIS) "t" MT "")
(setq STPT(nth COUNT VPTS) COUNT(1+ COUNT) SS(ssadd(entlast)SS))
)
(setq COUNT 2)
(while(< COUNT COLS)
(command "copy" SS "" "0,0" "0,0" "change" SS "" "p" "elev"
(+ BOT MT2(* COUNT MDIS)) "t" MT "")
(setq COUNT(1+ COUNT))
)
(setvar "HIGHLIGHT" 1)
(setvar "CMDECHO" 1)
(setvar "BLIPMODE" 1)
```

```
(princ"\nFINISHED!")
(terpri)
)
```

TO INVOKE: Create this macro as an AutoLISP file (**.lsp**).

LET'S TRY IT: Get into a drawing and load **MACRO18** (**Load "MACRO18"**). Type **WIN1.** When prompted, indicate the first and second glass lines (lines through glass, or "middle" of window). You might try typing **WIN1 0,0 36,0** to create a 36"-long window, or pointing to two points at any angle you choose. When prompted, supply the number of panes in the direction of the glass lines (**ROWS**), in the vertical or **Z** direction (**COLS**), the frame thickness and the bottom and top elevations (not thickness! this is calculated for you!). If you typed **4 3 1.0 30.0 45.0**, you would build a window with four panes across, three panes vertically (total 12 panes), a 1"-thick and 15"-high frame, raised to 30" off the ground (0). For each of the "distance" prompts, indicate your choice by picking two points.

After responding to these prompts, the macro will build a completed 3D window to your specifications. You can use the macro repeatedly to create sets of unique rectangular windows.

Macro
19 Parametric 3D Windows Revisited

PURPOSE: After experimenting with **MACRO18,** you might want to use a macro with fewer picks and prompts. Once you've supplied the variables for frame and mullion thickness (**FT** and **MT**), **ROWS** and **COLS** of panes, bottom (**BOT**) and top (**TOP**) heights, you could "knock out" a series of variable-width and variable-angle windows by merely picking two points. This macro, when used with a set-up macro or screen menu, will accomplish this.

TO CREATE:

```
(defun C:WIN2 (/ VARLIST S PT1 PT2 FT2 MT2
LEN HT ANG COUNT MID VPTS MDIS SS STPT)
(defun *ERROR* (s)
(setvar "HIGHLIGHT" 1)
(setvar "CMDECHO" 1)
(setvar "BLIPMODE" 1)
(princ s)
(setq *ERROR* nil)
(terpri)
)
(setq VARLIST(list ROWS COLS BOT TOP FT MT))
(if(member nil VARLIST)
(progn
(princ"\n*/Invalid/* NOT ALL VARIABLES SET!\n")
(princ "ROWS: ")(princ ROWS)(princ " COLS:")
(princ COLS)(princ " BOT:")(princ BOT)
(princ " TOP:")(princ TOP)(princ " FT:")
(princ FT)(princ " MT:")(princ MT)
)
(progn
(setvar "HIGHLIGHT" 0)
(setvar "CMDECHO" 0)
(setvar "BLIPMODE" 1)
(graphscr)
(setq PT1(getpoint "\nINDICATE 1st END OF GLASS LINE: ")
    PT2(getpoint PT1 "\nINDICATE 2nd END OF GLASS LINE:"))
(setvar "BLIPMODE" 0)
(setq FT2(/ FT 2.0)
  MT2(/ MT 2.0)
  LEN(distance PT1 PT2) HT(abs(- TOP BOT (* 2.0 FT)))
  ANG(angle PT1 PT2))
(princ"\nBUILDING 3D WINDOW...PLEASE WAIT!")
;
; build bottom rail and top rail
```

```
;
(princ"\nBUILDING BOTTOM AND TOP RAILS:")
(command "solid"
(polar PT1(- ANG(/ PI 2.0))FT2)
(polar PT1(+ ANG(/ PI 2.0))FT2)
(polar PT2(- ANG(/ PI 2.0))FT2)
(polar PT2(+ ANG(/ PI 2.0))FT2) ""
"change" (entlast) "" "p" "elev" BOT "t" FT ""
"copy" (entlast) "" "0,0" "0,0"
"change" (entlast) "" "p" "e" (- TOP FT) "t" FT "")
;
; build end verticals
;
(princ"\nBUILDING END VERTICALS:")
(command "solid"
(polar PT1(- ANG(/ PI 2.0))FT2)
(polar PT1(+ ANG(/ PI 2.0))FT2)
(polar PT1(- ANG(atan 0.5))
(sqrt(+(expt FT 2.0)(expt FT2 2.0))))
(polar PT1(+ ANG(atan 0.5))
(sqrt(+(expt FT 2.0)(expt FT2 2.0))))
"" "change" (entlast) "" "p" "elev"
(+ BOT FT) "t" HT "" "solid"
(polar PT2(- ANG PI (atan 0.5))
(sqrt(+(expt FT 2.0)(expt FT2 2.0))))
(polar PT2(+ ANG PI (atan 0.5))
(sqrt(+(expt FT 2.0)(expt FT2 2.0))))
(polar PT2(+ ANG(/ PI 2.0))FT2)
(polar PT2(- ANG(/ PI 2.0))FT2) ""
"change" (entlast) "" "p" "elev"
(+ BOT FT) "t" HT ""
)
;
; build middle verticals
;
```

```
(princ"\nBUILDING MIDDLE VERTICALS:")
(setq COUNT 1 MDIS(/ LEN ROWS) STPT PT1 VPTS nil)
(while(< COUNT ROWS)
(setq MID(polar PT1 ANG (* MDIS COUNT))
    VPTS(cons MID VPTS))
(command "solid" (polar MID(- ANG(* 0.75 PI))
(sqrt(* 2(expt MT2 2.0))))
(polar MID(+ ANG(* 0.75 PI))(sqrt(* 2(expt MT2 2.0))))
(polar MID(- ANG(/ PI 4.0))(sqrt(* 2(expt MT2 2.0))))
(polar MID(+ ANG(/ PI 4.0))(sqrt(* 2(expt MT2 2.0)))) ""
"change" (entlast) "" "p" "elev" (+ BOT FT) "t" HT "")
(setq COUNT(1+ COUNT))
)
;
; build horizontals
;
(princ"\nBUILDING HORIZONTALS:")
(setq VPTS(cons(polar PT2(- ANG PI)(- FT MT2))VPTS)
  VPTS(reverse VPTS) MDIS(/ HT COLS)
  STPT(polar PT1 ANG(- FT MT2)) SS(ssadd) COUNT 0)
(while(< COUNT ROWS)
(command "solid"
(polar STPT(+ ANG(/ PI 4.0))
(sqrt(* 2(expt MT2 2.0))))
(polar STPT(- ANG(/ PI 4.0))(sqrt(* 2(expt MT2 2.0))))
(polar (nth COUNT VPTS) (+ ANG(* 0.75 PI))
(sqrt(* 2(expt MT2 2.0))))
(polar (nth COUNT VPTS) (- ANG(* 0.75 PI))
(sqrt(* 2(expt MT2 2.0)))) ""
"change" (entlast) "" "p" "elev" (+ BOT MT2 MDIS) "t" MT "")
(setq STPT(nth COUNT VPTS) COUNT(1+ COUNT) SS(ssadd(entlast)SS))
)
(setq COUNT 2)
(while(< COUNT COLS)
```

```
(command "copy" SS "" "0,0" "0,0" "change" SS "" "p" "e"
   (+ BOT MT2(* COUNT MDIS)) "t" MT "")
(setq COUNT(1+ COUNT))
)
(setvar "HIGHLIGHT" 1)
(setvar "CMDECHO" 1)
(setvar "BLIPMODE" 1)
(princ"\nFINISHED!")
)
)
(terpri)
)
```

TO INVOKE: Create this macro as an AutoLISP file (**.lsp**).

LET'S TRY IT: Get into a drawing and load **MACRO19** (Load "MACRO19"). Before calling the macro into play, set the variables **ROWS**, **COLS**, **MT**, **BOT** and **TOP** by typing:

```
(setq ROWS 4 COLS 3 MT 1.0 FT 2.0 BOT 30.0 TOP 84.0)
```

Now, type **WIN2**. When prompted, select two points, either by typing or by indicating them with your cursor. The macro then builds a complete 3D window with no further prompts. If any of the necessary variables aren't set, the macro will detect this, stop execution and prompt you with a list of their current status. In this example, the window will have four rows and three columns of panes, a mullion thickness of 1", a frame thickness of 2", a bottom height of 30" and a top height of 84". Type **WIN2** again and choose two more points. Another window, with the same pane count, thicknesses, bottom and top will be created.

TIPS: You can set the variables in several ways. You can put the prompts into a separate macro, called only when you need to create a new window type:

MACRO 19A: WINDOW SET

```
(defun C:WINSET ()
(initget 7)
(setq ROWS(getint "\nHOW MANY PANES IN DIRECTION OF
    GLASS LINE (ROWS) ?"))
(initget 7)
(setq COLS(getint "\nHOW MANY PANES IN Z DIR (COLS)?"))
(setq MT(getdist "\nINDICATE THICKNESS OF FRAME: "))
(setq BOT(getdist "\nWHAT IS BOTTOM (SILL) HEIGHT ?"))
(setq TOP(getdist "\nWHAT IS TOP HEIGHT OF WINDOW? "))
)
```

This routine, if you load (Load "MACRO19A") and run it by typing WINSET, will prompt you for the variables. Then you can run WIN2 repeatedly by typing WIN2, followed by picking window "glass-line" endpoints.

You could also put the data into a screen menu format. For instance:

```
[*BOTTOM*]
[36"]^C^C(setq BOT 36.0)
[42"]^C^C(setq BOT 42.0)
[*TOP*]
[72"]^C^C(setq TOP 72.0)
[78"]^C^C(setq TOP 78.0)
[*FR WID*]
[1" FRAME]^C^C(setq FT 1.0)
[2" FRAME]^C^C(setq FT 2.0)
[*MULWID*]
[1" MULL]^C^C(setq MT 1.0)
[1.5" MUL]^C^C(setq MT 1.5)
[*PANES*]
[2x2]^C^C(setq ROWS 2 COLS 2)
[3x2]^C^C(setq ROWS 3 COLS 2)
[3x3]^C^C(setq ROWS 3 COLS 3)
```

```
[3DWINDOW]^C^C(if(null C:WIN2)(load "MACRO19"));WIN2
```

This menu is available on the optional diskette. Create this file as an AutoCAD menu file (**3dwindow.mnu**) or copy it from the diskette. Load the menu by typing **MENU 3DWINDOW**. You can now set and reset variables and execute **WIN2** from the screen menu by selecting the appropriate areas. You could expand or alter this application to provide a wide range of 3D windows, and it would be easy to expand it to include arched windows, brick facing, decorative 3D doors and doorframes, and more. We hope that other developers will create other "point-and-shoot" construction macros.

Macro 20 Save/Retrieve Complete View and Construction Setup

PURPOSE: In Release 10, you can request multiple viewports, change the view in each and save the configuration. You can also save the view in the current active viewport and save the current active **UCS**. These three actions are the "construction setup." This macro has two parts. When used together, they let you save **VIEW**, **VPORT** and **UCS** information as a unit, and restore them as a unit. You can have multiple construction setups in one drawing, since the macros actually store the information using standard commands.

TO CREATE:

MACRO 20A: SAVE CURRENT CONSTRUCTION PORT INFO

```
(defun C:SAVPRT (/ STR SAVNAM)
;
; function saves current UCS with VPORTS configuration and
```

```
; current active window so they can all be restored
; together
(setq STR "")
(while(null SAVNAM)
(setq SAVNAM
   (getstring"\nWHAT IS NAME FOR SAVING CURRENT VIEW
     CONFIGURATION? "))
(if(tblsearch "ucs" SAVNAM)
    (setq STR(strcat STR " UCS")))
(if(tblsearch "vport" SAVNAM)
    (setq STR(strcat STR " VPORTS")))

(if(tblsearch "view" SAVNAM)
    (setq STR(strcat STR " VIEW")))
(if(not(equal STR ""))
  (progn
    (princ(strcat"\nSORRY, THE FOLLOWING CONFIGURATIONS:"
    STR " ARE ALREADY SAVED WITH THE NAME: " SAVNAM))
    (setq SAVNAM nil STR "")
)
(command "UCS" "S" SAVNAM "VPORTS" "S" SAVNAM "VIEW" "S" SAVNAM)
)
)
)
```

MACRO 20B: RETRIEVE CONSTRUCTION PORT INFO

```
(defun C:GETPRT (/ STR GETNAM)
;
; function saves current UCS with VPORTS configuration and
; current active window so they can all be restored
; together
(setq STR "")
(while(null GETNAM)
(setq GETNAM
   (getstring"\nWHAT IS NAME OF VIEW CONFIGURATION TO RETRIEVE? "))
```

```
(if(null(tblsearch "ucs" GETNAM))
    (setq STR(strcat STR " UCS")))
(if(null(tblsearch "vport" GETNAM))
    (setq STR(strcat STR " VPORTS")))
(if(null(tblsearch "view" GETNAM))
    (setq STR(strcat STR " VIEW")))
(if(not(equal STR ""))
  (progn
    (princ(strcat"\nSORRY, THE FOLLOWING CONFIGURATIONS:"
      STR " ARE NOT SAVED WITH THE NAME: " GETNAM))
    (setq GETNAM nil STR "")
  )
  (command "UCS" "R" GETNAM "VPORTS" "R" GETNAM "VIEW" "R" GETNAM)
)
)
)
```

TO INVOKE: Create these two macros as AutoLISP files (**.lsp**).

LET'S TRY IT: Get into a new drawing and load **MACRO20A** (**Load "MACRO20A"**) and **MACRO20B** (**Load "MACRO20B"**). Create a simple object such as a cube. Set the viewports to a vertical two-view screen by typing **VPORTS 2 VERTICAL**. Now rotate the current active view by typing **VPOINT 1,1,1**. Rotate the current **UCS** by typing **UCS X 90**. Now invoke the "saving" macro by typing **SAVPRT**. When prompted, choose a name for saving the **UCS, VIEW** and **VPORT** configurations; the same name will be applied to all three. You could type **SPECIAL**, for instance. If any configurations of this name already exist, you'll be prompted for a new name.

Now return to a "generic" construction setup to test the retrieval macro. Type **VPORTS SI** to return to a single viewport. Type **UCS W** to return to the "world" **UCS**. Return to a plan view by typing **VPOINT 0,0,1**. To save this generic construction, type **SAVPRT** and when prompted for a name, type **GENERIC**.

To test the retrieval process, type **GETPRT**. When prompted for a construction set name, type **SPECIAL**. The viewport, **UCS** and view will change to return you to the "special" setup. Type **GETPRT** again and the name **GENERIC** to return to the generic setup. If you type the name of a nonexistent construction setup, the macro will tell you which construction datum, **VPORTS**, **UCS** or **VIEW**, doesn't exist, and prompt for a new name.

Macro 21 DVIEW with Preset Object Selection

PURPOSE: The **DVIEW** command asks you to choose objects for display during dynamic view selection. Unfortunately, you must choose your view set every time you use the **DVIEW** command. Since **DVIEW** is a display-only command, turning off automatically when construction commands or **VPOINT** is invoked, this macro was created to save the view set for automatic recall. In a typical drawing, it will let you select important entities such as outside lines or main structures, and display these each time you use **DVIEW**. This macro consists of two parts: the "selecting" macro, and a variation on the **DVIEW** command — a macro that calls **DVIEW** using the selection set.

TO CREATE:

MACRO 21A: DVIEW SELECTION SET CREATION

```
(defun C:DVSS ()
(prompt"\nSETTING SELECTION SET FOR DVIEWS.")
(setq DVSET(ssget))
)
```

MACRO 21B: DVIEW USING SELECTION SET

```
(defun C:DV ()
(while(null DVSET)
(princ"\nNO SELECTION SET EXISTS...")
```

```
(C:DVSS)
)
(command "DVIEW" DVSET "")
)
```

TO INVOKE: Create these two macros as AutoLISP files (**.lsp**).

LET'S TRY IT: Get into a simple drawing, or create a new one of your design. Load **MACRO21A** (**Load "MACRO21A"**) and **MACRO21B** (**Load "MACRO21B"**). Type **DVSS**. When prompted, select a group of display objects for use in **DVIEW**; if the model is small, you can select the entire model.

Type **DV**. This will invoke the **DVIEW** command, using the previous selection set for displaying. Once in the **DVIEW** command, you can select **DISTANCE**, **POINTS**, etc., to adjust the current view as usual. If you want to change the current display set, type **DVSS** from the **Command**: prompt and select a new group.

TIPS: These two AutoLISP macros could have been written as simple menu macros as follows:

```
^C^C(setq DVSET(ssget))

^C^CDVIEW;DVSET;;
```

However, we think that the AutoLISP solution is usually the better one. New AutoCAD commands created through AutoLISP can be inserted into any area of the menu interface without modification, as if they were "usual" commands. Also, if you call a menu macro, then type < RETURN > or space to repeat the macro, only the last AutoCAD command will be repeated — some of the utility may be lost.

To insert the **DV** and **DVSS** commands into a menu, use these macros:

```
^C^C(if(null C:DVSS)(load "MACRO21A"));DVSS

^C^C(if(null C:DV)(load "MACRO21B"));DV
```

In this style, a < **RETURN** > would repeat the entire **DV** variation or **DVSS** setup for you.

Hidden Line Removal (and Other Tasks) Without Text

Macro 22

PURPOSE: Text poses peculiar problems in 3D. While it's very useful for creating 2D charts and marking areas in plan view, it often clutters the 3D viewports. In wireframe views, it generally obscures an already complicated image; and because AutoCAD doesn't perform hidden-line removal on text, during a **HIDE** command or **DVIEW HIDE** it will still be written through the displayed objects.

These two macros remove and replace text in a drawing. You can use them with commands such as **HIDE** in a menu application.

TO CREATE:

MACRO 22A: TEXT BLOCKING OUT

```
(defun C:TOUT (/ TXT)
(setvar "EXPERT" 3)
(setvar "CMDECHO" 0)
(setq TXT(ssget "X" '((0 . "TEXT"))))
(if TXT
(progn
(prompt"\nTHIS DRAWING CONTAINS TEXT...BLOCKING IT...\n")
(command "BLOCK" "TEXTXXXX" "0,0" (ssget "X" '((0 .
  "TEXT"))) "")
(prompt(strcat"\nUSE " (chr 34) "TRET" (chr 34)
  " TO RE-INSERT TEXT..."))
)
(progn
(prompt"\nTHIS DRAWING DOESN'T CONTAIN TEXT...")
```

```
(setq BLOCKED nil)
)
)
(setvar "EXPERT" 0)
(setvar "CMDECHO" 1)
(setq BLOCKED 1)
(terpri)
)
```

MACRO 22B: TEXT RETRIEVAL

```
(defun C:TRET ()
(setvar "CMDECHO" 0)
(if(not(null BLOCKED))
(progn
(prompt"\nREINSERTING BLOCKED-OUT TEXT...")
(command "insert" "*TEXTXXXX" "0,0" "1" "0")
)
(prompt"\nNO FURTHER TEXT HAS BEEN BLOCKED OUT...")
)
(setq BLOCKED nil)
(setvar "CMDECHO" 1)
(terpri)
)
```

TO INVOKE: Create these two macros as AutoLISP files (**.lsp**).

LET'S TRY IT: Get into an existing drawing with text, or create a new drawing with text. Load **MACRO22A** (**Load "MACRO22A"**) and **MACRO22B** (**Load "MACRO22B"**). Type **TOUT**.

If there's text in the drawing, it will disappear. The macro has created a block named **TEXTXXXX** containing all the "free" text in the drawing (text that isn't part of an associated dimension or nested in another block).

You can now use **HIDE** or other commands, knowing that you can return the blocked text at will. To do this, type **TRET**. **MACRO22B** will re-insert an exploded version of the block **TEXTXXXX**.

TIPS: The block name **TEXTXXXX** was chosen at random, in the hope that the macro won't redefine an existing block in your drawing. Avoid using the name for another block, or, if you use the name **TEXTXXXX** frequently for a standard block, replace the name in both **MACRO22A** and **MACRO22B** with another of your choice.

The first macro has a "bug catcher" that will not make a block if there's no text in the drawing. The second macro will avoid making multiple inserts of the text into your drawing. The macros use the variable **BLOCKED** as a flag to indicate if a text block exists, and they check and reset this variable to avoid trouble.

You can use these macros in a menu, as follows:

```
^C^C(if(null C:TOUT)(load "MACRO22A"));TOUT

^C^C(if(null C:TRET)(load "MACRO22B"));TRET
```

Macro
23 Dual Viewports

PURPOSE: By using the **UCS** (User Coordinate System) and the **VPORTS** commands, you can manipulate your 3D construction more easily, but working in 3D may involve setting up standard viewport configurations. This macro presents one standard view configuration, in which the left-hand view is an orthogonal plan view, the right-hand view is rotated **45** degrees, and you work in the left viewport.

TO CREATE:
```
(defun C:2PORTS (/ UCSF VP LPRT RPRT)
; this function produces 2 standard vertical
; viewports.
;
(setvar "CMDECHO" 0)
(setvar "EXPERT" 3)
(setq UCSF(getvar "UCSFOLLOW"))
```

```
(command "vports" "si" "vports" "2" "V")
(setq VP(vports)
    RPRT(car(nth 0 VP))
    LPRT(car(nth 1 VP)))
(setvar "CVPORT" RPRT)
(command "VPOINT" "1,1,1")
(setvar "CVPORT" LPRT)
(command "VPOINT" "0,0,1")
(setvar "CMDECHO" 1)
(setvar "EXPERT" 0)
(setvar "UCSFOLLOW" UCSF)
(terpri)
)
```

TO INVOKE: Create this macro as an AutoLISP file (**.lsp**).

LET'S TRY IT: Get into an existing drawing and load **MACRO23** (**Load "MACRO23"**). Type **2PORTS**. The macro will create a dual viewport. If you want to save the configuration for automatic recall, use the **VPORTS SAVE** command and give it a name. You can also choose your active window by picking with your cursor, and manipulate your view using the **VPOINT** or **DVIEW** commands.

Macro
24 Quadruple Viewports

PURPOSE: Presents another standard view configuration, in which there are four viewports. The upper left window is an orthogonal plan view, the lower left window is a front view, the upper right window is a right-side view, and the lower right window is an isometric view rotated **45** degrees around the **Z** axis. You work in the upper left (plan) view. This is a standard layout adopted by many engineering firms for standard drafting.

TO CREATE:

```
(defun C:4PORTS ()
; this function produces 4 standard
; viewports.
;
(setvar "CMDECHO" 0)
(setvar "EXPERT" 3)
(setq UCSF(getvar "UCSFOLLOW"))
(command "vports" "si" "vports" "4")
(setq VP(vports)
    LRPRT(car(nth 0 VP))
    URPRT(car(nth 1 VP))
    ULPRT(car(nth 2 VP))
    LLPRT(car(nth 3 VP)))
(setvar "CVPORT" LLPRT)
(command "VPOINT" "0,-1,0")
(setvar "CVPORT" URPRT)
(command "VPOINT" "1,0,0")
(setvar "CVPORT" LRPRT)
(command "VPOINT" "1,1,1")
(setvar "CVPORT" ULPRT)
(command "VPOINT" "0,0,1")
(setvar "CMDECHO" 1)
(setvar "EXPERT" 0)
(setvar "UCSFOLLOW" UCSF)
(terpri)
)
```

TO INVOKE: Create this macro as an AutoLISP file (**.lsp**).

LET'S TRY IT: Get into an existing drawing and load **MACRO23** (**Load "MACRO23"**). Type **4PORTS**. The macro will create a quadruple viewport. If you want to save the configuration for automatic recall, use the **VPORTS SAVE** command and give it a name. You can also choose your active window by picking with your cursor, and manipulate your view using the **VPOINT** or **DVIEW** commands.

Macro
25 Solid-to-3DFACE Transformation

PURPOSE: An easy way to construct 3D objects is by extruding them using the techniques available in "2 1/2 D" prior to Release 10. For instance, many models are constructed using extruded solids; **3DFACES** would be more practical. For example, if two solids touch on an edge, those two faces will require additional computation time during the **HIDE** command. In addition, if you wanted to remove those common edges or any edge on the solids, you'd have to reconstruct the cubes as sets of 3DFACES. This routine transforms them for you, on either a selected set of solids or on all solids in the drawing file.

TO CREATE:

```
(defun C:SF (/ LA HI BL SEL SOLIDS COUNTER SOL DESCR TYP
   THIK ELEV LAY PT1 PT2 PT3 PT4 PT5 PT6 PT7 PT8 FL)
(setvar "CMDECHO" 0)
(setq FL (getvar "FLATLAND"))
(setvar "FLATLAND" 0)
(setq EL(getvar "ELEVATION") TH(getvar "THICKNESS")
   LA (getvar "CLAYER")
   HI(getvar"HIGHLIGHT") BL(getvar "BLIPMODE"))
(initget 1 "A S")
(setq SEL(getkword"\nCONVERT ALL SOLIDS OR A SELECTION ? (A S)"))
(if(equal SEL "A")(setq SOLIDS(ssget "X" '((0 . "SOLID"))))
(progn
(princ"\nPLEASE CHOOSE SOLIDS: ")
(setq SOLIDS(ssget))
)
)
(setvar "HIGHLIGHT" 0)
(setvar "BLIPMODE" 0)
(princ"\nCONVERTING SOLIDS TO 3DFACES...PLEASE WAIT!")
```

```
(setq COUNTER 0)
(if SOLIDS
(progn
(while(< COUNTER(sslength SOLIDS))
  (setq SOL(ssname SOLIDS COUNTER)
     DESCR(entget SOL)
     TYP(cdr(assoc 0 DESCR)))
  (if(equal TYP "SOLID")  .
     (progn
     (setq THIK(cdr(assoc 39 DESCR))
       ELEV(cadddr(assoc 10 DESCR))
       LAY(cdr(assoc 8 DESCR))
       PT1(cdr(assoc 10 DESCR))
       PT2(cdr(assoc 11 DESCR))
       PT3(cdr(assoc 12 DESCR))
       PT4(cdr(assoc 13 DESCR)))
(if THIK(setq PT5(list(car PT1)(cadr PT1)
     (+ THIK(caddrPT1)))
     PT6(list(car PT2)(cadr PT2)
     (+ THIK(caddr PT2)))
       PT7(list(car PT3)(cadr PT3)
       (+ THIK(caddr PT3)))
       PT8(list(car PT4)(cadr PT4)
       (+ THIK(caddr PT4))))
       )
       (setq PT1(trans PT1 SOL 1)
       PT2(trans PT2 SOL 1)
       PT3(trans PT3 SOL 1)
       PT4(trans PT4 SOL 1)
       PT5(trans PT5 SOL 1)
       PT6(trans PT6 SOL 1)
       PT7(trans PT7 SOL 1)
       PT8(trans PT8 SOL 1))
       (command "layer" "s" LAY ""
       "erase" SOL "" "3dface" PT1 PT2 PT4 PT3 "")
```

```
        (if THIK
        (command "3dface" PT5 PT6 PT8 PT7 ""
        "3dface" PT1 PT3 PT7 PT5 ""
        "3dface" PT2 PT4 PT8 PT6 ""
        "3dface" PT1 PT2 PT6 PT5 ""
        "3dface" PT3 PT4 PT8 PT7 "")
        )
        )
        )
        (setq COUNTER(1+ COUNTER))
        )
  )
(princ"\nTHERE ARE NO SOLIDS IN THIS DRAWING!")
)
        (command "layer" "s" LA "")
        (setvar "CMDECHO" 1)
        (setvar "HIGHLIGHT" HI)
        (setvar "BLIPMODE" BL)
        (princ "\nFINISHED!")
        (setvar "FLATLAND" FL)
        (terpri)
        )
```

TO INVOKE: Create this macro as an AutoLISP file (**.lsp**).

TO USE: This macro includes a **UCS** transformation routine that lets it operate on solids created on different **User Coordinate Systems**. It also transforms both extruded and unextruded solids to **3DFACES**.

Get into a new drawing. Type **SOLID 0,0 1,0 0,1 1,1 CHPROP L <RETURN> T 1**. This will create a one-unit extruded cube. Create another cube on another **UCS** by typing: **UCS X 45 SOLID 0,0 1,0 0,1 1,1 CHPROP L <RETURN> T 1**. To view the model, type **VPOINT 1,1,1**. You'll see two rotated cubes that intersect. Load **MACRO25** (**Load "MACRO25"**). Type **SF**. At the prompt, "Convert all solids or a selection? (A S)," type **A**. The macro will erase each of the extruded solids and replace them with **3DFACES** in the appropriate coordinates and layers. You can check them by using the **LIST** command.

Appendix: New System Variables

A large number of new system variables are available with Release 10. Here's a list of them and how they're used.

ACADPREFIX A read-only system variable. It contains a string value that indicates the directory name set by the **ACAD** environment variable. By using **SET ACAD =** you can specify an additional path for drawing files, LISP programs, etc.

ACADVER A read-only system variable. It contains a string that tells you the AutoCAD version being used.

AFLAGS Controls the status of the attributes in effect for the **ATTDEF** command. It uses an integer code as follows:

1 Invisible
2 Constant
4 Verify
8 Preset

Any time the *AutoCAD Reference Manual* indicates that a system variable is **(sum of the following)**, as it does for this variable, you can have more than one code in effect. Therefore, if you wanted **Invisible** and **Constant**, you'd use their sum (**3**).

ATTDIA   Causes the **INSERT** command to use either a dialogue box or regular command prompts. If it's set to 1, it uses the dialogue box. If it's set to 0, it uses the prompts.

ATTREQ   When set to 0, this always uses the defaults for the values of all attributes during block insertion. If it's set to 1, it uses prompts or the dialogue box, depending on how **ATTDIA** is set.

BACKZ   A read-only system variable that has meaning only if back clipping in **VIEWMODE** is on. It measures the back clipping plane offset for the current viewport, using the current drawing units. If you need to know the distance of the back clipping plane from the camera point, subtract **BACKZ** from the camera-to-target distance.

CVPORT   The identification number for the current viewport.

FLATLAND   This system variable guarantees compatibility with Release 9. If it's set to 1, then **OBJECT SNAP**, **DXF** and **AutoLISP** operate as they did in Release 9. If it's set to 0, then all the functions of Release 10 are available. This is a temporary variable that will be removed on the next major update.

FRONTZ   A read-only system variable that has meaning only if front clipping in **VIEWMODE** is on and "Front clip not at eye" is on. This is similar to the **BACKZ** system variable. It measures the front clipping plane offset for the current viewport using the current drawing units. To find the distance of the front clipping plane from the camera point, subtract **FRONTZ** from the camera-to-target distance.

LENSLENGTH   A read-only system variable that measures the length of the lens in millimeters. It's used when **PERSPEC-TIVE** is **ON**.

MENUNAME   A read-only system variable that contains the name of the current menu.

POPUPS   A read-only system variable that indicates whether the display driver supports pull-down menus. If it's set to 1, the driver supports pull-down menus. If it's set to 0, then the driver doesn't support pull-down menus.

SPLFRAME   This system variable controls whether the following will be displayed. If it's set to 1, then:

1. The control polygon for spline-fitted polylines is displayed.

2. The defining mesh of a surface-fitted polygon is displayed and not the fitted surface.

3. Invisible edges of **3DFACES** are displayed.

If it's set to 0, then:

1. The control polygon for spline-fitted polylines isn't displayed.

2. The defining mesh of a surface-fitted polygon isn't displayed and the fitted surface is.

3. Invisible edges of **3DFACES** aren't displayed.

SPLINESEGS   Determines the number of line segments to be generated for each **SPLINE** patch.

SPLINETYPE   Determines the type of **SPLINE** curve to be generated. 5 = aquadratic B-spline and 6 = acubic **B-spline**.

SURFTAB1   Controls the mesh density in the **M** direction. This is used by **TABSURF** and **RULESURF** for their primary density. **REVSURF** and **EDGESURF** also use this variable for one of the directions of the mesh.

SURFTAB2   Controls the mesh density in the **N** direction. This is used only by **REVSURF** and **EDGESURF**.

TARGET   A read-only system variable that contains the **UCS** coordinates for the target point for the current view-port.

TEMPPREFIX   A read-only system variable that contains the directory name for placement of temporary files.

TEXTEVAL   If its value is 0, then all text and attributes are taken literally. If it's set to 1, then text that begins with "!" or "(" is interpreted as an AutoLISP expression.

TEXTSTYLE   A read-only system variable that contains the name of the current **TEXT** style in effect.

UCSFOLLOW   If this is set to 1, then any change in **UCS** causes an automatic change to the plan view of the current **UCS**. If it's set to 0, then plan view doesn't change.

UCSICON   This system variable positions the **UCS** icon or turns it off and on.

                  0 = Off

                  1 = Place in lower left-hand corner

                  2 = Off

                  3 = Place at point of origin

                  Any number larger than 3 is converted to 1 and will place the icon in the lower left-hand corner.

UCSNAME	A read-only system variable that gives the name of the current **UCS**.
UCSORG	A read-only system variable that gives the coordinates of the point of origin, always in the **WCS**.
UCSXDIR	A read-only system variable that gives the X-direction of the current **UCS**.
UCSYDIR	A read-only system variable that gives the Y-direction of the current **UCS**.
VIEWDIR	A read-only system variable that provides the current viewport's viewing direction. This defines the camera point as an offset from the target point expressed in **WCS**.
VIEWMODE	A read-only system variable that displays a variety of modes. It uses (**sum of the following**), which means that you can establish multiple modes by adding them and using the sum as the code number.

> 1   Perspective is active
> 2   Front clipping is on
> 4   Back clipping is on
> 8   UCS FOLLOW mode is on
> 16 Front clip "not at eye" is on. If this is on, **FRONTZ** determines the front clipping plane. If it's off, **FRONTZ** is ignored.

VIEWTWIST	A read-only system variable that provides the view twist angle for the current viewport.
VSMAX	A read-only system variable that provides the upper right corner of the current viewport's virtual screen expressed in **UCS**.

VSMIN   A read-only system variable that provides the lower left corner of the current viewport's virtual screen expressed in **UCS**.

WORLDUCS   This is a read-only system variable. If it's 1, then the current **UCS** is the same as the **WCS**. If it's 0, then it's not.

WORLDVIEW   Since the **DVIEW** and **VPOINT** commands are relative to the current **UCS**, this variable will change the current **UCS** equal to the **WCS** for the duration of a **DVIEW** or **VPOINT** command. If it's set to 1, then the change will occur. If it's set to 0, the default, then it won't change.

The following are dimension variables new to Release 10:

DIMTOFL   If this variable is on, then a dimension line is drawn between the extension lines, even if the text is forced outside them.

DIMTIX   If this variable is on, then the text is forced between the extension lines, even if AutoCAD would normally place it outside.

DIMSOXD   This variable keeps AutoCAD from drawing lines outside the extension lines. If **DIMTIX** is on and AutoCAD would normally draw the dimension lines outside the extension lines, you can suppress the dimension line by setting **DIMSOXD** to **ON**. If **DIMTIX** is **OFF**, there's no effect.

DIMSAH   If this variable is on, then **DIMBLK1** and **DIMBLK2** are used as the arrowheads for each end of the dimension line. If it's off, then **DIMBLK** is used for both ends.

DIMTVP   Controls where text is placed, relative to the dimension line. **DIMTAD** must be set to **OFF**. **DIMTVP** uses positive or negative numbers. The distance from the dimension line is **DIMTVP * DIMTXT**. If it's positive, it's placed above the line. If negative, it's placed below.

DIMBLK1   Define the blocks used as the arrowheads at each
DIMBLK2   end of the dimension line. These are active only if **DIMSAH** is **ON**. If either is unspecified, then **DIMBLK** is used for that end.

Index

Y

Z

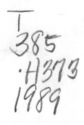